THE FRENCH IN
THE HEART OF AMERICA

THE FRENCH IN
THE HEART OF AMERICA

BY

JOHN FINLEY

COMMISSIONER OF EDUCATION AND PRESIDENT OF THE UNIVERSITY OF
THE STATE OF NEW YORK

A FIREBIRD PRESS BOOK

PELICAN PUBLISHING COMPANY
Gretna 1998

ISBN 1-56554-448-x
Manufactured in the United States of America

Published by Pelican Publishing Company, Inc.
1000 Burmaster Street, Gretna, Louisiana 70053

PREFACE

Most of what is here written was spoken many months ago in the Amphithéâtre Richelieu of the Sorbonne, in Paris, and some of it in Lille, Nancy, Dijon, Lyons, Grenoble, Montpellier, Toulouse, Bordeaux, Poitiers, Rennes, and Caen; and all of it was in the American publisher's hands before the great war came, effacing, with its nearer adventures, perils, sufferings, and anxieties, the dim memories of the days when the French pioneers were out in the Mississippi Valley, "The Heart of America."

As it was spoken, the purpose was to freshen and brighten for the French the memory of what some of them had seemingly wished to forget and to visualize to them the vigorous, hopeful, achieving life that is passing before that background of Gallic venturing and praying. It was planned also to publish the book simultaneously in France; and, less than a week before the then undreamed-of war, the manuscript was carried for that purpose to Paris and left for translation in the hands of Madame Boutroux, the wife of the beloved and eminent Émile Boutroux, head of the Fondation Thiers, and sister of the illustrious Henri Poincaré. But wounded soldiers soon came to fill the chambers of the scholars there, and the wife and mother has had to give all her thought to those who have hazarded their all for the France that is.

But it was my hope that what was spoken in Paris might some day be read in America, and particularly in that valley which the French evoked from the unknown, that those who now live there might know before what a valorous background they are passing, though I can tell them less of it than they will learn from the Homeric Parkman, if they will but read his immortal story.

My first debt is to him; but I must include with him many who made their contributions to these pages as I wrote them in Paris. The quotation-marks, diligent and faithful as they have tried to be, have, I fear, not reached all who have assisted, but my gratitude extends to every source of fact and to every guide of opinion along the way, from the St. Lawrence to the Gulf of Mexico, even if I have not in every instance known or remembered his name.

As without Parkman's long labors I could not have prepared these chapters, so without the occasion furnished by the Hyde Foundation and the nomination made by the President of Harvard University to the exchange lectureship, I should not have undertaken this delightful filial task. The readers' enjoyment and profit of the result will not be the full measure of my gratitude to Mr. James H. Hyde, the author of the Foundation, to President Lowell, and to him whose confidence in me persuaded me to it. But I hope these enjoyments and profits will add something to what I cannot adequately express.

That what was written could, in the midst of official duties, be prepared for the press is due largely to the patient, verifying, proof-reading labors of Mr. Frank L. Tolman, my young associate in the State Library.

The title of this book (appearing first as the general
title for some of these chapters in *Scribner's Magazine*
in 1912) has a purely geographical connotation. But
I advise the reader, in these days of bitterness, to go
no further if he carry any hatred in his heart.

JOHN FINLEY.

STATE EDUCATION BUILDING, ALBANY, N. Y.
Washington's Birthday, 1915.

CONTENTS

CONTENTS

THE FRENCH IN
THE HEART OF AMERICA

FROM "a series of letters to a friend in England," in 1793, "tending to shew the probable rise and grandeur of the American Empire":

"It struck me as a natural object of enquiry to what a future increase and elevation of magnitude and grandeur the spreading empire of America might attain, when a country had thus suddenly risen from an uninhabited wild, to the quantum of population necessary to govern and regulate its own administration."

G. IMLAY

("A captain in the American Army during the late war, and a commissioner for laying out land in the back settlements").

CHAPTER I

INTRODUCTION

I ADDRESS the reader as living in the land from which the pioneers of France went out to America; first, because I wrote these chapters in that land, a few steps from the Seine; second, because I should otherwise have to assume the familiarity of the reader with much that I have gathered into these chapters, though the reader may have forgotten or never known it; and, third, because I wish the reader to look at these new-world regions from without, and, standing apart and aloof, to see the present restless life of these valleys, especially of the Mississippi Valley, against the background of Gallic adventure and pious endeavor which is seen in richest color, highest charm, and truest value at a distance.

But, while I must ask my readers in America to expatriate themselves in their imaginations and to look over into this valley as aliens, I wish them to know that I write, though myself in temporary exile, as a son of the Mississippi Valley, as a geographical descendant of France; that my commission is given me of my love for the boundless stretch of prairie and plain whose virgin sod I have broken with my plough; of the lure of the waterways and roads where I have followed the boats and the trails of French voyageurs and coureurs de bois; and of the possessing interest of the epic story of the development of that most virile democracy known to the world. The "Divine River," discovered by the French, ran near the place of my birth. My county was that of "La Salle," a division of the land of the Illinois, "the land of men." The Fort, or the Rock, St. Louis, built by La Salle and Tonty, was only a few miles distant. A little farther, a town, Marquette, stands near the place where the French priest and explorer, Père Marquette, ministered to the Indians. Up-stream, a busy city keeps the name of Joliet on the lips of thousands, though the brave explorer would doubtless not recognize it as his own; and below, the new-made Hennepin Canal makes a shorter course to the Mississippi River than that which leads by the ruins of La Salle's Fort Crèvecœur. It is of such environment that these chapters were suggested, and it has been by my love for it, rather than by any profound scholarship, that they have been dictated. I write not as a scholar—since most of my life has been spent in action, not in study—but as an academic coureur de bois and of what I have known and seen in the Valley of Democracy, the fairest and most fruitful of the regions where France was pioneer in America.

There should be written in further preface to all the chapters which follow a paragraph from the beloved historian to whom I am most indebted and of whom I shall speak later at length. I first read its entrancing sentences when a youth in college, a quarter of a century ago, and I have never been free of its spell. I would have it written not only in France but somewhere at the northern portals of the American continent, on the cliffs of the Saguenay, or on that Rock of Quebec which saw the first vessel of the French come up the river and supported the last struggle for formal dominion of a land which the French can never lose, *except by forgetting:* "Again their ghostly camp-fires seem to burn, and the fitful light is cast around on lord and vassal and black-robed priest, mingled with wild forms of savage warriors, knit in close fellowship on the same stern errand. A boundless vision grows upon us; an untamed continent; vast wastes of forest verdure; mountains silent in primeval sleep; river, lake, and glimmering pool; wilderness oceans mingling with the sky. Such was the domain which France conquered for Civilization. Plumed helmets gleamed in the shade of its forests, priestly vestments in its dens and fastnesses of ancient barbarism. Men steeped in antique learning, pale with the close breath of the cloister, here spent the noon and evening of their lives, ruled savage hordes with a mild, parental sway, and stood serene before the direst shapes of death. Men of courtly nurture, heirs to the polish of a far-reaching ancestry, here, with their dauntless hardihood, put to shame the boldest sons of toil." [1]

These are the regions we are to explore, and these are the men with whom we are to begin the journey.

[1] Parkman: "Pioneers of France in the New World." New library edition. Introduction, xii–xiii.

CHAPTER II

FROM LABRADOR TO THE LAKES

WE shall not be able to enter the valley of the Mississippi in this chapter. There is a long stretch of the nearer valley of the St. Lawrence that must first be traversed. Just before I left America in 1910 two men flew in a balloon from St. Louis, the very centre of the Mississippi Valley, to the Labrador gate of the St. Lawrence, the vestibule valley, in a few hours, but it took the French pioneers a whole century and more to make their way out to where those aviators began their flight. We have but a few pages for a journey over a thousand miles of stream and portage and a hundred years of time. I must therefore leave most of the details of suffering from the rigors of the north, starvation, and the Iroquois along the way to your memories, or to your fresh reading of Parkman, Winsor, Fiske, and Thwaites in English, or to Le Clercq, Lescarbot, Champlain, Charlevoix, Sagard, and others in French.

The story of the exploration and settlement of those valleys beyond the cod-banks of Newfoundland begins not in the ports of Spain or Portugal, nor in England, but in a little town on the coast of France, standing on a rocky promontory thrust out into the sea, only a few hours' ride from Paris, in the ancient

4

town of St. Malo, the "nursery of hardy mariners,"
the cradle of the spirit of the West.[1]

For a son of France was the first of Europeans, so
far as we certainly know, to penetrate beyond the tide-
water of those confronting coasts, the first to step over
the threshold of the unguessed continent, north, at any
rate, of Mexico.   Columbus claimed at most but an
Asiatic peninsula, though he knew that he had found
only islands.   The Cabots, in the service of England,
sailing along its mysterious shores, had touched but
the fringe of the wondrous garment.   Ponce de Leon,
a Spaniard, had floundered a few leagues from the sea
in Florida searching for the fountain of youth.   Narvaez had found the wretched village of Appalache but
had been refused admission by the turbid Mississippi
and was carried out to an ocean grave by its fierce
current; Verrazano, an Italian in the employ of France,
living at Rouen, had entered the harbor of New York,
had enjoyed the primitive hospitality of what is now
a most fashionable seaside resort (Newport), had seen
the peaks of the White Mountains from his deck, and,
as he supposed, had looked upon the Indian Ocean, or
the Sea of Verrazano, which has shrunk to the Chesa-
peake Bay on our modern maps and now reaches not
a fiftieth part of the way to the other shore.

It was a true son of France who first had the persistence of courage and the endurance of imagination
to enter the continent and see the gates close behind
him—Jacques Cartier, a master pilot of St. Malo,
commissioned of his own intrepid desire and of the

---

[1] After reaching Paris on my first journey, the first place to which I made
a pilgrimage, even before the tombs of kings and emperors and the galleries of art, was this gray-bastioned town of St. Malo.

jealous ambition of King Francis I to bring fresh tidings of the mysterious "square gulf," which other Frenchmen, Denys and Aubert, may have entered a quarter of a century earlier, and which it was hoped might disclose a passage to the Indies.

It was from St. Malo that Cartier set sail on the highroad to Cathay, as he imagined, one April day in 1534 in two ships of sixty tons each.[1] There is preserved in St. Malo what is thought to be a list of those who signed the ship's papers subscribed under Cartier's own hand. It is no such instrument as the "Compact" which the men of the *Mayflower* signed as they approached the continent nearly a century later, but it is none the less fateful.

The autumn leaves had not yet fallen from the trees of Brittany when the two ships that started out in April appeared again in the harbor of St. Malo, carrying two dusky passengers from the New World as proofs of Cartier's ventures. He had made reconnoissance of the gulf behind Newfoundland and returned for fresh means of farther quest toward Cathay.

The leaves were but come again on the trees of Brittany when, with a larger crew in three small vessels (one of only forty tons), he again went out with the ebb-tide from St. Malo; his men, some of whom had been gathered from the jails, having all made their confession and attended mass, and received the benediction of the bishop. In August he entered the great river St. Lawrence, whose volume of water was so great as to brighten Cartier's hopes of having found the

---

[1] I crossed back over the same ocean, nearly four hundred years later, to a French port in a steamship of a tonnage equal to that of a fleet of four hundred of Cartier's boats; so has the sea bred giant children of such hardy parentage.

northern way to India. On he sailed, with his two dusky captives for pilots, seeing with regret the banks of the river gradually draw together and hearing unwelcome word of the freshening of its waters—on past the "gorge of the gloomy Saguenay with its towering cliffs and sullen depths, depths which no sounding-line can fathom, and heights at whose dizzy verge the wheeling eagle seems a speck"; on past frowning promontory and wild vineyards, to the foot of the scarped cliff of Quebec, now "rich with heroic memories, then but the site of a nameless barbarism"; thence, after parley with the Indian chief Donnacona and his people, on through walls of autumn foliage and frost-touched meadows to where the Lachine Rapids mocked with unceasing laughter those who dreamed of an easy way to China. There, entertained at the Indian capital, he was led to the top of a hill, such as Montmartre, from whose height he saw his Cathay fade into a stretch of leafy desert bounded only by the horizon and threaded by two narrow but hopeful ribbons of water. There, hundreds of miles from the sea, he stood, probably the only European, save for his companions, inside the continent, between Mexico and the Pole; for De Soto had not yet started for his burial in the Mississippi; the fathers of the Pilgrim Fathers were still in their cradles; Narvaez's men had come a little way in shore and vanished; Cabeça de Vaca was making his almost incredible journey from the Texas coast to the Pacific; Captain John Smith was not yet born; and Henry Hudson's name was to remain obscure for three quarters of a century. Francis I had sneeringly inquired of Charles V if he and the King of Portugal had parcelled out the world between them, and asked to see the last will and testament of the patriarch Adam. If King Francis had been permitted to see it, he would have found a codicil for France written that day against the bull of Pope Alexander VI and against the hazy English claim of the Cabots. For the river, "the greatest without comparison," as Cartier reported later to his king, "that is known to have ever been seen," carried drainage title to a realm larger many times than all the lands of the Seine and the Rhône and the Loire, and richer many times than the land of spices to which the falls of Lachine, "the greatest and swiftest fall of water that any where hath beene seene," seemed now to guard the way.

"Hochelaga" the Indians called their city—the capital of the river into which the sea had narrowed, a thousand miles inland from the coasts of Labrador which but a few years before were the dim verge of the world and were believed even then to be infested with griffins and fiends—a city which vanished within the next three quarters of a century. For when Champlain came in 1611 to this site to build his outpost, not a trace was left of the palisades which Cartier describes and one of his men pictures, not an Indian was left of the population that gave such cordial welcome to Cartier. And for all Champlain's planning it was still a meadow and a forest—the spring flowers "blooming in the young grass" and birds of varied plumage flitting "among the boughs"—when the mystic and soldier Maisonneuve and his associates of Montreal, forty men and four women, in an enterprise conceived in the ancient Church of St. Germain-des-Prés and consecrated to the Holy Family by a solemn ceremonial at Notre-Dame, knelt upon this same ground in 1642 before the hastily reared and decorated altar while Father Vimont, standing in rich vestments, addressed them. "You are," he said, "a grain of mustard-seed that shall rise and grow till its branches overshadow the earth. You are few, but your work is the work of God. His smile is on you and your children shall fill the land."[1] Parkman (from the same French authority) finishes the picture of the memorable day: "The afternoon waned; the sun sank behind the western forest, and twilight came on. Fireflies were twinkling over the darkened meadow. They caught them, tied them with threads into shining festoons and hung them before the altar, where the Host remained exposed. Then they pitched their tents, lighted their bivouac fires, stationed their guards and lay down to rest. Such was the birth-night of Montreal."[2]

On the 10th of September in 1910 two hundred thousand people knelt in that same place before an out-of-door altar, and the incandescent lights were the fireflies of a less romantic and a more practical age.

[1] François Dollier de Casson, "Histoire du Montreal," quoted in Parkman's "Jesuits in North America," p. 209, a free rendering of the original. "Voyez-vous, messieurs, dit-il, ce que vous voyez n'est qu'un grain de moutarde, mais il est jeté par des mains si pieuses et animées de l'esprit de la foi et de la religion que sans doute il faut que le ciele est de grands desseins puisqu'il se sert de tels ouvriers, et je ne fais aucun doute que ce petit grain ne produise un grand arbre, ne fasse un jour des merveilles, ne soit multiplié et ne s'étende de toutes parts."

[2] François Dollier de Casson, "Histoire du Montreal," quoted in Parkman's "Jesuits in North America," p. 209, a free rendering of the original. "On avait point de lampes ardentes devant le St. Sacrement, mais on avait certaines mouches brillantes qui y luisaient fort agréablement jour et nuit étant suspendues par des filets d'une façon admirable et belle, et toute propre a honorer selon la rusticité de ce pays barbare, le plus adorable de nos mystères."

Maisonneuve and Mademoiselle Mance would have
been enraptured by such a scene, but it would have
given even greater satisfaction to the pilot of St. Malo
if he could have seen that commercial capital of the
north lying beneath the mountain which still bears
the name he gave it, and stretching far beyond the
bounds of the palisaded Hochelaga. It should please
France to know that nearly two hundred thousand
French keep the place of the footprint of the first
pioneer, Jacques Cartier. When a few weeks before
my coming to France I was making my way by a trail
down the side of Mount Royal through the trees—
some of which may have been there in Cartier's day—
two lads, one of as beautiful face as I have ever seen,
though tear-stained, emerged from the bushes and
begged me, in a language which Jacques Cartier would
have understood better than I, to show them the way
back to "rue St. Maurice," which I did, finding that
street to be only a few paces from the place where
Champlain had made a clearing for his "Place Royale"
in the midst of the forest three hundred years ago.
That beautiful boy, Jacques Jardin, brown-eyed, bare-
kneed, in French soldier's cap, is to me the living incarnation of the adventure which has made even that
chill wilderness blossom as a garden in Brittany.

But to come back to Cartier. It was too late in the
season to make further explorations where the two
rivers invited to the west and northwest, so Cartier
joined the companions who had been left near Quebec
to build a fort and make ready for the winter. As if
to recall that bitter weather, the hail beat upon the
windows of the museum at St. Malo on the day when
I was examining there the relics of the vessel which

Cartier was obliged to leave in the Canadian river, because so many of his men had died of scurvy and exposure that he had not sufficient crew to man the three ships home. And probably not a man would have been left and not even the *Grande Hermine* would have come back if a specific for scurvy had not been found before the end of the winter—a decoction learned of the Indians and made from the bark or leaves of a tree so efficacious that if all the "doctors of Lorraine and Montpellier had been there, with all the drugs of Alexandria, they could not have done so much in a year as the said tree did in six days; for it profited us so much that all those who would use it recovered health and soundness, thanks to God."

Cartier appears again in July, 1536, before the ramparts of St. Malo with two of his vessels. The savages on the St. Charles were given the *Petite Hermine*,[1] its nails being accepted in part requital for the temporary loss of their chief. Donnacona, whom Cartier kidnapped.

A cross was left standing on the shores of the St. Lawrence with the fleur-de-lis planted near it. Donnacona was presented to King Francis and baptized, and with all his exiled companions save one was buried, where I have not yet learned, but probably somewhere

---

[1] James Phinney Baxter, "A Memoir of Jacques Cartier," p. 200, writes: "The remains of this ship, the *Petite Hermine*, were discovered in 1843, in the river St. Charles, at the mouth of the rivulet known as the Lairet. These precious relics were found buried under five feet of mud, and were divided into two portions, one of which was placed in the museum of the Literary and Historical Society of Quebec, and destroyed by fire in 1854. The other portion was sent to the museum at St. Malo, where it now remains. For a particular account *vide Le Canadien* of August 25, and the *Quebec Gazette* of August 30, 1843; 'Transactions of the Quebec Literary and Historical Society for 1862'; and 'Picturesque Quebec,' Le Moine, Montreal, 1862, pp. 484-7."

out on that headland of France nearest Stadacone, the seat of his lost kingdom.

Cartier busied himself in St. Malo (or Limoilou) till called upon, in 1541, when peace was restored in France to take the post of captain-general of a new expedition under Sieur de Roberval, "Lord of Norembega, Viceroy and Lieutenant-General of Canada, Hochelaga, Saguenay, Newfoundland, Belle Isle, Carpunt, Labrador, the Great Bay and Baccalaos,"[1] with a commission of discovery, settlement, and conversion of the Indians, and with power to ransack the prisons for material with which to carry out these ambitious and pious designs, thereby, as the king said, employing "clemency in doing a merciful and meritorious work toward some criminals and malefactors, that by this they may recognize the Creator by rendering Him thanks, and amending their lives." Again Cartier (Roberval having failed to arrive in time) sets out; again he passes the gloomy Saguenay and the cliff of Quebec; again he leaves his companions to prepare for the winter; again he ascends the river to explore the rapids, still dreaming of the way to Asia; again after a miserable winter he sails back to France, eluding Roberval a year late, and carrying but a few worthless quartz diamonds and a little sham gold. Then Roberval, the Lord of Norembega, reigns alone in his vast and many-titled domain, for another season of snows and famine, freely using the lash and gibbet to keep

---

[1] Baxter, "Memoir of Jacques Cartier," note, p. 40, writes: "These titles are given on the authority of Charlevoix, 'Histoire de la Nouvelle France,' Paris, 1744, tome I, p. 32. Reference, however, to the letters patent of January 15, 1540, from which he professes to quote and which are still preserved and can be identified as the same which he says were to be found in the Etat Ordinaire des Guerres in the Chambre des Comptes at Paris, does not bear out his statement."

his penal colonists in subjection; and then, according to some authorities, supported by the absence of Cartier's name from the local records of St. Malo for a few months, Cartier was sent out to bring the Lord of Norembega home.

So Cartier's name passes from the pages of history, even if it still appears again in the records of St. Malo, and he spends the rest of his days on the rugged little peninsula thrust out from France toward the west, as it were a hand. A few miles out of St. Malo the Breton tenants of the Cartier manor, Port Cartier, to-day carry their cauliflower and carrots to market and seemingly wonder at my curiosity in seeking Cartier's birthplace rather than Châteaubriand's tomb. It were far fitter that Cartier instead of Châteaubriand should have been buried out on the "Plage" beyond the ramparts, exiled for a part of every day by the sea, for the amphibious life of this master pilot, going in and out of the harbor with the tide, had added to France a thousand miles of coast and river, had opened the door of the new world, beyond the banks of the Baccalaos, to the imaginations of Europe, and unwittingly showed the way not to Asia, but to a valley with which Asia had nothing to compare.

For a half century after Cartier's home bringing of Roberval—the very year that De Soto's men quitted in misery the lower valley of the Mississippi—there is no record of a sail upon the river St. Lawrence. Hochelaga became a waste, its tenants annihilated or scattered, and Cartier's fort was all but obliterated. The ambitious symbols of empire were alternately buried in snows and blistered by heat. France had too much to think of at home. But still, as Parkman says, "the wandering Esquimaux saw the Norman and Breton sails hovering around some lonely headland or anchored in fleets in the harbor of St. John, and still through salt spray and driving mist, the fishermen dragged up the riches of the sea." For "codfish must still be had for Lent and fast-days." Another authority pictures the Breton babies of this period playing with trinkets made of walrus tusks, and the Norman maidens decked in furs brought by their brothers from the shores of Anticosti and Labrador.

Meanwhile in Brouage on the Bay of Biscay a boy is born whose spirit, nourished of the tales of the new world, is to make a permanent colony where Cartier had found and left a wilderness, and is to write his name foremost on the "bright roll of forest chivalry" —Samuel Champlain.

Once the sea, I am told, touched the massive walls of Brouage. There are still to be seen, several feet below the surface, rings to which mariners and fishermen moored their boats—they who used to come to Brouage for salt with which to cure their fish, they whose stories of the Newfoundland cod-banks stirred in the boy Champlain the desire for discovery beyond their fogs. The boys in the school of Hiers-Brouage a mile away—in the Mairie where I went to consult the parish records—seemed to know hardly more of that land which the Brouage boy of three centuries before had lifted out of the fogs by his lifelong heroic adventures than did the boy Champlain, which makes me feel that till all French children know of, and all American children remember Brouage, the story of France in America needs to be retold. The St. Lawrence Valley has not forgotten, but I could not learn that a citizen of the Mississippi Valley had made recent pilgrimage to this spot.[1]

In the year of Champlain's birth the frightful colonial tragedy in Florida was nearing its end. By the year 1603 he had, in Spanish employ, made a voyage of two years in the West Indies, the unique illustrated journal[2] of which in his own hand was for two centuries and more in Dieppe, but has recently been acquired by a library in the United States[3]—a journal most precious especially in its prophecy of the Panama Canal:[4] "One might judge, if the territory four leagues in extent, lying between Panama and the river were cut thru, he could pass from the south sea to that on the other side, and thus shorten the route by more than fifteen hundred leagues. From Panama to Magellan would constitute an island, and from Panama to Newfoundland would constitute another, so that the whole of America would be in two islands."

He had also made one expedition to the St. Lawrence, reaching the deserted Hochelaga, seeing the Lachine Rapids, and getting vague reports of the unknown West. He must have been back in Paris in time to see the eleven survivors of La Roche's unsuccessful expedition of 1590, who, having lived twelve years and more on Sable Island, were rescued and brought before King Henry IV, "standing like river gods" in their long beards and clad in shaggy skins. During the next

[1] For an interesting account of Brouage to-day, see "Acadiensis," 4 : 226.

[2] "Brief Discours des Choses plus remarquables que Sammuel Champlain de Brouage, reconnues aux Indies Occidentalles au voiage qu'il en a faict en icelles en l'annee V°IIIJ˟˟XIX (1599) et en l'annee VJ°J (1601) comme ensuite." Now in English translation by Hakluyt Society, 1859.

[3] The John Carter Brown Library at Providence, R. I.

[4] Several earlier Spanish suggestions for a canal had been made. See M. F. Johnson, "Four Centuries of the Panama Canal."

three years this indefatigable, resourceful pioneer assisted in founding Acadia and exploring the Atlantic coast southward. Boys and girls in America are familiar with the story of the dispersion of the Acadians, a century and more later, as preserved in our literature by the poet Longfellow. But doubtless not one in a hundred thousand has ever read the earlier chapters of that Æneid.

The best and the meanest of France were of the company that set out from Dieppe to be its colonists: men of highest condition and character, and vagabonds, Catholic priests and Huguenot ministers, soldiers and artisans. There were theological discussions which led to blows before the colonists were far at sea. Fiske, the historian, says the "ship's atmosphere grew as musty with texts and as acrid with quibbles as that of a room at the Sorbonne." There was the incident of the wandering of Nicolas Aubry, "more skilled in the devious windings of the [Latin Quarter] than in the intricacies of the Acadian Forest," where he was lost for sixteen days and subsisted on berries and wild fruits; there was the ravage of the relentless maladie de terre, scurvy, for which Cartier's specific could not be found though the woods were scoured; there were the explorations of beaches and harbors and islands and rivers, including the future Massachusetts Bay and Plymouth, and the accurate mapping of all that coast now so familiar; there were the arrivals of the ship *Jonas*, once with temporal supplies and again, as the *Mayflower of the Jesuits*, with spiritual teachers; there was the "Order of Good Times," which flourished with as good cheer and as good food at Port Royal in the solitude of the continent as the gourmands at the

Rue aux Ours had in Paris and that, too, at a cheaper rate;[1] there was later the news of the death of Henry IV heard from a fisherman of Newfoundland; and there was, above all else except the "indomitable tenacity" of Champlain, the unquenchable enthusiasm, lively fancy, and good sense of Lescarbot, the verse-making advocate from Paris.

There is so much of tragic suffering and gloom in all this epic of the forests that one is tempted to spend more time than one ought, perhaps, on that bit of European clearing (the only spot, save one, as yet in all the continent north of Florida and Mexico), in the jolly companionship of that young poet-lawyer who had doubtless sat under lecturers in Paris and who would certainly have been quite as capable and entertaining as any lecturers on the new world brought in these later days from America to Paris, a man "who won the good-will of all and spared himself naught," "who daily invented something for the public good," and who gave the strongest proof of what advantage "a new settlement might derive from a mind cultivated by study and induced by patriotism to use its knowledge and reflections."

It cannot seem unworthy of the serious purpose of this book to let the continent lie a few minutes longer in its savage slumber, or, as the Jesuits thought it, "blasted beneath the sceptre of hell," while we accompany Poutrincourt and Champlain, returning wounded and weather-beaten from inspecting the

---

[1] "Though the epicures of Paris often tell us we have no Rue aux Ours over there, as a rule we made as good cheer as we could have in this same Rue aux Ours and at less cost." Lescarbot, "Champlain Society Publication," 7 : 342.

coast of New England, to find the buildings of Port Royal, under Lescarbot's care, bright with lights, and an improvised arch bearing the arms of Poutrincourt and De Monts, to be received by Neptune, who, accompanied by a retinue of Tritons, declaimed Alexandrine couplets of praise and welcome, and to sit at the sumptuous table of the Order of Good Times, of which I have just spoken, furnished by this same lawyer-poet's agricultural industry. We may even stop a moment longer to hear his stately appeal to France, which, heeded by her, would have made Lescarbot's a name familiar in the homes of America instead of one known only to those who delve in libraries:

"France, fair eye of the universe, nurse from old of letters and of arms, resource to the afflicted, strong stay to the Christian religion, Dear Mother . . . your children, our fathers and predecessors, have of old been masters of the sea. . . . They have with great power occupied Asia. . . . They have carried the arms and the name of France to the east and south. . . . All these are marks of your greatness, . . . but you must now enter again upon old paths, in so far as they have been abandoned, and expand the bounds of your piety, justice and humanity, by teaching these things to the nations of New France. . . . Our ancient practice of the sea must be revived, we must ally the east with the west and convert those people to God before the end of the world come. . . . You must make an alliance in imitation of the course of the sun, for as he daily carries his light hence to New France, so let your civilization, your light, be carried thither by your children, who henceforth, by the frequent voyages they shall make to these western lands, shall be called children of the sea, which is, being interpreted, children of the west."[1]

"Children of the west." His fervid appeal found as little response then as doubtless it would find if made to-day, and the children of the sea were interpreted as the children of the south of Africa. The sons of France have ever loved their homes. They have, except the adventurous few, preferred to remain children of the rivers and the sea of their fathers, and so it is that few of Gallic blood were "spawned," to use Lescarbot's metaphor, in that chill continent, though the venturing or missionary spirit of such as Cartier and Champlain, Poutrincourt and De Monts gave spawn of such heroism and unselfish sacrifice as have made millions in America whom we now call "children of the west," geographical offspring of Brittany and Normandy and Picardy.

The lilies of France and the escutcheons of De Monts and Poutrincourt, painted by Lescarbot for the castle in the wilderness, faded; the sea which Lescarbot, as Neptune, impersonated in the pageant of welcome, and the English ships received back those who had not been gathered into the cemetery on land; and the first agricultural colony in the northern wilds lapsed for a time at least into a fur traders' station or a place of call for fishermen.

It was only by locating these points on Champlain's map of Port Royal that I was able to find in 1911 the site of the ancient fort, garden, fish-pond, and cemetery. The men unloading a schooner a few rods away seemed not to know of Lescarbot or Poutrincourt or even Champlain, but that was perhaps because they were not accustomed to my tongue.

[1] Lescarbot, "Histoire de la Nouvelle France," 1618, pp. 15-22.

The unquiet Champlain left Acadia in the summer of 1607, the charter having been withdrawn by the king. In the winter of 1607-8 he walked the streets of Paris as in a dream, we are told, longing for the northern wilderness, where he had left his heart four years before. In the spring of 1608 the white whales are floundering around his lonely ship in the river of his dreams. At the foot of the gray rock of Quebec he makes the beginning of a fort, whence he plans to go forth to trace the rivers to their sources, discover, perchance, a northern route to the Indies, and make a path for the priests to the countless savages "in bondage of Satan." Parkman speaks of him as the "Æneas of a destined people," and he is generally called the "father of Canada." But I think of him rather as a Prometheus who, after his years of bravest defiance of elements and Indians, is to have his heart plucked out day by day, chained to that same gray rock—only that death instead of Herculean succor came.

There is space for only the briefest recital of the exploits and endurances of the stout heart and hardy frame of the man of whom any people of any time might well be proud. The founding of Quebec, the rearing of the pile of wooden buildings where the lower town now stretches along the river; the unsuccessful plot to kill Champlain before the fort is finished; the death of all of the twenty-eight men save eight before the coming of the first spring—these are the incidents of the first chapter.

The visit to the Iroquois country; the discovery of the lake that bears his name; the first portentous collision with the Indians of the Five Nations, undertaken to keep the friendship of the Indian tribes along the St. Lawrence; a winter in France; the breaking of ground for a post at Montreal; another visit to France to find means for the rescue and sustenance of his fading colony, make a depressing second chapter.

Then follows the journey up the Ottawa with the young De Vignau, who had stirred Paris by claiming that he had at last found the northwest passage to the Pacific, when he had in fact spent the winter in an Indian lodge not two hundred miles from Montreal; the noble forgiveness of De Vignau by Champlain; his crestfallen return and his going forth from France again in 1615 with four Récollet friars (Franciscans of the strict observance) of the convent of his birthplace (Brouage) inflamed by him with holy zeal for the continent of savages. For a little these "apostolic mendicants" in their gray robes girt with the white cord, their feet naked or shod in wooden sandals, tarried beneath the gray rock and then set forth east, north, and west, soon (1626) to be followed and reinforced by their brothers of stronger resources, the Jesuits, the "black gowns," upon a mission whose story is as marvellous as a "tale of chivalry or legends of lives of the saints."

Meanwhile Champlain, exploring the regions to the northwest, is the first of white men to look upon the first of the Great Lakes—the "Mer Douce" (Lake Huron) being discovered before the lakes to the south—the first after the boy Étienne Brûlé and Friar Le Caron: the latter having gone before him, celebrated the first mass on Champlain's arrival the 12th of August, 1615, a day "marked with white in the friar's calendar," and deserving to be marked with red in the calendar of the west.

There follow twenty restless years in which Champlain's efforts are divided between discovery and strengthening the little colony, and his occupations between holding his Indian allies who lived along the northern pathway to the west, fighting their enemies to the south, the Iroquois, restraining the jealousies of merchants and priests, trade and missions, reconciling Catholics and Huguenots, going nearly every year to France in the interests of the colony, building and repairing, yielding for a time to the overpowering ships of the English. The grizzled soldier and explorer, restored and commissioned anew under the fostering and firm support of Richelieu, struggled to the very end of his life to make the feeble colony, which eighteen years after its founding "could scarcely be said to exist but in the founder's brain," not chiefly an agricultural settlement but a spiritual centre from which the interior was to be explored and the savage hordes won—at the same time to heaven and to France—subdued not by being crushed but by being civilized, not by the sword but by the cross. It was a far different colony that was beginning to grow fronting the harbor of Plymouth, where men quite as intolerant of priests as Richelieu was intolerant of Huguenots were building homes and making firesides in enjoyment of religious and political freedom.

Champlain lay dying as the year 1635 went out, asking more help from his patron Richelieu, but his great task had been accomplished. The St. Lawrence had been opened, the first two of the Great Lakes had been reached, and explorer and priest were already on the edge of that farther valley of the "Missipi," which we are to enter in the next chapter.

CHAPTER III

THE PATHS OF THE GRAY FRIARS AND BLACK GOWNS

IT was exactly a hundred years, according to some authorities, after Jacques Cartier opened and passed through the door of the St. Lawrence Valley that another son of France, Jean Nicolet, again the first of Europeans so far as is now certainly known, looked over into the great valley of the Mississippi from the north.

Champlain, dying beneath the Rock of Quebec, had touched two of the Great Lakes twenty years before. He never knew probably that another of those immense inland seas lay between, though, as his last map indicates, he had some word several years before his death of a greater sea beyond, where now two mighty lakes, the largest bodies of fresh water on the globe, carry their sailless fleets and nourish the life of millions on their shores.

From the coureurs de bois, "runners of the woods," whom he, tied by the interests of his feeble colony to the Rock, had sent out, enviously no doubt, upon journeys of exploration and arbitration among the Indians, and from the Gray Friars and Black Gowns who, inflamed of his spirit, had gone forth through the solitudes from Indian village to village, from suffering to suffering, reports had come which he must have been frequently translating with his practised hand into river and shore line of this precious map, the original of which is still kept among the proud archives of France. He was disappointed the while, I have no doubt, that still the fresh water kept flowing from the west, and that still there was no word of the salt sea.

The straight line which makes the western border of his map is merciful of his ignorance, but merciless of his hopes. It admits no stream that does not flow into one of the lakes or into the St. Lawrence. But it was made probably four years before his death and it is possible, indeed probable, that just before paralysis came upon him, he had heard through the famous coureur de bois, Jean Nicolet, whom he had despatched the year previous, of a river which this man of the woods had descended so far that "in three days more" he would have reached what the Indians called the "Great Water."[1] There is good reason, in the appointment of this same coureur de bois as a commissioner and interpreter at Three Rivers, for thinking (as one wishes to think) that like Moses, Champlain had, through him a vision of the valley which he himself might not enter, but which his compatriots were to possess.

The historian Bancroft said of that land: "Not a cape was turned, not a river entered, but a Jesuit led the way." But the men of sandalled feet had not yet penetrated so far in 1635. It is an interesting tribute to these spiritual pioneers, however, that the particular rough coureur de bois who first looked into that far valley of solitude, inhabited only by Indians and buf-

---

[1] The Mississippi. Nicolet probably did not go beyond the Fox portage. See C. W. Butterfield, "The Discovery of the Northwest by Jean Nicolet."

faloes and other untamed beasts, would doubtless never have left his Indian habits and returned to civilization if he could have lived without the sacraments of the church.

This coureur de bois Nicolet presents a grotesque appearance as he mounts the rims of the two valleys where the two bowls touch each other, bowls so full that in freshet the water sometimes overflows the brim and makes one continuous valley.

Nicolet would not be recognized for the Frenchman that he was, as he appears yonder; for, having been told that the men whom he was to meet were without hair upon their faces and heads, and thinking himself to be near the confines of China, he had attired himself as one about to be received at an Oriental court. Accordingly, he stands upon the edge of the prairies in a robe of Chinese damask embroidered with flowers and birds—but with a pistol in each hand. Having succeeded in his mission to these barbarians (for such he found them to be, wearing breech-clouts instead of robes of silk), he was impelled or lured over into the great valley, it is believed. He passed from the lake on the border of Champlain's map[1] up a river (the Fox) that by and by became but a stream over which one might jump. He portaged from this stream or creek across a narrow strip of prairie, only a mile wide, to the Wisconsin River, a tributary of the Mississippi. The statement over which I have pondered, walking along that river, that he might have reached the "great water" in three more days, is intelligible only in this interpretation of his course.

The next Europeans to look out over the edge of

[1] Lake Michigan.

the basin of the lakes were two other sons of France, one a man of St. Malo, Radisson, a voyageur and coureur de bois, the other his brother-in-law, Groseilliers (1654). It is thought that these companions went all the way to the Mississippi and so became the discoverers of her northern waters. The journal of the voyage is unfortunately somewhat obscure. The great "rivers that divide themselves in two" are many in that valley, and no one can be certain of the identity of that river "called the forked" mentioned in the "relation" of Radisson, which had "two branches, one towards the west, the other towards the south," and, as the travellers believed, ran toward Mexico.[1]

Then came the Hooded Faces, the friars and the priests. To the four Récollet friars whom Champlain brought out with him in 1615 from the convent of his native town (Brouage), Jamay, D'Olbeau, Le Caron, and a lay brother, Du Plessis, others were added, but there were not more than six in all for the missions extending from Acadia to where Champlain found Le Caron in 1615 in the vicinity of Lake Huron. Their experiences and ardor (not unlike those of other missionaries in other continents and in our own times) have illustration in this extract from a letter written by Le Caron: "It would be difficult to tell you the fatigue I have suffered, having been obliged to have my paddle in hand all day long and row with all my strength with the Indians. I have more than a hundred times walked in the rivers over the sharp rocks, which cut my feet, in the mud, in the woods, where I

[1] See Warren Upham. Groseilliers and Radisson, the first white men in Minnesota, 1655-6 and 1659-60, and their discovery of the Upper Mississippi River, in Minn. Historical Society Collections, 10 : 449-594.

carried the canoe and my little baggage, in order to avoid the rapids and frightful waterfalls. I say nothing of the painful fast which beset us, having only a little sagamity, which is a kind of pulmentum composed of water and the meal of Indian corn, a small quantity of which is dealt out to us morning and evening. Yet I must avow that amid my pains I felt much consolation. For alas! when we see such a great number of infidels, and nothing but a drop of water is needed to make them children of God, one feels an ardor which I cannot express to labor for their conversion and to sacrifice for it one's repose and life."[1]

"Six months before the Pilgrims began their meeting-house on the burial hill at Plymouth," he and his brother priests laid the corner-stone of "the earliest church erected in French-America." It was a bitter disappointment when, in 1629, he was carried away by the English from his infant mission to spend his latter days far from his savage converts, perhaps in his white-washed cell in the convent of Brouage, and to administer before an altar where it was not necessary to have neophytes wave green boughs to drive off the mosquitoes—those pestiferous insects from whose persecutions a brother Récollet said he suffered his "worst martyrdom" in America. But more bitter chagrin was in store for Le Caron, for when the French returned to Quebec, in 1632, after the restoration under the treaty, the Gray Apostles of the White Cord (who had invited the Black Gowns to join them in their missions years before and had so hospitably entertained them when denied shelter elsewhere in Quebec) were

---

[1] Le Clercq, "First Establishment of the Faith in New France (Shea)," 1 : 95.

not permitted to be of the company.[1] The Jesuits went alone. Repairing their dilapidated buildings of Notre Dame des Anges, a little way out of Quebec on the St. Charles River, where Cartier had spent his first miserable winter in America, they began their enterprises *ad majorem Dei gloriam* in a field of labor whose vastness "might," as Parkman says, "tire the wings of thought itself." Le Jeune left the convent at Dieppe, De Nouë that at Rouen, and they went out from Havre together to begin their labors among a people whose first representatives came aboard the vessel at Tadoussac with faces variously painted, black and red and yellow, as a party of "carnival maskers." One cannot well conjecture a more hopeless undertaking than that of making those half-naked, painted barbarians understand the mystery of the Trinity, for example, or the significance of the cross. Think of this gentle, holy father, Le Jeune, seated in a hovel beside one of these savages, whose language he is trying to learn, bribing his Indian tutor with a piece of tobacco at every difficulty to make him more attentive, or with half-frozen fingers writing his Algonquin exercises, or making translations of prayers for the tongues of his prospective converts—and you will be able to appreciate the beginnings of the task to which these men without the slightest question set themselves.

It was a life, once these men left the mission house of Notre Dame des Anges, that was without the slight-

---

[1] Le Caron, says Le Clercq, when he "saw all his efforts were useless, experienced the same fate as Saint Francis Xavier, who when on the point of entering China, found so many secret obstacles to his pious design that he fell sick and died of chagrin. So was Father Joseph a martyr to the zeal which consumed him, and of that ardent charity which burned in his heart to visit his church again."—Le Clercq, l. c. 1 : 324.

est social intercourse, that was beyond the prizes of any earthly ambition, that was frequently in imminence of torture and death, and that was usually in physical discomfort if not in pain.   Obscure and constant toil for tender hands, solitude, suffering, privation, death— these made up the portion of the messengers of the faith who turned their faces toward the wilderness, their steps into the gloom of the forests, pathless except for the traces of the feet of savages and wild beasts.

For it is twenty-five years after that memorable day when Le Caron first said mass on the shores of one of the Great Lakes (Champlain being present) before the farthermost shore of the farthest lake is reached by these patient and valorous pilgrims of the west.   The story of that heroic journey, of the consecration of those forests and waters and clearings by suffering and unselfish ministry, fills many volumes (forty in the French edition and seventy-two in the edition recently published in the United States, the English translation being presented on the pages opposite the Latin or French originals).   There is material in them for many chapters of a new-world "Odyssey." To these "Relations," as they were called, we owe the great body of information we have concerning New France, from 1603 in Acadia to the early part of the eighteenth century in the Mississippi and St. Lawrence Valleys; for they who wrote them were not priests alone, they were at the same time explorers, scientists, historical students, ethnologists (the first and best-fitted students of the North American Indian), physicians to the bodies as well as ministers to the souls of those wild creatures.

There was a time when these "Relations," as they came from the famous press of Cramoisy, were eagerly awaited and devoured, and were everywhere the themes of enthusiastic discussion in circles of high devotion in Paris and throughout France, where it is doubtless believed by many to-day that the borders of the lakes which the authors of these "Relations" traversed are still possessed by Indians, or at best by half-civilized, half-barbaric peoples who would stand agape in the Louvre as the Goths stood before the temples and the statues of Rome.

The "Relations" of Jesuits are among our most precious chronicles in America. With these the history of the north—the valleys of the St. Lawrence, the Great Lakes, and the Mississippi—begins. The coureurs de bois may have anticipated the priests in some solitary places, but they seldom made records. Doubtless, like Nicolet, they told their stories to the priests when they went back to the altars for sacrament, so that even their experiences have been for the most part preserved. But when we know under what distracting and discouraging conditions even the priest wrote, we wonder, as Thwaites says, that anything whatever has been preserved in writing. The "Relations" were written by the fathers, he reminds us,[1] in Indian camps, the aboriginal insects buzzing or crawling about them, in the midst of a chaos of distractions, immersed in scenes of squalor and degradation, overcome by fatigue and improper sustenance, suffering from wounds and disease, and maltreated by their hosts who were often their jailers. What they wrote under these circumstances is simple and direct. There is no

[1] "Jesuit Relations," 1 : 39, 40.

florid rhetoric; there is little self-glorification; no un-
necessary dwelling on the details of martyrdom; and
there is not a line to give suspicion "that one of this
loyal band flinched or hesitated."

"I know not," says one of these apostles[1] in an
epistle to the Romans (for this particular letter went
to Rome), "I know not whether your Paternity will
recognize the letter of a poor cripple, who formerly,
when in perfect health was well known to you. The
letter is badly written, and quite soiled because in
addition to other inconveniences, he who writes it
has only one whole finger on his right hand; and it is
difficult to avoid staining the paper with the blood
which flows from his wounds, not yet healed: he uses
arquebus powder for ink, and the earth for a table."
This particular early American writer, besides having
his hand split and now one finger-nail or joint burned
off and now another, his hair and beard pulled out,
his flesh burned with live coals and red-hot stones,
was hung up by the feet, had food for dogs placed
upon his body that they might lacerate him as they
ate, but finally escaped death itself through sale to
the Dutch.

Two other chroniclers of that life of which they were
a part, were two men of noble birth: the giant Brébeuf,
"the Ajax of the mission," a man of vigorous passions
tamed by religion (as Parkman says, "a dammed-up
torrent sluiced and guided to grind and saw and weave
for the good of man"); and in marked and strange contrast with him, Charles Garnier, a young man of
thirty-three, of beardless face—laughed at by his
friends in Paris, we are told, because he was beardless

---

[1] Fr. Francesco Gioseppe Bressani, "Jesuit Relations" (Thwaites), 39 : 55.

but admired by the Indians for the same reason—of a delicate nature but of the most valiant spirit.

It was Brébeuf who kept the westernmost outpost for many years. A man of iron frame and resoluteness, the only complaint of his that I have found, is one which would furnish a study for a great artist: it was that he had "no moment to read his breviary, except by moonlight or the fire, when stretched out to sleep on a bare rock by some savage cataract,—or in a damp nook of the adjacent forest." There is another picture of him in action, crouched in a canoe, barefoot, toiling at the paddle, hour after hour, day after day, week after week, behind the lank hair and brown shoulders and long, naked arms of his aboriginal companion. Still another simple "Relation" shows him teaching the Huron children to chant and repeat the commandments under reward of beads, raisins, or prunes. In 1637, accused of having bewitched the Huron nation and having brought famine and pest, he was doomed to death; he wrote his farewell letter to his superior, gave his farewell dinner to his enemies, taking that opportunity to preach a farewell sermon concerning the Trinity, heaven and hell, angels and fiends—the only real things to him—and so wrought upon his guests that he was spared to labor on, though often in peril, until the Iroquois (1649), still following the Hurons, found him with a brother priest giving baptism and absolution to the savages dying in that last struggle this side of the Lakes against their ancient enemies. They tied him to a stake, hung a collar of "hatchets heated red-hot" about his neck, baptized him with boiling water, cut strips of flesh from his limbs, drank his blood as if to inherit of his valiance, and finally tore out and ate his heart for supreme courage. Such cannibalism seems poetically justifiable in tribute to such unflinching constancy of devotion.

His brother priest, Lalemant, who was tortured to death at the same time, had thought it no good omen ten years before (1639) that no martyr's blood had yet furnished seed for the church in that new soil, though consoling himself with the thought that the daily life amid abuse and threats, smoke, fleas, filth, and dogs might be "accepted as a living martyrdom." There was ample seed by now, and still more was soon to be added, for very soon, the same year, the gentle Garnier is to die the same death ministering to these same Hurons, whose refugees, flying beyond two lakes to escape from their murderous foes, are to lure the priests on still farther westward till, even in their unmundane thoughts, the great, mysterious river begins to flow toward a longed-for sea.

It was by such a path of danger and suffering, a path which threads gloomy forests, that the first figures clad in black gowns came and peered over the edge of the valley of this mysterious stream, even before Radisson and Groseilliers wandered in that wooded and wet and fertile peninsula which, beginning at the junction of three lakes, widens to include the whole northwest of what is now the United States. You may travel in a day and a night now up the Ottawa River, above Lake Nipissing, around Huron to the point of that peninsula, from Montreal, and if you go in the season of the year in which I once made the journey you will find this path (the path on which Champlain came near losing his life, where Récollet and Jesuit, coureur de bois and soldier toiled up hundreds of portages) bordered as a garden path much of the way by wild purple flowers (that doubtless grew red in the blood-sodden ground of the old Huron country), with here and there patches of gold.

The first of these was Father Raymbault and with him Father Isaac Jogues, who was later to knock with mutilated hands for shelter at the Jesuit college in Rennes. Jogues was born at Orleans; he was of as delicate mould as Garnier, modest and refined, but "so active that none of the Indians could surpass him in running." In the autumn of 1641 he stood with his companion at the end of the peninsula between the Lakes, their congregation to the number of two thousand having been gathered for them from all along the southern shore of Lake Superior, the land of the Chippewas. Father Raymbault died at Quebec from exposure and hardship encountered here, the first of the Christian martyrs on that field, and Jogues was soon after sent upon an errand of greater peril. While on his way from Quebec to the new field (the old Huron station) with wine for the eucharist, writing materials, and other spiritual and temporal supplies, he was captured by the Iroquois and with his companions subjected to such torture as even Brébeuf was not to know. Journeying from the place of his capture on the St. Lawrence to that of his protracted torture he, first of white men, saw the Lake Como of America which bears the name of "George," a king of England, instead of "Jogues," whom the holy church may honor with canonization, but who should rather be canonized by the hills and waters where he suffered. His fingers were lacerated by the savages before the journey was begun; up the Richelieu River he went, suffering from his wounds and "the clouds of mosquitoes." At the south end of Lake Champlain this gentle son of France was again subjected to special tortures for the gratification of another band of Iroquois; his hands were mangled, his body burned and beaten till he fell "drenched in blood." Where thousands now land every summer at the head of Lake George for pleasure he staggered forth under his portage burden to the shores of the Mohawk, where again the chief called the crowd to "caress" the Frenchmen with knives and other instruments of torture, the children imitating the barbarity of their elders. I should not repeat such details of this horrible story here except to give background to one moment's act in the midst of it all, illustrative of the motive which was back of this unexampled endurance. While he and his companions were on the scaffold of torture, four Huron prisoners were brought in and put beside the Frenchmen: whereupon Father Jogues began his ministry anew, for when an ear of green corn was thrown him for food, discovering a few rain-drops clinging to the husks, he secretly baptized two of his eleventh-hour converts.

This was not the end, but after months of pain and privation, which make one wonder at what a frail body, fitted with a delicate organism, can endure, he escaped by the aid of the Dutch at Fort Orange (now the capital of the State of New York), whither the Iroquois had gone to trade, and after six weeks in hiding there, was sent to New Amsterdam—then a "delapidated fort garrisoned by sixty soldiers" and a village of only four or five hundred inhabitants, but even at that time so cosmopolitan that, as one of my friends who has recently revived a census of that day shows, nearly twenty different languages were spoken.

It is thus that a little French father of the wilderness comes from a thousand miles behind the mountains, from the shores of the farthest lake, in the middle of the continent, at a time when New York and Boston had together scarcely more inhabitants than would fill a hall in the Sorbonne.

If only Richelieu (who died in the very year that Jogues was exemplifying so faithfully the teaching of Him whose brother he called himself) had permitted the Huguenot who wanted to go, to follow this little priest into those wilds, instead of trying in vain to persuade those to go who would not, who shall say that American visitors from that far interior might not be speaking to-day in a tongue which Richelieu, were he alive, could best understand.

The little father, who has always seemed to me an old man, though he was then only thirty-six, was carried back to England, suffering from nature and pirates almost as much as from the Iroquois, and at last reached Rennes, where, after his identity was disclosed, the night was given to jubilation and thanksgiving, we are told. He was summoned to Paris, where the queen "kissed his mutilated hands" and exclaimed: "People write romances for us—but was there ever a romance like this, and it is all true?" Others gladly did him honor. But all this gave no satisfaction to his soul bent upon one task, and as soon as the Pope, at the request of his friends, granted a special dispensation[1] which permitted him, though deformed by the "teeth

---

[1] The answer of Pope Urban VIII was: "Indignum esset martyrem Christi, Christi non bibere sanguinem."

and knives of the Iroquois," to say mass once more, he
returned to the wilderness where within a few months
the martyrdom was complete and his head was displayed from the palisades of a Mohawk town.

So vanished the face of the first priest of France
from the edge of the great valley, he, too, as Raymbault, perhaps, hoping "to reach China across the
wilderness" but finding his path "diverted to heaven."

It was not until 1660 that another came into that
peninsula at whose point Jogues had preached, the
aged Ménard, who after days among the tangled
swamps of northern Wisconsin was lost, and only his
cassock, breviary, and kettle were ever recovered. A
little later came Allouez and Dablon, and Druilletes
who had been entertained at Boston by Winslow and
Bradford and Dudley and John Eliot, and last of those
to be selected from the increasing number of that
brotherhood for mention, the young Père Marquette,
"son of an old and honorable family at Laon," of
extraordinary talents as a linguist (having learned, as
Parkman tells us, to speak with ease six Indian languages) and in devotion the "counterpart of Garnier
and Jogues." When he first appears in the west it is
at the mission of Pointe de St. Esprit, near the very
western end of Lake Superior. There he heard, from
the Illinois who yearly visited his mission, of the great
river they had crossed on their way, and from the
Sioux, who lived upon its banks, "of its marvels."
His desire to follow its course would seem to have been
greater than his interest in the more spiritual ends of
his mission, for he disappointedly, it is intimated, followed his little Huron flock suddenly driven back
toward the east by the Iroquois of the West—the

Sioux. At Point St. Ignace, a place midway between the two perils, the Sioux of the West and the Iroquois of the East, they huddled under his ministry.

It was there in the midst of his labors among his refugees, that Louis Joliet, the son of a wagon-maker of Quebec, a grandson of France, found him on the day, as he writes in his journal, of "the Immaculate Conception of the Holy Virgin, whom I had continually invoked since I came to this country of the Ottawas to obtain from God the favor of being enabled to visit the Nations on the river Missisipi." Joliet carried orders from Frontenac the governor and Talon the intendant, that Marquette should join him—or he Marquette—upon this voyage of discovery, so consonant with Marquette's desire for divine ordering. Marquette quieted his morbid conscience, which must have reproved his exploring ambitions, by reflecting upon the "happy necessity of exposing his life" for the salvation of all the tribes upon that particular river, and especially, he adds, as if to silence any possible lingering remonstrance, "the Illinois, who when I was at St. Esprit, had begged me very earnestly to bring the Word of God among them."

So the learned son of Laon and the practical son of the wagon-maker of Quebec set out westward upon their journey under the protection of Marquette's particular divinity, but provided by Joliet with supplies of smoked meat and Indian corn, and furnished with a map of their proposed route made up from rather hazy Indian data. Through the strait that leads into Lake Michigan, and along the shores of this wonderful western sea they crept, stopping at night for bivouac on shore; then up Green Bay to the old

mission; and then up the Fox River, where Nicolet had
gone, in his love not of souls but of mere adventure.
What interests one who has lived in that region, is to
hear the first word of praise of the prairies extending
farther than the eye can see, interspersed with groves
or with lofty trees.[1]

I have spoken of the little river, dwindling into a
creek of perplexed channel before the trail is found
that ties the two great valleys together.   One cannot
miss it now, for when I last passed over it it was being
paved, or macadamized, and a steam-roller was doing
in a few days what the moccasined or sandalled feet
of the first travellers there would not have accomplished in a thousand thousand years.   I shall speak
later of what has grown upon this narrow isthmus
(now crossed not merely by trail and highway, but
by canal as well), but I now must hasten on where
the impatient priest and his sturdy, practical companion are leading, toward the Wisconsin.

Nicolet may have put his boat in this same Wisconsin River, but if he did he did not go far below the
portage.   La Salle may even have walked over this
very path only a year or two before.   But, after all, it
is only a question as to which son of France it was, for
we know of a certainty that on a day in June of 1673
Joliet and Marquette did let their canoes yield to
the current of this broad, tranquil stream after their
days of paddling up the "stream of the wild rice."

I have walked in the wide valley of the Wisconsin
River and have seen through the haze of an Indian
summer day the same dim bluffs that Marquette
looked upon, and by night the light of the same stars

[1] "Jesuit Relations" (Thwaites), 59 : 103.

that Marquette saw reflected from its surface. But having never ridden upon its waters, I take the description of one who has followed its course more intimately if not more worshipfully. "They glided down the stream," he writes, "by islands choked with trees and matted with entangling grape-vines, by forests, groves and prairies, the parks and pleasure-grounds of a prodigal nature; by thickets and marshes and broad bare sand-bars; under the shadowing trees between whose tops looked down from afar the bold brow of some woody bluff. At night, the bivouac, the canoes inverted on the bank, the flickering fire, the meal of bison-flesh or venison, the evening pipes, and slumber beneath the stars; and when in the morning they embarked again, the mist hung on the river like a bridal veil, then melted before the sun, till the glassy water and the languid woods basked breathless in the sultry glare."[1]

But to those first voyagers it had a charm, a lure which was not of stars or shadows or wooded bluffs or companionable bivouac. It led to the great and the unknown river, which in turn led to a sea remote from that by which the French had come out of Europe into America. They were travelling over the edge of Champlain's map, away from Europe, away from Canada, away from the Great Lakes. As far as that trail which led through the grass and reeds up from the Fox, one might have come every league of the way from Havre or even from a quay of the Seine, by water, except for a few paces of portage at La Chine and at Niagara. But that narrow strip of prairie which they crossed that June day in 1673 was in a sense the coast

[1] Parkman, "La Salle," pp. 63 and 64.

of a new sea, they knew not what sea—or, better, it was
the rim of a new world.

On the 17th of June they entered the Mississippi
with a joy which they could not express, Marquette
naming it, according to his vow, in honor of the Virgin
Mary, Rivière de la Conception, and Joliet, with an
earthly diplomacy or gratitude, in honor of Frontenac,
"La Buade." For days they follow its mighty current southward through the land of the buffalo, but
without sight for sixty leagues of a human being,
where now its banks are lined with farms, villages, and
towns. At last they come upon footprints of men, and
following them up from the river they enter a beautiful prairie where a little way back from the river lay
three Indian villages.   There, after peaceful ceremonies and salutations, they, the first Frenchmen on
the farther bank, their fame having been carried westward from the missions on the shores of the lakes, were
received.

"I thank thee," said the sachem of the Illinois,
addressing them; "I thank thee, Black Gown, and thee,
O frenchman," addressing himself to Monsieur Jollyet,
"for having taken so much trouble to come to visit
us.   Never has the earth been so beautiful, or the sun
so Bright, as to-day; Never has our river been so Calm,
or so clear of rocks, which your canoes have Removed
in passing; never has our tobacco tasted so good, or
our corn appeared so fine, as We now see Them.   Here
is my son, whom I give thee to Show thee my Heart.
I beg thee to have pity on me, and on all my Nation.
It is thou who Knowest the great Spirit who has made
us all.   It is thou who speakest to Him, and who
hearest his word.   Beg Him to give me life and health,

and to come and dwell with us, in order to make us Know him."[1]

Knowing the linguistic attainments of Marquette and his sincerity, one must credit this first example of eloquence and poetry of the western Indians, cultivated of life amid the elemental forces of the water, earth, and sky.[2] A beautiful earth, sprinkled with flowers, a bright sun, a calm river free of rocks, sweet-flavored tobacco, thriving corn, an acquaintance with the Great Spirit—well might the old man who received the Frenchman say: "thou shalt enter all our cabins in peace."

Indian eloquence is not of the lips only. It is a poor Indian speech indeed that is not punctuated by gifts. And so it was that the French travellers resumed their journey laden with presents from their prairie hosts, and a slave to guide them, and a calumet to procure peace wherever they went.

It is enough now, perhaps, to know that the voyagers passed the mouth of the Illinois, the Missouri, the Ohio, and reached the mouth of the Arkansas, when thinking themselves near the gulf and fearing that they might fall into the hands of the Spaniards if they ventured too near the sea, and so be robbed of the fruits of their expedition, they turned their canoes up-stream. Instead, however, of following their old course they entered the Illinois River, known sometimes as the "Divine River." I borrow the observing father's description of that particular valley as it was just two centuries before I first remember seeing it. "We have seen nothing like this river for the fertility of the

---

[1] Jesuit Relations" (Thwaites), 59 : 121.

[2] It was of these same prairies, rivers, and skies, these same elemental ever-present forces, that Abraham Lincoln learned the simple, rugged eloquence that made him the most powerful soul that valley has known.

land, its prairies, woods, wild cattle, stag, deer, wild-cats, bustards, swans, ducks, parrots, and even beaver; its many little lakes and rivers."[1] Through this para-dise of plenty they passed, up one of the branches of the Illinois, till within a few miles of Lake Mich-igan, where they portaged a thousand paces to a creek that emptied into the lake of the Illinois.   If they were following that portage path and creek to-day they would be led through that city which stands next to Paris in population—the city of Chicago, in the commonwealth that bears the name of the land through which the French voyagers passed, "Il-linois."

At the end of September, having been absent four months, and having paddled their canoes over twenty-five hundred miles, they reached Green Bay again. There these two pioneers, companions forever in the history of the new world, separated—Joliet to bear the report of the discovery of the Rivière de Buade to Count Frontenac, Marquette to continue his devotions to his divinity and recruit his wasted strength, that he might keep his promise to return to minister to the Illinois, whom he speaks of as the most promising of tribes, for "to say 'Illinois' is in their language to say 'the men.'"

By most unhappy fate Joliet's canoe was upset in the Lachine Rapids, when almost within sight of Mon-treal, and all his papers, including his precious map, were lost in the foam.   But several maps were made under his direction or upon his data.

Marquette's map, showing nothing but their course

[1] B. F. French, "Historical Collections of Louisiana," 4 : 51.   "Jesuit Relations" (Thwaites), 59 : 161.

and supplying nothing from conjecture, was found
nearly two hundred years later in St. Mary's College
in Montreal, furnishing, I have thought, a theme and
design for a mural painting in the interesting halls of
the Sorbonne, where so many periods, personages, and
incidents of the world's history are worthily remembered. The art of that valley has sought to reproduce
or idealize the faces of these pioneers. The more elo-
quent, visible memorial would be the crude map from
the hand of the priest Jacques Marquette, son of Rose
de la Salle of the royal city of Rheims.

Of his setting out again for the Illinois, where he
purposed establishing a mission, of his spending the
winter, ill, in a hut on the Chicago portage path, of his
brief visit to the Illinois, of his journey northward, of
his death by the way, and of the Indian procession
that bore his bones up the lake to Point St. Ignace—of
all this I may not speak in this chapter.

Here let me say only the word of tribute that comes
to him out of his own time, as the first stories of history came, being handed down from generation to
generation by word of mouth, till a poet or a historian
should make them immortal. The story of Marquette
I had known for many years from the blind Parkman,
but not long ago I met one day an Indian boy, with
some French blood of the far past in his veins, the son
of a Chippewa chief, a youth who had never read
Parkman or Winsor but who knew the story of Marquette better than I, for his grandmother had told
him what she had heard from her grandmother, and
she in turn from her mother or grandmother, of listening to Marquette speak upon the shores of Superior, of going with other French and Indians on that

missionary journey to the Illinois to prepare food for him, and of hearing the mourning among the Indians when long after his death the report of his end reached their lodges.

The grim story of the labors of the followers of Loyola among the Indians has its beatific culmination in the life of this zealot and explorer. Pestilence and the Iroquois had ruined all the hopes of the Jesuits in the east. Their savage flocks were scattered, annihilated, driven farther in the fastnesses, or exiled upon islands. The shepherds who vainly followed their vanishing numbers found themselves out upon the edge of a new field. If the Iroquois east and west could have been curbed, the Jesuits would have become masters of that field and all the north. We shall, thinking of that contingency, take varying views, beyond reconciliation, as to the place of the Iroquois in American history; but we shall all agree, whatever our religious and political predilection, men of Old France and men of New France alike, in applauding the sublime disinterestedness, fearless zeal, and unquestioned devotion to something beyond the self, which have consecrated all that valley of the Lakes and have, in the person of Marquette, the son of Laon, made first claim upon the life of the valley, whose great water he helped to discover.

CHAPTER IV

FROM THE GREAT LAKES TO THE GULF

PÈRE MARQUETTE was still in a convent in Rheims when a French wood-ranger and fur trader was out in those western forests making friends for the French, one Sieur Nicolas Perrot, who would doubtless have been forgotten with many another of his craft if he had not been able—as few of them were—to read and write. And Marquette was but on his way from France to Canada when Sieur Perrot was ministering with beads and knives and hatchets and weapons of iron to these stone-age men on the southern shore of Superior, where the priest was later to minister with baptismal water and mysterious emblems. It was Perrot, whom they would often have worshipped as a god, who prepared the way for the altars of the priests and the forts of the captains; for back of the priests there were coming the brilliantly clad figures of the king's representatives. Once when Perrot was receiving such adoration, he told the simple-minded worshippers that he was "only a Frenchman, that the real Spirit who had made all, had given the French the knowledge of iron and the ability to handle it as if it were paste"; that out of "pity for His creatures He had permitted the French nation to settle in their country."[1] At another time he

[1] Emma H. Blair, "Indian Tribes of the Upper Mississippi Valley," I : 310.

said: "I am the dawn of that light, which is beginning to appear in your lands," and having learned by experience the true Indian eloquence, he proceeded in his oration with most impressive pauses: "It is for these young men I leave my gun, which they must regard as the pledge of my esteem for their valor. They must use it if they are attacked. It will also be more satisfactory in hunting cattle and other animals than are all the arrows that you use. To you who are old men I leave my kettle (pause); I carry it everywhere without fear of breaking it" (being of copper or iron instead of clay). "You will cook in it meat that your young men bring from the chase, and the food which you offer to the Frenchmen who come to visit you."[1] And so he went on, throwing iron awls to the women to be used instead of their bone bodkins, iron knives to take the place of pieces of stone in killing beavers and cutting their meat, till he reached his peroration, which was punctuated with handfuls of round beads for the adornment of their children and girls.

Do not think this a petty relation. It is a detail in the story of an age of iron succeeding, in a single generation, an age of stone. The splendor of the court and age of Louis XIV was beginning to brighten the sombreness of the northern primeval forests.

It is this ambassador Perrot, learned in the craft of the woods rather than in that of the courts, more effective in his forest diplomacy than an army with banners, who soon after (1671) appears again on those shores, summoning the nations to a convocation by the side of that northern tumultuous strait, known everywhere now as the "Soo," then as the Sault Ste.

[1] Blair, "Indian Tribes of the Upper Mississippi Valley," 1 : 330, 331.

Marie, there to meet the representatives of the king who lived across the water and of the Onontio who governed on the St. Lawrence.

This convocation, of which Perrot was the successful herald, was held in the beginning of summer in the year 1671 (the good fishing doubtless assisting the persuasiveness of Perrot's eloquence in procuring the great savage audience). When the fleets of canoes arrived from the west and the south and east, Daumont de St. Lusson and his French companions, sent out the previous autumn from Quebec, having wintered in the Mantoulin Island, were there to meet them. It is a picture for the Iliad. Coureur de bois and priest had penetrated these regions, as we have seen; but now was to take place the formal possession by the crown of a territory that was coming to be recognized as valuable in itself, even if no stream ran though it to the coasts that looked on Asia.

The scene is kept for us with much detail and color. On a beautiful June morning the procession was formed, the rapids probably furnishing the only music for the stately march of soldier and priest. After St. Lusson, four Jesuits led the processional: Dablon, Allouez, whom we have already seen on the shores of Superior, André from the Mantoulin Island, and Druilletes; the last, familiar from his long visit at Plymouth and Boston with the character of the Puritan colonies and doubtless understanding as no one else in that company, the menace to the French of English sturdiness and industry and self-reliant freedom. He must have wondered in the midst of all that formal vaunt of possession, how long the mountains would hold back those who were building permanent

bridges over streams, instead of traversing them in
ephemeral interest, or as paths to waters beyond; who
were working the iron of the bogs near by, instead of
hunting for the more precious ores or metals on remote
shores; who were sawing the trees into lumber for
permanent homes and shops, instead of adapting themselves to the more primitive life and barter in the woods;
who were getting riches from the cleared fields, instead
of from the backs of beavers in the sunless forests; who
were raising sheep and multiplying cattle, instead of
hunting deer and buffaloes; who were beginning to trade
with European ports not as mere voyageurs but as
thrifty merchants; who were vitally concerned about
their own salvation first, and then interested in the
fate of the savage; and who, above all, were learning
in town meetings to govern themselves, instead of
having all their daily living regulated from Versailles
or the Louvre. Druilletes, remembering New England
that day, must have wondered as to the future of this
unpeopled, uncultivated empire of New France, without ploughs, without tame animals, without people,
even, which St. Lusson was proclaiming.[1] Was its
name indeed to be written only in the water which
their canoes traversed ?

   There were fifteen Frenchmen with St. Lusson,
among them the quiet, practical, unboastful Joliet,
trained for the priesthood, but turned trader and explorer, who had already been two years previous out
on the shores of Superior looking for copper. Marquette was not with the priests but was urging on the
reluctant Hurons and Ottawas who did not arrive
until after the ceremony.

[1] See Justin Winsor "Pageant of St. Lusson," 1892.

The French were grouped about a cross on the top of a knoll near the rapids, and the great throng of savages, "many-tinted" and adorned in the mode of the forest, sat or stood in wider circle. Father Dablon sanctified a great wooden cross. It was raised to its place while the inner circle sang *Vexilla Regis*. Close to the cross a post bearing a plate inscribed with the royal arms, sent out by Colbert, was erected, and the woods heard the *Exaudiat* chanted while a priest said a prayer for the king. Then St. Lusson (a sword in one hand and "crumbling turf in the other") cried to his French followers who applauded his sentences, to the savages who could not understand, to the rapids which would not heed, and to the forests which have long forgotten the vibrations of his voice, the words in French to which these words in English correspond:

"'In the name of the most high, most mighty and most redoubtable monarch Louis, the XIVth of the name, most Christian King of France and Navarre, we take possession of the said place of Ste Mary of the Falls as well as of Lakes Huron and Supérieur, the Island of Caientoton and of all other Countries, rivers, lakes and tributaries, contiguous and adjacent thereunto, as well discovered as to be discovered, which are bounded on the one side by the Northern and Western Seas and on the other side by the South Sea, including all its length or breadth;' Raising at each of the said three times a sod of earth whilst crying Vive le Roy, and making the whole of the assembly as well French as Indians repeat the same; declaring to the aforesaid Nations that henceforward as from this moment they were dependent on his Majesty, subject to be controlled by his laws and to follow his customs, promising them all protection and succor on his part against the incursion or invasion of their enemies, declaring unto all other Potentates, Princes and Sovereigns, States and Republics, to them and their subjects, that they cannot or ought not seize on, or settle in, any places in said Country, except with the good pleasure of his said most Christian Majesty and of him who will govern the Country in his behalf, on pain of incurring his hatred and the effects of his arms; and in order that no one plead cause of ignorance, we have attached to the back the Arms of France thus much of the present our Minute of the taking possession."[1]

Then the priest Allouez (as reported by his brother priest Dablon), after speaking of the significance of the cross they had just raised, told them of the great temporal king of France, of him whom men came from every quarter of the earth to admire, and by whom all that was done to the world was decided.

"But look likewise at that other post, to which are affixed the armorial bearings of the great Captain of France whom we call King. He lives beyond the sea; he is the Captain of the greatest Captains, and has not his equal in the world. All the Captains you have ever seen, or of whom you have ever heard, are mere children compared with him. He is like a great tree, and they, only like little plants that we tread under foot in walking. You know about Onnontio, that famous Captain of Quebec. You know and feel that he is the terror of the Iroquois, and that his very name makes them tremble, now that he has laid waste their country and set fire to their Villages. Beyond the sea there are ten thousand Onnontios like him,

[1] "Wisconsin Historical Collections," 11 : 28.

who are only the Soldiers of that great Captain, our Great King, of whom I am speaking. When he says, 'I am going to war,' all obey him; and those ten thousand Captains raise Companies of a hundred soldiers each, both on sea and on land. Some embark in ships, one or two hundred in number, like those that you have seen at Quebec. Your Canoes hold only four or five men—or, at the very most, ten or twelve. Our ships in France hold four or five hundred, and even as many as a thousand. Other men make war by land, but in such vast numbers that, if drawn up in a double file, they would extend farther than from here to Mississaquenk, although the distance exceeds twenty leagues. When he attacks, he is more terrible than the thunder: the earth trembles, the air and the sea are set on fire by the discharge of his Cannon; while he has been seen amid his squadrons, all covered with the blood of his foes, of whom he has slain so many with his sword that he does not count their scalps, but the rivers of blood which he sets flowing. So many prisoners of war does he lead away that he makes no account of them, letting them go about whither they will, to show that he does not fear them. No one now dares make war upon him, all nations beyond the sea having most submissively sued for peace. From all parts of the world people go to listen to his words and to admire him, and he alone decides all the affairs of the world. What shall I say of his wealth? You count yourselves rich when you have ten or twelve sacks of corn, some hatchets, glass beads, kettles, or other things of that sort. He has towns of his own, more in number than you have people in all these countries five hundred leagues around; while in each town there are warehouses containing enough hatchets to cut down all your forests, kettles to cook all your moose, and glass beads to fill all your cabins. His house is longer than from here to the head of the Sault"—that is, more than half a league—"and higher than the tallest of your trees; and it contains more families than the largest of your Villages can hold."[1]

This remarkable proclamation and this extraordinary speech are to be found in the records. And the historian would end the incident here. But one may at least wonder what impressions of Louis the Great and Paris and France these savages carried back to their lodges to ponder over and talk about in the winter nights; and one must wonder, too, what impression the proclamation and pantomime of possession made upon their primitive minds. Perrot translated the proclamation for them, and asked them to repeat "Long live the king!" but it must have been a free translation that he made into their idioms; he must have softened "vassals" to "children," and "king" to "father," and made them understand that the laws and customs of Versailles would not curb their freedom of coiffure or attire, of chase or of leisure, on the shores of Superior.

The speech of Allouez may seem full of hyperbole to those who know, in history, the king, and, by sight, the palace employed in the priest's similes; but if we think of Louis XIV not in his person but as a representative of the civilization of Europe that was asserting its first claim there in the wilderness, and give to the word of the priest something of the import of prophecy, the address becomes mild, indeed. Through those very rapids a single fleet of boats carries every year enough iron ore to supply every man, woman, and child in the United States (97,000,000) with a new iron kettle every year; another fleet bears enough to meet the continent's, if not the world's, need of hatchets. Trains laden with golden grain, more precious than beads, trains that would encircle the palace at Versailles or the Louvre now cross that narrow strait every day. A track of iron, bearing the abbreviated name of the rapids and the mission, penetrates the forests and swamps from which that savage congregation was gathered in the first great non-religious convocation on the shores of the western lakes where men with the scholarship of the Sorbonne now march every year with emblems of learning on their shoulders.

As to the proclamation, Parkman asks, what now remains of the sovereignty it so pompously announced? "Now and then," he answers, "the accents of France on the lips of some straggling boatman, or vagabond half-breed—this and nothing more."

But again I would ask you to think of St. Lusson not as proclaiming merely the sovereignty of Louis XIV or of France, but as heralding the new civilization, for if we are to appreciate the real significance of that pageant and of France's mission, we must associate with that day's ceremony, not merely the subsequent wanderings of a few men of French birth or ancestry in all those "countries, rivers, lakes and streams," "bounded on the one side by the seas of the north and west and on the other by the South Sea," but all that life to which they led the adventurous, perilous way.

The Iroquois and disease had thinned the Indian

populations of the northeast, but here was a new and a friendly menace to that stone-age barbarism whose dusky subjects found their way back to their haunts by the stars, lighted their fires by their flint, and gluttonously feasted in plenty, or stoically fasted in famine.

For the French it was a challenge to "those countries, lakes and islands bounded by the seas." They must now "make good the grandeur of their hopes." And a brave beginning is soon to be made. This highly colored scene becomes frontispiece of another glorious chapter, in the midst of whose hardship one will turn many a time to look with a sneer or smile, or with pity, at the figures in court garments, burnished armor, and "cleansed vestments," standing where the east and the west and the far north and the south meet.

From the shores of a seigniory on the St. Lawrence, eight or nine miles from Montreal, just above those hoarse-voiced, mocking rapids which had lured and disappointed Cartier and Champlain and Maisonneuve, and which were to get their lasting name of derision from the disappointment of the man who now (1668) stands there, Robert René Cavelier, Sieur de la Salle, looks across the waters of Lake St. Louis (into which the St. Lawrence for a little way widens) to the "dim forests of Chateauguay and Beauharnois." His thoughts look still farther, for they are out in that valley of his imagination through which a river "must needs flow," as he thinks, "into the 'Vermilion Sea' " —the Gulf of California. The old possessing dream!

This young man (but twenty-five years of age) was a scion of an old and rich family of Rouen. As a youth he showed unusual traits of intellect and character and

(it is generally agreed) doubtless because of his promise, he was led to the benches of the Jesuits. Whether
this be true or not, he was an earnest Catholic. But
his temperament would not let him yield unquestioned
submission to any will save his own. For it was will
and not mere passion that mastered his course. "In
his faults," says a sympathetic historian, "the love of
pleasure had no part." At twenty-three he had left
Rouen, and securing a seigniory, where we have just
seen him, in the "most dangerous place in Canada,"
he made clearing for the settlement which he named
the Seigniory of St. Sulpice (having received it from the
seminary of St. Sulpice), but which his enemies named,
as they named the rapids, "La Chine."

There tutored in the Indian languages and inflamed
of imagination as he looked day after day off to the
west, his thoughts "made alliance with the sun," as
Lescarbot would have said, and dwelt on exploration
and empire.

It was ten years later that those who were keeping
the mission and the trading-post on Point St. Ignace,
where to-day candles burn before the portrait of Père
Marquette, saw a vessel equipped with sails, as large
as the ships with which Jacques Cartier first crossed the
Atlantic, come ploughing its way through waters that
had never before borne such burdens without the
beating of oars or paddles. Its commander is Sieur
de la Salle, now a noble and possessed of a seigniory
two hundred miles west of that on which we left him
—two hundred miles nearer his goal. This galleon,
called the *Griffin* because it carried on its prow the
carving of a griffin, "in honor of the armorial bearings
of Count Frontenac," was the precursor of those

mighty fleets that now stir those waters with their commerce.

These ten years of disaster and disappointment, but also of inflexible purpose and indomitable persistence, must not be left to lie unremembered, though the recital must be the briefest. In 1669, in company with some Sulpitian priests and others, twenty-four in all, he sets forth from his seigniory. Along the south shore of Ontario they coast, stopping on the way to visit the Senecas, La Salle, at least, hoping to find there a guide to the headwaters of what is now known as the Ohio River. Disappointed, he with them journeyed on westward past the mouth of the Niagara River, hearing but the sound of the mighty cataract. At the head of Lake Ontario they have the astounding fortune to meet Louis Joliet, who with a companion was returning from Superior (two years before the pageant of St. Lusson) and who had just discovered that great inland lake between the two lakes, Ontario and Huron (which had been shown on French maps as connected by a river only). This lake, Erie, now the busiest perhaps of all that great chain, had been avoided because of the hostility of the Iroquois, and so it was that it was last to rise out of the geographic darkness of that region. Even Joliet's Iroquois guide, although well acquainted with the easier route, had not dared to go to the Niagara outlet but had followed the Grand River from its northern shores and then portaged to Lake Ontario.

The Sulpitian priests and their companions followed to the west the newly found course, but La Salle, the goal of whose thought was still the Ohio, feigning illness (as it is believed), received the sacrament from the priests (an altar being improvised of some paddles), parted from them, and, as they at the time supposed, went back to Montreal. But it was not of such fibre that his purposes were knit. Just where he went it is not with certainty known, but it is generally conceded that he reached and followed the Ohio as far at least as the site of Louisville, Ky. It is claimed by some that he coasted the unknown western shores of Lake Huron; that he reached the site of Chicago; and that he even saw the Mississippi two years at least before Marquette and Joliet. What Parkman says in his later edition, after full and critical acquaintance with the Margry papers in Paris, is this: "La Salle discovered the Ohio, and in all probability the Illinois also; but that he discovered the Mississippi has not been proved, nor, in the light of the evidence we have, is it likely." Winsor argues that in the minds of those who knew him in Montreal, La Salle's projects had failed, since it was then that the mocking name was given to his estate— a name which, by the way, has been made good, as some one remarks, "by the passage across La Salle's old possessions of the Canadian Pacific Railway," a new way to China.

I think we must admit, with his enemies of that day and hostile authorities of this, despite Margry's documents, that except for his increased knowledge of the approaches and his acquaintance with Indians and the conditions of nature in that valley, La Salle's expedition was a failure. It was his first defiance of the wilderness before him and the first victory of his enemies behind him.

While Marquette is spending the winter, sick of a mortal illness, in the hut on the Chicago portage, La

Salle is in Paris, bearing a letter from Frontenac, in which he is recommended to Minister Colbert as "the most capable man I know to carry on every kind of enterprise and discovery" and as having "the most perfect knowledge of the state of the country,"[1] that is, of the west. A letter I find was sent to Colbert under the same or proximate date[2] acquainting Colbert with the discovery made by Joliet. La Salle must therefore have known of the Mississippi and its course, even if he himself had not beheld it with his own eyes or felt the impulse of its current.

He goes back to Canada possessed of a new and valuable seigniory (having spent the proceeds of the first in his unsuccessful venture) under charge to garrison Fort Frontenac (on the north shore of Ontario) and to gather about it a French colony. For two years he labors there, bringing a hundred acres of sunlight into the forests, building ships for the navigation of the lake, and establishing a school under the direction of the friars. He might have stayed there and become rich "if he had preferred gain to glory"—there where he had both solitude and power. "Feudal lord of the forest around him, commander of a garrison raised and paid by himself, founder of the mission and patron of the church, he reigned the autocrat of his lonely little empire." But this does not satisfy him. It is but a step toward the greater empire still farther to the west.

In 1677 he comes back again to Paris with a desire not for land, but for authority to explore and open up the western country, which he describes in a letter to

---

[1] Margry, "Découvertes et établissements des Français," I : 227.
[2] Winsor dates letter November 14, 1674. Margry, November 11.

Colbert. It is nearly all "so beautiful and fertile; so free from forests and so full of meadows, brooks and rivers; so abounding in fish, game, and venison that one can find there in plenty, and with little trouble, all that is needful for the support of powerful colonies. The soil will produce anything that is raised in France."[1] He says that cattle may be left out all winter, calls attention to some hides he has brought with him of cattle whose wool is also valuable, and again expresses confidence that colonies would become prosperous, especially as they would be increased by the tractable Indians, who will readily adapt themselves to the French way of life, as soon as they taste the advantages of French friendship. He does not fail to mention the hostility of the Iroquois and the threatened rivalry of the English, who are beginning to covet that country —all of which only animates him the more to action. Lodged in Paris in an obscure street, Rue de la Truanderie, and attacked as a visionary or worse, he is yet petitioning Louis XIV for the government of a realm larger than the king's own, and holding conference with Colbert.

In the early summer, after his winter of waiting somewhere in the vicinity in which I have written this chapter, a patent comes to him from the summer palace at St.-Germain-en-Laye, which must have been to him far more than his patent of nobility or title to any estate in France:

"Louis, by the grace of God King of France and Navarre, to our dear and well-beloved Robert Cavelier, Sieur de la Salle, greeting. We have received with favor the very humble petition made us in your name

[1]Parkman, "La Salle," p. 122. Margry, 1 : 331.

to permit you to undertake the discovery of the western parts of New France; and we have the more willingly consented to this proposal, since we have nothing more at heart than the exploration of this country, through which, to all appearances, a way may be found to Mexico."[1] La Salle, accordingly, was permitted to build forts at his own expense, to carry on certain trade in buffalo-hides, and explore to his heart's content.

This lodger in Rue de la Truanderie now sets about raising funds for his enterprise and, having succeeded chiefly among his brothers and relations, he gathers materials for two vessels, hires shipwrights, and starts from Rochelle for his empire, his commission doubtless bound to his body, taking with him as his lieutenant Henri de Tonty—son of the inventor of the Tontine form of life insurance who had come to France from Naples—a most valuable and faithful associate and possessed of an intrepid soul to match his own.

From Fort Frontenac, an outpost, La Salle's company pushes out to build a fort below Niagara Falls near the mouth of the Niagara River, the key to the four great lakes above, and to construct a vessel of fifty tons above the Falls for the navigation of these upper lakes. It is on this journey that the world makes first acquaintance of that mendacious historian Friar Hennepin, who, equipped with a portable altar, ministered to his companions and the savages along the way and wrote the chronicles of the expedition. It is he who has left us the first picture of Niagara Falls unprofaned by tourists; of the buffalo, now extinct except for a few scrawny specimens in parks, and of

---

[1] Various translations.   Original in Margry, 1 : 337.

St. Anthony Falls. After loss by wreck of a part of
the material intended for the vessel and repeated de-
lays, due to La Salle's creditors at Frontenac and the
Indians on his way, the vessel was at last completed,
launched with proper ceremonies, and started on her
maiden trip up those lakes where sail was never seen
before.

It is this ship that found temporary haven in the
cove back of Point St. Ignace in 1679 while La Salle,
"very finely dressed in his scarlet cloak trimmed with
gold lace," knelt, his companions about him, and again
heard mass where the bones of Marquette were doubtless even then gathered before the Jesuit altar. Thence
they pushed on to Green Bay, where some of his advance agents had gathered peltries for his coming. The
Griffin, loaded with these, her first and precious cargo,
was sent back to satisfy his creditors, and La Salle
with fourteen men put forth in their canoes for the
land of his commission, of "buffalo-hides," and of
"the way toward Mexico."

I will "make the *Griffin* fly above the crows," La
Salle is recorded to have said more than once in his
threat toward those of the Black Gowns who were
opposing his imperious plans, because they aimed at the
occupation, fortification, and settlement of what the
order still hoped to keep for itself. But the flight of
this aquatic griffin gave to La Salle no good omen of
triumph. The vessel never reached safe port, so far
as is known. Tonty searched all the east coast of Lake
Michigan for sight of her sail, but in vain. And those
whom in America we call "researchers"—those who
hunt through manuscripts in libraries—have not as
yet had word of her. Many have doubtless walked,

as I, the shores of that lake with thoughts of her, but
no one has found so much as a feather of her pinions.
Whether she foundered in a storm or was treacherously
sunk and her cargo stolen, no one will probably ever
know.

La Salle and his men in their heavily laden canoes
had a tempestuous voyage up the west shore of Lake
Michigan.[1] They passed the site of Chicago, deciding
upon another course (which persuades me that La
Salle must have been in that region before) and on
till they reached the mouth of the St. Joseph River,
where precious time was lost in waiting for Tonty
and his party coming up the other shore. I take space
to speak in such detail of this voyage because it traces
another important route into the valley.

About seventy miles up the stream there stands an
old cedar-tree bearing, as it is believed by antiqua-
rians, the blaze marks of the old French broadaxes
and marking the beginning of another of those historic
portage paths over the valley's low rim. I have visited
this portage more than once, and when last there I
dug away the sand and soil about the trunk of the
tree till I could trace the scar left by the axe of the
French. It is only about two miles from this tree at
the bend of the St. Joseph to where a mere ditch in the
midst of the prairie, a tributary of the Illinois, soon
gathers enough eager water to carry a canoe toward the
Gulf of Mexico.

[1] It will illustrate what a change has come over a bit of that shore along
which he passed if I tell you that when I landed there one day from a later
lake *Griffin*, at a place called Milwaukee—in La Salle's day but another
"nameless barbarism"—the first person whom I encountered chanced to
be reading a copy of the *London Spectator*—the ultimate symbol of civilization some would think it.

I have read in the chronicles, with a regret as great as that of the hungry Hennepin, that the Illinois, from whom La Salle expected hospitality at their village farther down the Illinois River, which had been visited by Marquette twice, were off on their hunting expeditions. But I have satisfaction in knowing that he took needful food from their caches in my own county, now named La Salle.

Early in January they passed on to a village four days beyond—the site of the second largest city in the State of Illinois. There La Salle, detained by Indian suspicions of his alliance with the Iroquois, discouraged by the desertion of some of his own men and by the certainty that the *Griffin* was lost beyond all question not only with its skins but with the materials for a vessel, which he purposed building for the Mississippi waters, stayed for the rest of the winter, building for shelter and protection a fort which he named Fort Crèvecœur, not to memorialize his own disheartenments as some hint, but, as we are assured by other historians, to celebrate the demolition of Fort Crèvecœur in the Netherlands by Louis XIV, in which Tonty had participated. The vessel for the Mississippi he bravely decides to build despite the desertion of his sawyers, who had fled to the embrace of barbarism and who, fortunately, did not return to prevent the employment of the unskilled hands of La Salle himself and some others of his men. And so the first settlement in Illinois begins.

On the last day of February Father Hennepin and two associates were sent down the Illinois River on a voyage of exploration, carrying abundant gifts with which to make addresses to the Indians along the way.

We may not follow their tribulations and experiences, but we have reason to believe that they reached the upper waters of the Mississippi. There, taken by the Sioux, they were in humiliating and even perilous captivity till rescued by the aid of Du Lhut. We almost wish that the rumor that Hennepin had been hung by his own waist-cord had been true, if only we could have had his first book without the second.

On the next day La Salle, leaving Tonty in command, set out amid the drifting ice of the river with four or perhaps six[1] men and a guide for Fort Frontenac, to replace at once the articles lost in the *Griffin*, else another year would be spent in vain. Having walked many, many miles along that particular river on those prairies, I can appreciate, as perhaps some readers cannot, what it means to enter upon a journey of a thousand miles when the "ground is oozy" and patches of snow lie about, and the ice is not strong enough to bear one's weight but thick enough to hinder one's progress. La Salle, moreover, was in constant danger of Indians of various tribes. In a letter to a friend he said that though he knew that they must suffer all the time from hunger, sleep on the open ground, and often without food, watch by night and march by day, loaded with baggage, sometimes pushing through thickets, sometimes wading whole days through marshes where the water was waist-deep; still he was resolved to go. Two of the men fell ill. A canoe was made for them and the journey continued. Two men were sent to Point St. Ignace to learn if any news had come of the *Griffin*. At Niagara, where he learned of further misfortune, he left the other two Frenchmen and the

[1] Margry, I : 488.

faithful Mohigan Indian as unfit for further travel and
pushed on with three fresh men to Fort Frontenac,
which he reached in sixty-five days from the day of
his starting from Fort Crèvecœur. This gives intimation and illustration of the will which possessed the
body of this "man of thought, trained amid arts and
letters." "In him," said the Puritan Parkman, "an
unconquerable mind held at its service a frame of
iron." And Fiske adds: "We may see here how the
sustaining power of wide-ranging thoughts and a lofty
purpose enabled the scholar, reared in luxury, to surpass in endurance the Indian guide and the hunter in-
ured to the hardships of the forest." I have wondered
how his petition to the king, if written after this journey, would have described this valley. But its attraction seems not to be less despite this experience,
for he was setting forth again, when word came to
him that his Fort Crèvecœur had been destroyed,
most of his men deserting and throwing into the river
the stores and goods they could not carry away!

All has to be begun again. Less than nothing is
left to him of all his capital. Nothing is left except
his own inflexible spirit and the loyalty of his Tonty
in the heart of the wilderness. Still undismayed, he
turns his hand to the giant task again, only to find
when he reaches the Illinois a dread foreboding of the
crowning disaster. The Iroquois, the scourge of the
east, had swept down the valley of the Illinois like
hyenas of the prairies, leaving total desolation in their
path. After a vain, anxious search for Tonty among the
ruins and the dead, he makes his way back, finding at
last at the junction of the two rivers that make the
Illinois a bit of wood cut by a saw.

I fear to tire the reader with the monotony of the mere rehearsal of difficulty and discouragement and despairful circumstance which I feel it needful to present in order to give faithful background to the story of the valley. I have by no means told all: of continued malevolence where there should have been help; of the conspiracy of every possible untoward circumstance to block his way. But the telling of so much will be tolerated in the knowledge that, after all, his master spirit did triumph over every ill and obstacle. With Tonty, who, as he writes, is full of zeal, he confounded his enemies at home, gathered the tribes of the west into a confederacy against the Iroquois, as Champlain had done in the east, gave up for the present the building of the vessel, and in 1681, the river being frozen, set out on sledges at Chicago portage and made a prosperous journey down the Illinois to Fort Crève-cœur. Re-embarking in his canoes, they paddled noise-lessly past tenantless villages into the Mississippi. He went beyond the mouth of the Arkansas, reached by Joliet and Marquette; he was entertained by the Indians of whom Châteaubriand has written with such charm in his "Atala"; and at last, in April, 1682, fifteen years from the days that he looked longingly from his seigniory above the Lachine Rapids, he found the "brackish water changed to brine," the salt breath of the sea touched his face, and the "broad bosom of the great gulf opened on his sight—limitless, voice-less, lonely as when born of chaos, without a sail, with-out a sign of life."

His French companions and his great company of Indians about him, he repeated there, in the subtropi-cal spring, the ceremony which ten years before had been performed two thousand miles and more by the water to the north, but in phrases which his inflexible purpose, valorously pursued, had given him a greater right to pronounce. "In the name of the most high, mighty, invincible and victorious prince, Louis the Great—I,—in virtue of the commission of his majesty which I hold in my hand, and which may be seen by all whom it may concern, have taken and do now take, in the name of his Majesty—possession of this country of Louisiana, the seas, harbors, ports, bays, adjacent straits, and all nations, peoples, provinces, cities, towns, villages, mines, minerals, fisheries, streams, and rivers, —from the mouth of the great river St. Louis, otherwise called the Ohio,—as also along the river Colbert, or Mississippi, and the rivers which discharge themselves thereinto, from its source beyond the Nadouessioux—as far as its mouth at the sea, or Gulf of Mexico, and also to the mouth of the River of Palms, upon the assurance we have had from the natives of these countries, that we are the first Europeans who have descended or ascended the river Colbert."[1]

None could have remembered the emaciated followers of De Soto, who cared not for the land since they had found no gold there and asked only to be carried back to the sea, whence they had so foolishly wandered. There were probably not even traditions of the white god who had a century and a half before been buried in the river that his mortality might be concealed. It was, indeed, a French river, from where Hennepin had been captured by the Sioux through the stretches covered by Marquette and Joliet to the very sea which La Salle had at last touched. The

---

[1] Margry, 2 : 191.

water path from Belle Isle, Labrador, to the Gulf of
Mexico was open, with only short portages at Lachine and Niagara and of a few paces where the Fox
all but touches the Wisconsin, the Chicago the Des
Plaines, or the St. Joseph the Kankakee. It took almost a century and a half to open that way, but every
league of it was pioneered by the French, and if not for
the French forever, is the credit the less theirs?

When the "weathered voyagers" that day on the
edge of the gulf planted the cross, inscribed the arms
of France upon a tree, buried a leaden plate of possession in the earth and sang to the skies "The banners of
heaven's king advance," La Salle in a loud voice read
the proclamation which I have in part repeated. Thus
"a feeble human voice, inaudible at half a mile,"[1] in
fact gave to France a river and a stupendous territory,
of which Parkman has made this description for the
title-deed: "The fertile plains of Texas, the vast basin
of the Mississippi, from its frozen springs to the sultry
borders of the gulf; from the wooded ridges of the
Alleghanies to the bare peaks of the Rocky Mountains
—a region of savannas and forests, sun-cracked deserts,
and grassy prairies, watered by a thousand rivers,
ranged by a thousand warlike tribes."[1] They gave it
to France. That, perhaps, the people of France almost
wish to forget. But it is better and more accurately
written: "On that day France, pioneer among nations,
gave this rich, wide region to the world."

[1] Parkman, "La Salle," p. 308.

CHAPTER V

THE RIVER COLBERT: A COURSE AND SCENE OF EMPIRE

A CHARACTERIZATION OF THE RIVER WHOSE EXPLORA-
TION AND CONTROL GAVE TO FRANCE LOUISIANA
AND THE LAND OF THE ILLINOIS

TO the red barbarian tribes, of which Parkman says there were a thousand, the river which passed through their valley was the "Mississippi," that is, the Great Water. They must have named it so under the compulsion of the awe in which they stood of some parts of it, and not from any knowledge of its length. They must have been impressed, especially they of the lower valley, as is the white man of to-day, by the "overwhelming, unbending grandeur of the wonderful spirit ruling the flow of the sands, the lumping of the banks, the unceasing shifting of the channel and the send of the mighty flood." No one tribe knew both its fountains and its delta, its sources and its mouth. To those midway of the valley it came out of the mystery of the Land of Frosts and passed silently on, or, in places, complainingly on, to the mystery of the Land of the Sun, into neither of which dared they penetrate because of hostile tribes. While the red men of the Mississippi lowlands were not able as the "swamp angel" of to-day to discern the rising of its Red River tributary by the reddish tinge of the water in his particular bayou, or to measure by changing hues, now the impulses of the Wisconsin or of the Ohio, and now of the richer-silted blood of the Rockies (as Mr. Raymond S. Spears, writing of the river, has graphically described),[1] yet as they gazed with wonderment at these changes of color, they must have had inward visions of hills of red, green, and blue earth somewhere above their own lodges or hunting-grounds, and must even have had at times some tangible message of their brothers of the upper waters, some fragments of their handiwork, such as a broken canoe, an arrow-shaft. But the men of the sources, up toward the "swamps of the nests of the eagles," on the low watersheds, heard only vague reports of the sea or gulf; even the Indians of Arkansas, as we read in the account of the De Soto expedition, could or would "give no account of the sea, and had no word in their language, or idea or emblem, that could make them comprehend a great expanse of salt water like the ocean."

So the river was not the source or father of running waters, but the great, awe-inspiring water. The French were misled, as we have seen, when they first heard Indian references to it, thinking it was what they were longing for—the western ocean, a great stretch of salt water instead of another and a larger Seine. And when they did discover that it was a river, their first concern was not as to what lay along its course, but as to where it led.

A prominent American historian, to whom we are

---

[1] "The Moods of the Mississippi," in *Atlantic Monthly*, 102 : 378–382. See also his "Camping on a Great River," New York, Harper, 1912, and numerous magazine articles.

much indebted, with Parkman, for the memorials of this period, praises by contrast those who kept within smell of tide-water along the Atlantic shore. But when we reach the underlying motives of the exploration and settlement of that continent, do they who sought the sources and the paths to the smell of other tide-waters deserve dispraise or less praise than those who sat thriftily by the Atlantic seashore?

The English colonists were struggling for themselves and theirs, not for the good or glory of a country across seas. They had no reason to look beyond their short rivers, so long as their valleys were fruitful and ample. Shall they be praised the more that they did not for a century venture beyond the sources of those streams? The first French followers of the river courses were, as we have seen, devotees of a religion for the salvation of others, bearers of advancing banners for the glory of France, and lovers of nature and adventure. And if there were, as there were, avaricious men among them, we must be careful not to blame them more than those whose avarice or excessive thrift was economically more beneficial to the world and to the community and the colony and to themselves. Economic values and moral virtues, as expressed in productivity of fields, mines, factories, church attendance, and obedience to the selectmen, are so easy of assessment that it is difficult to get just appraisement for those who endured everything, not for their own freedom or gain but for others' glory, and accomplished so little that could be measured in the terms of substantial, visible, tangible, economic, or ecclesiastical progress.

Who first of Europeans looked upon this river at the gulf we do not know, but on a Ptolemy map, published

in Venice in 1513, it is thought by some that the delta
is traced with distinctness, as less distinctly in Waldseemüller's map of 1507. Five years later (1518) on
Garay's map of Alvarez de Pineda's explorations, there
descends into the gulf a sourceless river, the Rio del
Espiritu Santo, which is thought by some to be the
same river that Marquette's map showed under the
name de la Conception, ending its course in the midst
of the continent; but it is more generally thought now
to be the Mobile River, and the Gulf del Espiritu Santo
to be the Bay of Mobile. Narvaez, as I have said,
tried a score of years after to enter the Mississippi,
but he was carried out to sea in his flimsy improvised
craft, by its resisting current. Cabeça de Vaca may have
seen it again after he left Narvaez, but we have no
record in his narrative that distinguishes it from any
other river. Then came the accredited discoverer De
Soto, who found it but another obstacle in his gold-
seeking path toward the Ozarks and who found it
his grave on his harassed, disappointed journey back
toward Florida.

It was more than a hundred years after "it pleased
God that the flood should rise," as the chronicle has it,
and carry the brigantines built by De Soto's lieutenant,
Moscoso, with his emaciated followers "down the
Great River to the opening gulf," before another white
face looked upon this great water. It was in 1543
that Moscoso and his men disappeared, sped on their
voyage by the arrows of the aborigines. It was a June
day in 1673 that Marquette and Joliet, coming down
the Wisconsin from Green Bay, saw before them,
"avec une joye que je ne peux pas expliquer," the slow,
gentle-currented Mississippi; or, as Mark Twain has

measured the time in a chronology of his own: "After
De Soto glimpsed the river, a fraction short of a
quarter of a century elapsed, and then Shakespeare was
born, lived a trifle more than a half a century,—then
died; and when he had been in his grave considerably
more than half a century, the second white man saw
the Mississippi."[1]

In 1682 La Salle followed it to where it meets the
great gulf, possessing with emblems of empire and his
indomitable spirit the lower reaches of the stream
whose upper waters had first been touched by the
gentle Marquette and the practical Joliet and the vainglorious Hennepin. Between that day and the time
when it became a course of regular and active commerce (again in Mark Twain's chronology), "seven
sovereigns had occupied the throne of England, America had become an independent nation, Louis XIV
and Louis XV had rotted—the French monarchy had
gone down in the red tempest of the Revolution—and
Napoleon was a name that was beginning to be talked
about."[2] Of what befell in that period, marked by
such figures and events, a later chapter will tell. Here
our thought is of the river itself, the river of "a hundred thousand affluents," as one has characterized
it; the river which for a little time bore through the
valley of Louisiana and of the Illinois the name of
the great French minister "Colbert."

To the Spanish the river was a hazard, a difficulty
to be gotten over. To the Indian it was the place of
fish and defense. To the Anglo-American empire of
wheels, that later came over the mountains, it was a

---

[1] "Life on the Mississippi," Hillcrest edition, pp. 19, 20.
[2] "Life on the Mississippi," p. 20.

barrier athwart the course, to be ferried or forded or bridged, but not to be followed. To be sure, it was (later) utilized by that empire, for a little while, as a path of dominant, noisy commerce in haste to get its products to market. And the keels of commerce may come again to stir its waters. But the river will never be to its later east-and-west migrants what it was to the French, whose evangelists, both of empire and of the soul, saw its significance, caught its spirit into their veins, and (from the day when Marquette and Joliet found their courage roused, and their labor of rowing from morning till night sweetened by the joy of their expedition) have possessed the river for their own and will possess it, even though all the land belongs to others, and the rivers are put to the uses of millions to whom the beautiful speech of the French is alien. Many a time in poling or paddling a boat in its tributaries in years gone by, have I thought and said to my companion: "How less inviting this stream would be if the French with valiant, adventurous spirit had not first passed over it!" And my companion was generally one who was always "Tonty" to me. It is still the river of Marquette and Joliet, Nicolet, Groseilliers and Radisson, La Salle and Tonty, Hennepin and Accau, Gray Gowns and Black Gowns, Iberville and Bienville, St. Ange and Laclede; for across every portage into the valley of that river, it was the men of France, so far as we know, who passed, first of Europeans, from Lake Erie up to Lake Chautauqua; or across to Fort Le Bœuf and down French Creek into the Alleghany and the Ohio (La Belle Rivière); or up the Maumee and across to the Wabash (the Appian Way); or from Lake Michigan up the St.

Joseph and across to the Kankakee, at South Bend; or, most trodden path of all, from Green Bay up the Fox River and across to the Wisconsin; or at Chicago from the Chicago River across to the Des Plaines (to which with the Illinois River the French seem to have given the name "Divine"), and so on to the Mississippi.

It is this last approach that I learned first and, though a smoke now hangs habitually over the entrance as a curtain, I have for myself but to push that aside to find the Divine River way still the best route into the greatest valley of the earth. Man has diverted this Divine River to very practical uses, and even changed its name, but it is hallowed still beyond all other approaches to the Great River. In a hut on the portage Père Jacques Marquette spent his last winter on earth in sickness; down the river the brave De la Salle built his Fort St. Louis on the great rock in the midst of his prairies, and still farther down his Fort Crèvecœur. On no other affluent stream are there braver and more stirring memories of French adventure and sacrifice than move along those waters or bivouac on those banks. And so I would have one's imagination take that trail toward the Mississippi and first see it glisten beneath the tall white cliffs which stand at the portal of the Divine River entry.

Its branches are reputed to have all borne at one time the names of saints, and it had like canonization itself. But these streams of the Mississippi, like the Seine, have none or few of the qualities that make this saintly terminology appropriate. It is anthropomorphism, not canonization, that befits its temper and its lure. Mystery no longer hangs over its waters. Now that all the prairie and plain have been occupied, the mystery has fled entirely from the valley or has hidden itself in the wilderness and "bad lands." All is translated into the values of a matter-of-fact, pragmatic, industrial occupation.

These are some of the pragmatic and other facts concerning it which I have gathered from the explorers and surveyors and lovers of this region, Ogg[1] and Austin[2] and Mark Twain[3] among them.

Its length lies wholly within the temperate zone. In this respect it is more fortunately situated than the more fertile-valleyed Amazon, since the climate here, varied and sometimes inhospitable as it is, offers conditions of human development there denied.

The main stream is two thousand five hundred and three miles in length, or more truly four thousand one hundred and ninety miles, if the Mississippi and Missouri be taken; that is, many times the length of the Seine. As Mark Twain, who is to be forever associated with its history, has said, it is "the crookedest river" in the world, travelling "one thousand three hundred miles to cover the same ground that a crow would fly over in six hundred and seventy-five." For a distance of several hundred miles the Upper Mississippi is a mile in width. Back in 1882 it was seventy miles or more[4] wide when the flood was highest, and in 1912 sixty miles wide. The volume of water discharged by it into the sea is second only to the Amazon, and is greater than that of all European rivers combined—Seine, Rhine, Rhône, Po, Danube, and all the rest, omitting

[1] Ogg, F. A., "Opening of the Mississippi," New York, 1904.
[2] Austin, O. P., "Steps in the Expansion of our Territory," New York, 1903.
[3] Mark Twain, "Life on the Mississippi," various editions.
[4] Mark Twain, "Life on the Mississippi," p. 456.

the Volga. The amount is estimated at one hundred and fifty-nine cubic miles annually—that is, it would fill annually a tank one hundred and fifty-nine miles long, a mile wide, and a mile high. With its tributaries it provides somewhat more than sixteen thousand miles of navigable water, more than any other system on the globe except the Amazon, and more than enough to reach from Paris to Lake Superior by way of Kamchatka and Alaska—about three-fourths of the way around the globe.

The sediment carried to the sea is estimated at four hundred million tons[1] annually. As one has put it, it would require daily for its removal five hundred trains of fifty cars, each carrying fifty tons, and would make two square miles each year over a hundred and thirty feet deep. Mark Twain in "Life on the Mississippi" is authority for the statement that the muddy water of the Missouri is more wholesome than other waters, until it has settled, when it is no better than that of the Ohio, for example. If you let a pint of it settle you will have three-fourths of an inch of mud in the bottom. His advice is to keep it stirred up.[2]

The area which it drains is roughly a million and a quarter square miles, or two-fifths of the United States. That is, as one graphic historian has visualized it in European terms, Germany, Austria-Hungary, France, and Italy could be set down within its limits and there would still be some room to spare.

The river has the strength (for the most part put to no use) of sixty million horses. The difference between high water and low water in flood conditions

[1] Humphrey's and Abbot's estimate.
[2] "Life on the Mississippi," p. 182.

is in some places fifty feet, which shows that it has a
wider range of moodiness than even the Seine.

The rim dividing the Mississippi basin from that of
the Great Lakes is, as we have seen, low and narrow;
in some places, especially in wet seasons, the watershed is indistinguishable. The waters know not which
way to go. This fact furnishes the explanation of the
ease with which the French explorers penetrated the
valley from the north. A high mountain range kept
the English colonists out of it from the east. The
Spanish found no physical barriers at the south (except the water, which gave the Frenchmen help), but, .
as we have seen, on the other hand, they found no adequate inducement.

The isotherm which touches the southern limits of
France passes midway between the source and mouth
of the river. In the northern half, it has the mean
annual temperature of France, England, and Germany;
in the southern half, of the Mediterranean coasts.

From the gulf into which it empties, a river (that is,
an ocean river, or current) runs through the ocean to
the western coasts of Europe; another runs out along
the northeastern coast of South America, and, still
another is in waiting at the western terminus of the
Panama Canal to assist the ships across the Pacific.

A fair regularity and reliability of rainfall have
made the rich soil of the valley tillable and productive
without irrigation, except in the far western stretches;
and these blessings are likely to continue, as one authority puts it, "so long as the earth continues to
revolve toward the east and the present relationship
of ocean and continent continues."

Including Texas and Alabama (which lie between the

same ranges of mountains with this valley, though their rivers run into the gulf and not into the Mississippi), this valley has perhaps one hundred and forty thousand miles of railway, or about sixty per cent of the total mileage of the country, or twenty-five per cent of the mileage of the entire globe.

. "In richness of soil, variety of climate, number and value of products, facilities for communication and general conditions of wealth and prosperity, the Mississippi Valley surpasses anything known to the Old World as well as the New." It produces the bulk of the world's cotton and oil; of corn it raises much more than all the rest of the world combined, and of each of the following (produced mainly in this same valley) the United States leads in quantity all the nations of the earth: wheat, cattle, hogs, oats, hay, lumber, coal, iron and steel, and other mineral products.

Its valley supports an estimated population of over fifty millions, or over half that of the whole United States; and has an estimated maintenance capacity of from 200,000,000[1] to 350,000,000,[2] or from four to seven times its present population. It has been tilled with "luxurious carelessness." A peasant in Brittany or a forester in Normandy would be scandalized by the extravagant, profligate use of its patrimony. That it is likely to have at least the 250,000,000 by the year 2100, and with intensive cultivation will be able to support them, is allowed by estimates of reliable statisticians. Europe had 175,000,000 at the beginning of the nineteenth century and North America 5,308,000.

[1] Justin Winsor, "Mississippi Basin," p. 4.
[2] A. B. Hart, "Future of the Mississippi Valley," *Harper's Magazine*, 100 : 419, February, 1900.

The former has somewhat more than doubled its population in the century since; America has increased hers about twenty times, and the Mississippi Valley several thousand times. It is not unreasonable to expect the doubling of the population of that valley in another century and its quadrupling in two.

Let De Tocqueville make summary of those prideful items in his description of the valley, embraced by the equator-sloping half of the continent: "It is upon the whole," he says, "the most magnificent dwelling-place prepared by God for man's abode"—a "space of 1,341,649 square miles—about six times that of France"—watered by a river "which, like a god of antiquity, dispenses both good and evil."[1]

And it was still another Frenchman who first gave to the world an accurate description of the sources of the river. On his own account, Nicollet, sometime professor in the Collège Louis le Grand, set out in 1831 to explore the river from its mouth to the source. He spent five years in these regions which he described as "a grand empire possessing the grandest natural limits on the earth." He then returned to a little Catholic college in Baltimore as a teacher, but the United States Government, hearing of his valuable service, commissioned him to make another expedition that would enable him to complete his map of the region of the sources. What he then accomplished has given him "distinct and conspicuous place among the explorers of the Mississippi." His map shows myriad lakes in the region of the sources (where the slightest jar of earth might turn in other directions the water of these brimming bowls), so many indeed, that there

[1] "Democracy in America," 1 : 22, 21, 20. New York, 1898.

would seem to be only lake and marsh and savannas. But we see him looking off toward plateaus "looming as if [they were] a distant shore." Another picture I shall always keep from his report is of his stolid half-breed guide (who usually waited for him and his companion with face toward them) sitting one day somewhat ahead of the party on a slight elevation, which makes the watershed between the rivers of the north and the rivers of the south, his face turned from them, gazing in silent rapture upon the boundless stretch of plains.

How their magical influence possessed him, as well as that child of forest and plain, Nicollet, a peasant boy of Savoy, a professor in Paris, interrupts his topographical report to tell: "It is difficult to express by words the varied impressions which the spectacle of these prairies produces. Their sight never wearies. To look a prairie up or down, to ascend one of its undulations, to reach a small plateau (or, as the voyageurs call it, a prairie planché), moving from wave to wave over alternate swells and depressions and finally to reach the vast, interminable low prairie that extends itself in front—(be it for hours, days or weeks)—one never tires; pleasurable and exhilarating sensations are all the time felt; ennui is never experienced. Doubtless there are moments when excessive heat, a want of fresh water, and other privations remind one that life is a toil; but these drawbacks are of short duration. There are no concealed dangers—no difficulties of road; a far-spreading verdure, relieved by a profusion of variously colored flowers, the azure of the sky above, or the tempest that can be seen from its beginning to its end, the beautiful modifications of the changing clouds, the curious looming of objects between earth and sky, taxing the ingenuity every moment to rectify —all, everything, is calculated to excite the perceptions and keep alive the imagination. In the summer season, especially, everything upon the prairies is cheerful, graceful, and animated. The Indians, with herds of deer, antelope and buffalo, give life and motion to them. It is then they should be visited; and I pity the man whose soul could remain unmoved under such a scene of excitement."[1]

It is a singular fortune that has made a son of France, a century and a half after the discovery of this mighty stream, the explorer and cartographer of its sources, a fortune that has its partial explanation at least in the lure of this stream for the Gallic heart.

Mrs. Trollope, a famous English traveller, found its lower valley depressing, as has many another: "Unwonted to European eyes and mystically heavy is the eternal gloom that seems to have settled upon that region. Whatever wind may blow, however bright and burning the southern sun may blaze in the unclouded sky, the stream is forever turbid and forever dark." Of the scene at its mouth, where La Salle and his men had sung with such joy, she says: "Had Dante seen it, he might have drawn images of another Bolgia from its horrors."[2] But no French visitor, so far as I know, has ever found it gloomy, even in flood or tempest on its subtropical stretches; nor has he found those level vastnesses desolate. A traveller, Paul Fountain by name, and so of French origin, I suspect,

[1] Report intended to illustrate a map of the hydrographical basin of the upper Mississippi River, Washington, 1843, 26th Cong., 2d Sess., Sen. Doc. 237, p. 52.
[2] "Domestic Manners of the Americans," p. 1.

wandering over those valley plains in the early days, tells of the sense of freedom, health, and strength that they give: "There is no air like the prairie air—not even the grand freshness of the boundless ocean itself.— The loveliness and variety of the prairie odors are quite indescribable, as are its superb wild flowers. It is a paradise. No man who has lived on it long enough to know it and love it (no great time, I can assure you) ever experiences real happiness after he has left it. There is a longing and eager craving to return to the life. The vulgar cowboys and hunters, uneducated and unpoetical past all degree, never leave it except to get drunk. Their money gone, back they go to get fresh strength and more pelf for another orgie; but if by chance they abandon the wild, free life, they soon drink themselves to lunacy or death, and their last babblings are of the glorious wilderness they all love."[1] This is the too exuberant expression of one who had probably never had a hearth of his own in France, but it gives some intimation of the charm of that great and seemingly infinite sweep of level ground, which many, and especially unimaginative minds, find so monotonous.

We cannot be quite sure, when we listen to some recent critics, that Châteaubriand ever saw this great valley. Certainly we who have grown up in it have never found his reindeer and moose about our homes (save in our Christmas-time imaginations). Paroquets that in the woods repeated the words learned of settlers are not of the fauna known to reputable Ohio naturalists, nor have two-headed snakes been found except in the vision of those who see double in their

[1] "The Great Deserts and Forests of North America," p. 22.

intoxication. The tamarind and the terebinth are not of its forest-trees. But whether or not Châteaubriand visited it in person, his imagination had frequent residence upon the Mississippi and its tributaries. His "Atala" put into French literature a country where many have loved to dwell, though its fauna and flora were not more accurate in some respects than the mineralogy and meteorology of the John Law scheme, known later as the "Mississippi Bubble," that made France wild with excitement once. However, I have recalled the fervid pen of Châteaubriand, not as that of a faunal or floral naturalist, but to have it rewrite these sentences: "Nothing is more surprising and magnificent than this movement and this distribution of the central waters of North America" (whence flows the Mississippi), "a river which the French first descended; a river which flowed under their power, and the rich valley of which," as the translator has rendered it, "still regrets their genius," but, as Châteaubriand doubtless meant it, and as it is better translated, "still grieves for their spirit," their "familiar" ("et dont la riche vallée regrette encore leur génie").[1]

I think that Châteaubriand had accurate instinct in divining the river's grieving for the spirit that (with all the practical genius which now inhabits the valley) is still needed to give an appreciation of that in the valley which lies beyond the counting of statistics or even the glowing rhetoric of the orators of liberty.

Hamlin Garland, reared in that valley, and first known in American letters as the author of remarkable stories of life on a Western farm, "Main Travelled

[1] "Travels in America and Italy," 1 : 72, 73, London, 1828.

Roads," has recently given expression to this grieving
(though he says no word of the French) in an essay on
"The Silent Mississippi," published a few years ago.
He speaks of the river's bold, blue-green bluffs "looking away into haze," of its golden bars of sand "jutting
out into the burnished stream," of its thickets of yellow-
green willows, of the splendid old trees and of its glades
opening away to the hills (all making a magical way
of beauty), only to use it as a background for the
statement that "not one beautiful building" is to be
seen on its banks "for a thousand miles." There are
many towns, but "without a single distinctive building; everything is a flimsy jumble, out of key, meaningless, impertinent, evanescent, too, thanks to climate."
"We took a wild land beautiful as a dream," he proceeds, "and we have made a refuse heap. The birds
of the trees have disappeared, the water-fowl have
gone, every edible creature has vanished. An era of
hopeless, distinctive vulgarity is upon us."

I have travelled down the smaller waterways of
the valley with like feeling, which, though it has led
to no such comprehensive generalization, yet gave me
a distinct consciousness of their "grieving," if not for
the French, at any rate for the silences that preceded
the French, and for their own riparian architecture.
The busy towns along the streams I have known have
turned their faces from these streams toward the
railroads. They have left the riverside to the thrift-
less men and the truant boys. Stables and outhouses
look upon their waters, and the sewers pollute them.
And if on some especially eligible bluff better buildings
do stand, their owners or builders show no appreciation of what the bluff or river cares for, but reproduce

the lines of some pretentious edifice that has no relation, historic or otherwise, to it or to the site. The
old mills, with their feet in the water, are almost the
only sympathetic structures—especially so when they
are in ruins.

I once followed the upper waters of the stream (the
Ohio) along which Céloron, of whom I shall speak
later, planted his emblems of French possession. He
would doubtless care to claim that valley even to-day,
though unsightly houses and sheds line it, and pipes
and shafts of iron, hastily rigged up and left to rust
when done with, run everywhere, and the scum of oil
is on the water. The profit of the hour was all that was
visible of motive or achievement in that smoky valley,
though I know it is not safe to generalize, for miracles
have been wrought in that very valley.

A change is coming in many of the towns and cities
of both the lesser and the larger rivers. In the town
that I knew best, thirty years ago only a few ventured
upon the water, and they were the fishermen or river-
men who had not much to do with the community life;
now the steam or gasolene launch is making these
streams highways of pleasure, and so is bringing them
within the daily life of thousands.

Waiting for a boat in St. Louis one beautiful summer
morning on the quay, where in Paris I should have
found the book-stalls, I saw a Pullman train just starting for New York, and at the water's edge under the
stately bridge one tramp "barbering" another. But,
reading the morning paper, I found by chance that
back in the city there was one man at least, a teacher
and artist, who had the old-time French feeling for
the grieving river. It was dark before I found him,

after my day on a steamboat whose most important passenger, pointed out to me with some apparent pride by the old-time captain, was a brewer, author of a brew more famous in those parts than the artist's river pictures which I saw by candle-light that night in his schoolroom.

The artist had his river studio upon one of the beautiful cliffs which La Salle must have seen when he came out of the Illinois into the Mississippi. And it was within a few miles of that studio, it may be added, that I found, too, one noteworthy exception to Mr. Hamlin Garland's statement concerning riparian architecture.

These are hopeful intimations succeeding the fading of the last traces in that region of the old French days, traces which I found a few hours' journey below St. Louis, in the village of Prairie du Rocher (locally pronounced Prary de Roosh); for Cahokia, where I stopped first, had no mark of the French régime except the "congregation," which was, as the priest told me, two hundred years old. The village had no distinctiveness. But Prairie du Rocher had its own atmosphere and charm. French skies never produced a more glorious August sunset than I saw through the Corot trees of that village, which stands or reclines beneath the cliffs and looks off toward the river that has receded far to the westward. I tried to find the old French records of which I had heard, but there was a new priest who knew not the French; yet I did not need them to assure me that the French had been there. At dawn, after such a peaceful night as one might have in upper Carcasonne, I found my way to the river near which are the ruins of Fort Chartres—

all that is left of the greatest French fortress in the Mississippi Valley, the last to yield to man and the last to surrender to nature. The town, Nouvelle Chartres, with all its color and gayety, has become a corn field, and only the magazine of the fort remains, hidden, a gunshot from the river, among the weeds, bushes, vines, and trees.

Fourteen miles below is the site of the oldest French village in the upper valley. But the river was jealous and took it all, foundation and roof, to itself. The charms of old Kaskaskia, the sometime capital of all that region, are "one with Nineveh and Tyre." Not a vestige is left of its first days and only a broken structure or two of its later glory.

Nor is there any other trace, so far as I could learn, anywhere down the winding stream till one reaches New Orleans. The red sun-worshippers in their white garments—familiar of old to the French—even they have followed their divinity toward its setting, and only among those with African shadows in their faces do they still sing, as I have heard, of the "brave days of D'Artaguette." The monuments do not remember beyond the bravery and carnage of the Civil War, or at farthest beyond the War of 1812. I was myself apprehended for a foreign spy one day while I was searching too near to the guns of a present fort for more ancient monuments.

The great river and some of its tributaries have a commerce, but it is of an inanimate and unappealing kind. They no longer draw the throngs daily to the wharfs as in the days of the glory of the steamboat. Everybody is in too much of a hurry to travel by water.

An old Mississippi River steamboat captain[1] has written a reminiscent book, in which he tells with sorrow of the departed majesty and glory of the river, the glamour remaining only in the memories of those who knew the river sixty years or more ago. He laments the passing of that mighty fleet, destroyed by the very civilization that built it—a civilization which cut down the impounding forests and so removed the great natural dams which must in time be replaced by artificial ones if the rivers are ever to run full again in the dry seasons and not overflow in the wet. It is that day of the Mississippi that is best known in our literature. Mark Twain has put forever on the map of letters (where the Euphrates, the Nile, the Ilyssus, the Tiber, the Seine, the Thames long have been) the Mississippi, the river which the French first traced upon the maps of geography. So we are especially indebted to the French for Mark Twain, who began his career as a "cub" pilot on the river which in turn gave him the name by which the world is ever to know him.

It was he who once wrote of this river: "The face of the water, in time, became a wonderful book—a book that was a dead language to the uneducated passenger, but which told its mind to me without reserve, delivering its most cherished secrets as clearly as if it uttered them with a voice. And it was not a book to be read once and thrown aside, for it had a new story to tell every day. Throughout the long twelve hundred miles there was never a page that was void of interest, never one that you could leave unread without loss, never one that you would want to skip, thinking you could

[1] George B. Merrick, "Old Times on the Upper Mississippi," Cleveland, A. H. Clark Co., 1909.

find higher enjoyment in some other thing. There never was so wonderful a book written by man; never one whose interest was so absorbing, so unflagging, so sparklingly renewed with every reperusal."[1]

When I was entering the English Channel on my way to Havre, the captain showed me what varied courses must be taken at different hours and different days to gain full advantage of tide and current and yet avoid all danger. But, as this Mississippi River pilot has observed, it is now a comparatively easy undertaking to learn to run these buoyed and lighted ship channels; it was then quite another matter to pilot a steamboat in the Mississippi or Missouri, "whose alluvial banks cave and change constantly, whose snags are always hunting up new quarters, whose sand-bars are never at rest, whose channels are forever dodging and shirking, and whose obstructions" had fifty years ago to be "confronted in all nights and all weathers without the aid of a single lighthouse or a single buoy."[2] And yet that man, who came to know, in age, the courses of human emotions the world over, could, as a young man, shut his eyes and trace the river from St. Louis to New Orleans, and read its face as one "would cull the news from a morning paper."

It was for years a wish of mine that when Mark Twain should come to die, he should lie not in an ordinary sepulchre of earth but in the river which he knew so well and loved, and of whose golden days he sang. I wished that the river might be turned aside from its wonted channel, as the River Busentinus for the interment of Alaric, and then, after his burial there, be let

---

[1] "Life on the Mississippi," pp. 82-83.
[2] "Life on the Mississippi," p. 86.

back into it again, that he might ever hear the sonorous voice of its waters above him, and, perhaps, now and then the call of the leadsman overhead, crying the depth beneath, as he himself in the pilot-house used once to hear the call "Mark Twain" from the darkness below. So it was a disappointment to me that when the world followed him to his grave it was to a little patch of earth outside the valley, beyond the reach of even the farthest tributary of the Mississippi.

The great river has been the course of one empire and the scene of many. Spain, France, England, and the United States have each claimed its mastery, as we have seen or shall see. The Germans once dreamed of a state on its banks, but could not agree as to the locality (Minnesota or Texas), so variedly tempting was the fertility of its upper and its lower waters. The sons of the Norsemen are now tilling the land around its sources. Indeed, it has now upon its banks and within the reach of its myriad streams a babel of earth's races, although the river has not, as the River of the Lotus Flower, conformed them to one uniform type.

We are beginning now to realize more keenly that the river has yet to be conquered. It has yielded complete sovereignty to no people. It has made light of the emblems of empire. It has even ignored the white, channel-marking signals of the government that now exercises lordship over all the land it drains. Its untamed spirit flaunts continual challenge in the face of all men. It has had in derision the building of cities and towns. One town, for example, has been left to choose between being left high and dry five miles from water, or of meeting the fate of old Kaskaskia.

And though the town has already thrown a million dollars to the river, as if to some unappeased god, the river is merciless. One town and another have been ostracized or destroyed, their wharfs left far inland or carried away to some commerceless bayou. The sentiment I have regarding the river makes it difficult to excuse its infidelity toward one little French town in particular, St. Genevieve. I can do so only by assuming that the river has cared less for its later inhabitants than it did for those who gave it name. It has laughed at the embankments on which hundreds of millions have been spent by nation, state, and private enterprise to keep its flood in restraint. Shorn of its trees, as Samson of his long hair, it has pulled down the pillars of man's raising into its own destroying waters. In 1912 a space nearly two and a half times the size of the State of New Jersey was devastated.[1] In 1913 the loss in a single year was one hundred and sixty million dollars.[2] In the last thirty years it is estimated the loss has been a half of a billion, and it would have been immensely greater, of course, if the river had not been given unchallenged freedom of great, unclaimed swamps. And yet the river has never at any one time massed its great army of waters. At one time it has been the Ohio, at another the Missouri, and then the Red that it has sent against the fortifications. If all these streams were to be brought in flood at once the lower valley would be swept clean.

So it is no martial simile that I am using. It is a real battle that is continuously on. The gaunt sharp-

[1] Seventeen thousand six hundred and five square miles.
[2] One hundred and sixty-three million, U. S. Weather Bureau estimate.

shooter, pacing the embankment with Winchester in hand to shoot any burrowing confederate of the river, a rat, or mole, is a real and not an imaginary figure. And the battles that have been fought along its course are as play by the side of those yet to be waged before it is subdued by man.

It is fitly the War Department of the government that has been watching its every movement, that has set the signals on its fitful tide, and that has recorded its every shift for years as if it were an animate enemy. Its changing area, velocity, discharge—items of infinite permutations—are all noted and analyzed. But the war department of the government is still almost as powerless to control the river as the Yazoo farmer who watches its changing moods, not by instruments but by the movement of an eddy in his own hidden bayou. The battle is with floods, shallows, and erosion, but it is essentially a battle with floods, for not until their strongholds are taken, controlled, is the complete conquest assured. It was control of the mouth of the river that seemed so important in early days. The effort to obtain that led ultimately to the purchase of Louisiana (that is, the west bank of the river) from the French by the United States. It was the confirmation of that security of navigation which gave the battle of New Orleans its high significance. Then the mouth (thus obtained) was found too shallow for the demands of commerce, and there followed what some one with poetic instincts has called the battle of the shoals, a battle in which General Eads, who had bridged the river at St. Louis, compelled the river by means of jetties to run deeper and carry heavier burdens.

But the future battle-fields are perceived to lie toward the sources, at the eaves, as it were, of the watersheds, the headwaters of its tributaries as well as its own. No deepening, embanking, straightening, canalization of the river is to be permanently effective until all danger of flood can be removed.

Wandering among those tributaries, seeing the trickling fountains of several of them, watching the timid stream in the naked, deforested fields (not knowing quite which way to go, east or west, north or south), I have been strongly appealed to by the plan of impounding in reservoirs these first waters, whose freedom (no longer restrained in youth by the sage forests) makes them libertines and wantons in the distant valleys below.

Such impounding has successful inauguration in five small reservoirs now in operation on the headwaters of the Mississippi out of forty-two planned. An ambitious plan for controlling the turbulent Ohio by a system of from seventeen to forty-three reservoirs at an estimated cost of from twenty to thirty-four millions of dollars has been suggested by Mr. M. O. Leighton of the United States Geological Survey, and received indorsement from the Pittsburgh Flood Commission, the Dayton Flood Commission, and the National Waterways Commission. These would suffice to keep the lawless waters within temperate bounds in the spring and to give more generous navigable currents in the summer and autumn. Against the great expense of such a project is set the tremendous possibilities in the development of water-power. Of the theoretical sixty millions of horse-power in the current of the Mississippi, it is estimated that about six and a half millions can be economically developed throughout the year, while twelve millions could be developed during six months or more without storage reservoirs. An adequate system of reservoirs might double or treble these totals, while a million or two would be immediately available to begin the payment of the debt, and more of the strength would be harnessed to that purpose in time. So, it is urged, the river would be made to meet the expense of its own conquest.[1]

And once that is done the river may be straightened, shortened, deepened, leveed, and made a docile, reliable carrier of commerce. It may then be compelled to a respect for cities and government signals and wharfs and mills. And the astute suggestion of the practical Joliet for the canalization of its waters, may be realized in the safe passage not merely of boats but of stately, giant, ocean-sized vessels from the Great Lakes to the gulf.

A hundred years ago (1809) one Nicholas Roosevelt, commissioned of Robert Fulton (the inventor of the steamboat) and others, was sent to Pittsburgh to build the first steamboat to be launched in western waters. So confident was this young man of the success of steamboat navigation of the Ohio and Mississippi that, on his journey of inspection, he purchased coal-mines along the way and arranged to have the coal piled up on the river bank against the time of its need by boats whose keels had not been laid and whose existence even depended upon the approval of eastern capitalists. It suggests the prevision of the nephew, Theodore

[1] See reports of the National Conservation Commission in 1909; National Waterways Commission, 1912; Report Commissioner of Corporations on Water-Power Development in the United States, 1912; J. L. Mathews "Remaking the Mississippi," Boston, 1909.

Roosevelt, in making provision for the coaling of ships in the east long before the Spanish War was in sight. I was on the Marquette-Joliet portage the very day that this same nephew was predicting with like confidence to the people of St. Louis that the Mississippi would be deepened till from the lakes to the gulf it should be a course for seagoing vessels. Champlain suggested the Panama Canal three hundred years before its building. Joliet, in 1673, suggested the lakes-to-the-gulf ship waterway,[1] and by the three-hundredth anniversary, perhaps, it will be completed.

I made a journey in 1911 that began at the first settlements of the French in Nova Scotia, touched the Bay of Chaleur and the lower St. Lawrence, and then followed the French water paths all the way to the mouth of the Mississippi, where the master of pilots, a descendant of France, carried me out into the Gulf of Mexico. Starting back before dawn in a little boat, I saw, just as the sun was coming up over the swamps where the river begins to divide, the hulk of a great seagoing vessel against the morning sky. It seemed then a gloomy apparition; but as I think of it now it was rather the presage of the new commerce than the ghost of that which has departed.

That the Valley of a Hundred Thousand Streams— streams that together touch every community of any size from the Alleghanies to the Rockies—streams whose waters all find their way sooner or later into the Mississippi—will ever give up battle till the great water itself is conquered, no one who knows the determined people in that valley will ever question. The sixty million people will not be resisted perma-

[1] Margry, I : 268.

nently by the sixty million horses of the river, though
the strength of the horses be driven by all the clouds
that the gulf sends up the valley to its aid. Some day
the great, free River Colbert will run vexed of impenetrable, unyielding walls to the sea. Its "titanic ambition for quiet flowing" down this beautiful, gently
sloping valley to the gulf (which, as one has said, "has
been its longing through ages") will have been turned
to human ministry. The spirit of the great water
will have become as patient, as thoughtless of its own
wild comfort or ambitions as that of the priest who
dedicated it to the honor of the mother of the most
patient of men.

CHAPTER VI

THE PASSING OF NEW FRANCE AND THE DREAM OF ITS REVIVAL

THE readers who have through these chapters been companions of Champlain, La Salle, Joliet, Marquette, and others in the discovery of the mighty rivers and the conquest of the mighty vastnesses of the new world will have, if they continue, yet before them even harder and more disheartening ventures, as La Salle himself had that April day in 1682, when he turned from the column which he had planted in sight of the Gulf of Mexico, four thousand miles from the Cape of Labrador, and began to drive his canoes up the river which he had traced forever, if too tortuously, on the maps of the earth.

During the chapter since we reached the shores of that lonely sea without a sail, we have, covering in prospect two centuries, contemplated the majesty of that river of a hundred thousand affluents.

Now, as we turn our faces toward the lakes and Canada again, a century of hardship confronts us. If the readers endure it with me, as I have endured it again and again, they will have added again to their France and their United States memories more precious than the titles to boundless prairies and trackless forests.

La Salle was not content with the discovery of the

great waterway to the gulf, the tracing of whose course had ended all dreams of a shorter route to China by aid of its current. In place of his La Chine dream grew another dream: to open this valley to France from the south instead of from the north, where the way was long and perilous, closed half the year by ice and storm, and beset all the year by hostile intrigue, envy, and dishonesty of colonial officials. A Franco-Indian colony was to be established along the Illinois under the protection of Fort St. Louis on the Rock. Ultimately a chain of forts and colonies would hold the watercourse all the way from gulf to gulf—from the Gulf of St. Lawrence to the Gulf of Mexico—maintained by revenues from the hides and wool of the buffalo then roaming the woods and prairies and plains from one side of the valley to the other; the Indians would gather about these centres for gain and protection; and in the midst of this wilderness he would hold for France the empire that the inscription on the column at the mouth of the river claimed. The crows might fly about his fields, but they could not then touch his rich crops. Griffins—flocks, fleets of griffins —would fly above them.

That was the vision with which he started northward from the mouth of the great river, the vision out of which he might at once have been starved except for the meat of alligators shot along the way. Seized of a dangerous illness, he sent Tonty on to Mackinaw to forward news of the discovery to Canada, and unable, even after months of Father Membré's care, to go to Paris to prepare for the carrying out of his great scheme, he, joined by Tonty, climbs the Rock St. Louis and lays out ramparts on its crest, of

which I thought I discovered traces many years ago.
It was another Rock of Quebec, rising sheer a hundred
and twenty-five feet above the river in the midst of
the prairie. About it gathered under his protection
many tribes of Indians, in common dread of the Iroquois, in common hope, doubtless, of gain from commerce with the French. La Salle, in a report to be
found in the archives of the Marine in Paris, states
that his extemporized colony numbered four thousand
warriors, or twenty thousand souls.[1] It had come up
as Jonah's gourd and might as quickly wither, as the
village of the Illinois but a few years previous had
withered into desolation in a few hours before the hot
breath of the terrorizing fame of the Iroquois. From
his seigniorial aerie he sent messages to the governor
of Canada, no longer the friendly Frontenac but a
Pharaoh who knew not this Joseph, praying for co-
operation, saying that he could not leave his red allies
lest, if the Iroquois should strike in his absence, they
would think him in league with their dread enemies;
asking that his men who go down with hides in exchange for munitions be not retained as outlaws;
urging that it is for the advantage of his creditors (for
his losses had amounted to forty thousand crowns)
that they do not seize his goods—since the means of
meeting all his debts would then be destroyed—and
begging for more men with whom to make this colony
permanent and gather the more remote Indian tribes
around the sheltering Rock St. Louis.[2]

But it was not such prayers that reached Louis XIV,
who, on May 10, 1682, before La Salle's report of the

[1] Margry, 2 : 363. Parkman, "La Salle," pp. 317, 318.
[2] Margry, 2 : 314. Parkman, "La Salle," pp. 320–324.

discovery of the Mississippi arrived at Versailles, had directed that no further permission should be given to make journeys of discovery toward the Mississippi, as the colonists might better be employed in cultivating the lands.

This is an example of the advice the king is receiving from his governor in Quebec: "You will see that . . . [La Salle] has been bold enough to give you intelligence of a false discovery and that, instead of returning to the colony to learn what the King wishes him to do, he does not come near me, but keeps in the backwoods, five hundred leagues off, with the idea of attracting the inhabitants to him, and building up an imaginary kingdom for himself, by debauching all the bankrupts and idlers of this country, . . . All the men who brought me news from him have abandoned him, and say not a word about returning, but sell the furs they have brought as if they were their own; so that he cannot hold his ground much longer."[1]

Meanwhile the king, the same king who five years before had said in La Salle's commission that he had "nothing more at heart" than the exploration of that country, writes to the governor of Canada from Fontainebleau: "I am convinced, as you, that the discovery of the Sieur de la Salle is very useless, and that such enterprises ought to be prevented in the future."[2]

In his extremity, his supplies cut off, his men sent to Quebec deserting with the profits of his hides, La Salle leaves Tonty on the Rock, starts for Quebec, intending to go to France, meets on the way an officer appointed to succeed him in all his wilderness author-

[1] Parkman, "La Salle," p. 323.   [2] Parkman, "La Salle," p. 324.

ity, and in the spring of 1684 is again a lodger in Rue de la Truanderie, a miserable little street in Paris where, as I have said before, I have tried to locate the lodging of the valiant soul who once dwelt upon the mysterious rock near my boyhood home.

Thence this man of "solitary disposition," whose life had been joined to savages, and who had for years had "neither servants, clothes nor fare which did not savor more of meanness than of ostentation," and who was of such natural timidity that it took him a week "to make up his mind to go to an audience" with Monseigneur de Conti, is summoned to an interview with the king himself.

La Salle's memorials, which recall by way of introduction his five journeys of upward of five thousand leagues, in great part on foot, through more than six hundred leagues of unknown country among savages and cannibals, and at the cost of one hundred and fifty thousand francs, and which propose projects that seem in some of their features quixotic and visionary, received favorable consideration of the king and his minister Colbert's son. La Salle's wilderness empire is restored to him and he is granted four ships in which to carry soldiers, mechanics, and laborers to establish a fort and colony at the mouth of the Mississippi, to open up all the interior of America from the south, and incidentally to make war on the Spaniards (who were claiming the gulf for their own), and to seize their valuable mines.

The quarrellings of this expedition (due in part to the divided command); the failure to find the mouth of the Mississippi since, we are told, La Salle had been unable in 1682 to determine its longitude; the landing on the shores of Texas, far beyond the mouth of the Mississippi; the loss of one of the vessels to the Spanish, the wreck of two others, and the return of the fourth to France; the miserable fate of the colony left on those desolate shores; the long search of La Salle and his companions for the "fatal river"—these make a dismal story whose details cannot be rehearsed here, a story whose tragic end was the murder of La Salle by one of his own disaffected followers in March, 1687, on the banks of the Trinity River.

There is time, as we hasten on, for only a few words over the body of this "iron man," left "a prey to the buzzards and wolves" of the wilderness in which he sacrificed all, as Champlain, for France.

"One of the greatest men of his age," said Tonty, who was nearest to him in all his labors save his last. "Without question one of the most remarkable explorers whose names live in history," writes Parkman.[1] His "personality is impressed in some respects more strongly than that of any other upon the history of New France," says another historian, Fiske.[2] "For force of will and vast conceptions; for various knowledge and quick adaptation of his genius to untried circumstances; for a sublime magnanimity, that resigned itself to the will of Heaven, and yet triumphed over affliction by energy of purpose and unfaltering hope—this daring adventurer had no superior among his countrymen," says Bancroft.[3] And further, in the estimate of a recent historian of the valley, "for all the qualities of rugged manhood, courage, persistency that could not be broken,

[1] Parkman, "La Salle," p. 430.
[2] "New France and New England," p. 132.
[3] "History of the United States," 3 : 173.

contempt of pain and hardship, he has never been surpassed."[1]

Let him who next to Tonty knew him better than
all the other chroniclers say a last word—one which
will justify the time that we have given to following
the fortunes and adversities of this spirit, unbroken to
the last: "He was a tower of adamant, against whose
impregnable front hardship and danger, the rage of
man and of the elements, the southern sun, the northern blast, fatigue, famine, disease, delay, disappointment and deferred hope, emptied their quivers in
vain. . . . Never under the impenetrable mail of
paladin or crusader beat a heart of more intrepid
mettle than within the stoic panoply that armed the
breast of La Salle. To estimate aright the marvels of
his patient fortitude, one must follow on his track
through the vast scene of his interminable journey-
ings. . . . America owes him an enduring memory;
for in this masculine figure she sees the pioneer who
guided her to her richest heritage."[2]

France had deserved well of that valley had she
done nothing more than to set that rugged, fearless
figure in the heart of America, a perpetual foil to
effeminacy and submission to softening luxury, to the
arts that seek merely popularity, to drunkenness and
other vices which he combated even in that wilderness, to sycophancy and demagogy—a perpetual example of the "vir" and virtue in the noblest sense in
which mankind has defined them.

In the grand amphitheatre in the Sorbonne, I witnessed one day in Paris a celebration of the conquests

[1] James K. Hosmer, "Short History of the Mississippi Valley," p. 140.
[2] Parkman, "La Salle," p. 432.

of the French language in lands outside of France: conquests in the islands of the West Indies, where La Salle suffered all but death; in Canada, where he had his first visions; and in Louisiana, where he perished. Though his name was not spoken, it were a reason for greater celebration in France that the spirit of such a Frenchman as La Salle had enduring memory in the severe ideals of manhood that are for all time to possess the men of that valley to which he guided the world.

There is a grave for which I wished to make search in Rouen, the grave of the mother of La Salle, to whom he wrote in 1684: "I hope . . . to embrace you a year hence with all the pleasure that the most grateful of children can feel with so good a mother as you have always been."[1] I wish I could have made her know—but since I could not, I tried to let France know instead—that there are millions who could speak to-day as the most "grateful of children" what her son and France's son was never permitted to utter.

La Salle's dream of New France did not fade with his last sight of his empire of Louisiana. But the century in which he was born and died had all but gone out before the stirring of his life's vision and sacrifice, strengthened by appeal of the gallant and faithful Tonty, resulted in the offer by one who has been called the "Cid of Canada," Le Moyne d'Iberville, to carry out the schemes of La Salle, and it was becoming clear that France must act at once or England would build the glorious structure which La Salle had designed. In the offer of this young Canadian and his brother Bienville were the purposes that gave substantial

[1] Parkman, "La Salle," p. 364.

foundation to Louisiana. Sailing with their two ships in 1699, they were caught in the "strong, muddy current of fresh water," which La Salle had unluckily passed without seeing. They entered this stream and, after several days of exploration, had verification of the identity of the river in a letter (or "speaking bark," as the Indians called it), dated the 20th of April, 1685, which Tonty, years before, when making the journey down the river in search of La Salle, had left in the hands of an Indian chief to be delivered to La Salle, or, as the chief called him, "the man who should come up the river."

The fortunes which befell those of this colony, trying to find a suitable site in that land of bushes and cane-brakes, are not agreeable to follow. For thirteen years the "paternal providence of Versailles" watched over them, sending them marriageable women, soldiers, priests, and nuns, but so little food that famine and pestilence often came to their miserable stockades. They were under injunction "to seek out pearl fisheries," "to catch bison-calves, tame them and take their wool," and "to look for mines." What employment for the founders of an empire![1]

One cannot resist the temptation to say again: If only Louis XIV had had the good sense, unblinded of pearls and gold and bigotry and some other things, to let the industrious, skilled Huguenots, flying from France after the revocation of the Edict of Nantes,

[1] In one of the branches of that river at whose mouth they settled I saw a summer or two ago, one of the men of that valley wading in its water, still in search of pearls. A pearl worth a thousand dollars had once been found near by, and so (in the same hope that animated the mind of King Louis XIV) man after man in that neighborhood had abandoned his fertile farm to search for pearls, only to be reduced, as the poor settlers of early Louisiana, to live upon the shell-fish in which the pearls refused to grow.

settle in Louisiana, instead of forcing them to swell the numbers of the English colonies on the Atlantic coast, and eventually assist them in taking the New France from which they had been debarred!

The French engineer of an English ship, appearing on the river one day, had furtively handed Bienville a petition of four hundred Huguenots in the Carolinas to be allowed to settle in Louisiana and to have the privilege of worship, such as is enjoyed to-day. The answer came from Versailles to the cane-brakes—from Versailles, where, amid scenes "which no European court could rival," the "greatest of France, princes, warriors, statesmen," were gathered week after week in the "Halls of Abundance, Venus, Mars and Apollo," from Versailles to the half-starved little group sitting in exile by the gulf, far from abundance, without love, in dread of Mars, and with no arts of Apollo save the sound of the wind in the trees and the moan of the sea: "Have I expelled heretics from France in order that they should set up a republic in America?"

One has reminded us that while Iberville was making almost futile attempts with the half-hearted support of his government to establish this colony at the mouth of the Mississippi, Peter the Great was beginning to lay the foundations of St. Petersburg in as unpromising a place—a barren, uncultivated island which was a frozen swamp in winter and a heap of mud in summer, in the midst of pathless forests and deep morasses haunted by wolves and bears. Peter the Great spent great treasure in clearing the forests, draining the swamps, and raising embankments for this future capital of an empire. Louis XIV had only to let certain Frenchmen settle on these less forbidding coasts, that might soon have become the capital of as fruitful a province as Peter the Great's; and the transformation would have been made, as in New England, without any assistance from the king except perhaps for defense.

It is due the memory of Iberville, often slandered as was La Salle before him, not that the story of his all but hopeless struggles should be repeated here but that the object toward which he so valiantly struggled should be clearly seen. He had read Father Membré's account of the La Salle voyage of discovery and Joutel's story of the last expedition. He had even had a conversation with La Salle, and had heard his own lips describe the river; and he had known Tonty of the Iron Hand, faithful to the last. Iberville had a mind capable of entertaining the vision, and he had a spirit capable of following it. He seems to have been for a time after La Salle's death his only great-minded follower. He wrote on reaching Rochelle after his first voyage that "if France does not immediately seize this part of America, which is the most beautiful, and establish a colony strong enough to resist any which England may have here, the English colonies (already considerable in Carolina) will so thrive that in less than a hundred years they will be strong enough to seize all America."[1]

But the answer from Versailles only hastened the fulfilment of Iberville's prophecy. It is as a page torn from a contemporaneous suburban villa prospectus that speaks of one of those migratory settlements of Iberville on the shores of the gulf as a "terrestrial paradise," a "Pomona," or "The Fortunate Island."

[1] Margry, *l. c.*, IV: 322.

And the reality which confronts the home seeker is usually more nearly true to the idealistic details than that which Governor Cadillac, wishing no doubt to discredit his predecessor, reported when he went to succeed Bienville for a time as governor: "I have seen the garden on Dauphin Island, which had been described to me as a terrestrial paradise. I saw there three seedling pear-trees, three seedling apple-trees, a little plum-tree about three feet high, with seven bad plums on it, a vine some thirty feet long, with nine bunches of grapes, some of them withered, or rotten, and some partly ripe, about forty plants of French melons and a few pumpkins."[1]

Bienville, the brother, also deserves remembrance both in France and America—dismissed once but exonerated, returning later to succeed the pessimistic Cadillac and to lay the foundations of New Orleans on the only dry spot he had found on his first journey up the river, there to plant the seed of the fruits and melons and pumpkins of the garden on Dauphin Island, that were to bring forth millionfold, though they have not yet entirely crowded out the cypress and the palmetto, and the fleur-de-lis that still grows wild and flowers brilliantly at certain seasons.

It was some time before this, however, that the king, nearing the end of his days, vexed with his wars, tired of his expensive and unproductive venture, gave over the colony into the hands and enterprise of a speculator, one Antoine Crozat, a French merchant whose purse had been open to Louis for his wars. There was a total population at this juncture (1712) of three hundred and eighty souls, about one half of whom were

[1] Parkman, "A Half Century of Conflict," I : 309.

"in the king's pay." Crozat, the king's deputy despot, finds no better fortune than the king, and soon (1717) resigns his charter, to be succeeded in his anxieties and privileges by that famous Scotch adventurer John Law, who organized the Mississippi Company in order to enjoy the varied monopolies assembled in its charter —monopolies which would make any inhabitant of that trust-hating valley to-day fume in denouncing. It was a tobacco trust, a coinage trust, a revenue trust, a slave-holding trust, a mining trust, a trade trust wrapped in one, with an unlimited license. It was, moreover, a conscience trust, a speech trust, a religion trust, a race trust. It was, in short, the ultimate, sublimated expression of a monopolistic theory made effective in a charter. Immigration, within these re- strictions, was not likely to be voluntary and eager, as was the case in New England, and, since the company was under the one compulsion of providing a certain number of colonists and slaves, immigration was forced. Every conceivable sound economic and philosophical principle was violated, and yet investors came from all parts of Europe. "Crowds of crazed speculators jostled and fought each other" before the offices of the company in the Rue Quincampoix[1] from morning till night to get their names inscribed among the stock- holders, and, though five hundred thousand foreigners were attracted to Paris by opportunities for speculation, scarcely a colonist went willingly to the Eldorado of the company, whose stock was capitalized in billions and "whose ingots of gold were displayed in Paris shop- windows." There were maps of that valley to be found

[1] A now disreputable street, or so it seemed as I walked through it one day in the dusk.

in abundance in Paris in those days with mines indi-
cated on them indiscriminately.   When the bubble
burst, Louisiana "became a name of disgust and terror" in Europe, and doubtless thousands hoped never
to hear the word "Mississippi" again, and yet it was
only time that was needed to make even such wild
prophecies true.

The monopolistic venture failed.   Many of the
colonists whom the company entered died or ran away;
millions of pounds had been spent, there was no return,
and there was little tangible to show for it all—a few
thousand white settlers, many of whom, in a phrase
current to-day in the States, were "undesirable
citizens," living in palisaded cabins.   So the little
settlement became a crown colony again and came
back to the king, but not to him in whose name it
had been originally taken, for that king was dead.
Louis XIV's name, kept in "Louisiana," claims now
but a fragment of that vast territory which might have
been his forever.   The little outcast colony was laid
on the steps of Versailles again, and was again subject
to "paternalistic nursing," because of or in despite of
which it began at last to show signs of growth.   It
was at the cost of a half-century of time, of eight or
more millions of livres to the king, Crozat and the
company, of millions upon millions more to those who
bought the worthless stock of the Mississippi Company,
and of ignominy and shame, that La Salle's dream
began to have realization, while on the Atlantic seaboard the English colonies were growing luxuriantly in
comparative neglect.

Meanwhile French explorers were traversing this
mighty interior valley with all the spirit of Cartier,

Joliet, Champlain, and La Salle. Pierre Charles le Sueur had ascended the Mississippi far toward its source in search of copper and lead. Bernard de la Harpe and Louis Juchereau, the Sieur de St. Denis, explored the Red River and penetrated as far as the Spanish settlement of St. Jean Baptiste on the Rio Grande. Each might have a volume. The turbid Missouri even (which Marquette and Joliet first saw heading great trees down into the Mississippi) was not passed by as impervious to the hardihood of undaunted, amphibious geographers such as La Harpe and Du Tisne.

Two brothers, Pierre and Paul Mallet, penetrated to the old Spanish settlement at Santa Fé and may have been the first of Frenchmen to see the farther boundary of the valley, the Rocky Mountains. Whether they did or not, it is certain that far to the northwest two other brothers did reach that mighty range and "discovered that part of it to which the name Rocky Mountains properly belongs."

The brothers La Vérendrye in 1735, two centuries after Cartier, were still looking for a way to the western sea (Mer de l'Ouest). With their father these sons ventured their lives and gave their fortunes to the exploration of the northwest out beyond Lake Superior, out past the ranch where a century and a half later President Roosevelt wrote the "Winning of the West," out to or beyond the edge of what is now the great Yellowstone National Park, anticipating by more than sixty years the first stages of the famous Lewis and Clark expedition. The snow covered the peaks of the Big Horn Mountains, but the party probably forced a way to the Wind River Range before they reluctantly turned back from the foot of the mountains, disappointedly fancying that they might have seen the Pacific if they could have reached the summits.

It is not far from the place where they began their homeward journey that I have seen two trickling streams, within a few yards of each other, start, one toward the gulf and one toward the Pacific—but the latter had seven or eight hundred miles of mountain and forest to pass before it could touch what the Vérendrye brothers hoped to see. Yet, though they, as Cartier, Champlain, Nicolet, La Salle, and scores of others did not find the way to the western sea, their unappreciated, heroic efforts made at their own expense stretched the line of French forts all the way across the valley from sea to mountain range, completing, as one historian has represented it, a T, but as it seems to me rather a cross, with a perpendicular column reaching from the gulf to Hudson's Bay, and its transverse strip from the Big Horn Mountains to Cape Breton. Or so it stood for a day in the world's history, raised by unspeakable suffering, a vision once seen never to be forgotten.

Chevalier de la Vérendrye, who had seen, first of white men, the snow-capped mountains, "sank into poverty and neglect," and finally perished in the shipwreck off the island of Cape Breton. So was the whole east and west line of French pioneering retraced and extended in the life of one hardy French family.[1]

And as to the north and south line, every year saw its foundations and strength increase as if it were a a growing tree. Along the Mississippi, forts were

[1] Parkman, "The Discovery of the Rocky Mountains," in *Atlantic Monthly*, 61 : 783-793. "A Half Century of Conflict," 2 : 4-43. Thwaites, "A Brief History of Rocky Mountain Exploration," pp. 26-36.

planted and Jesuit and Sulpician missions grew. The Illinois country enjoyed a "boom," as we say in America, even in those days, and became known for a time as the Garden of New France; but only for a time, for it was so easy to earn a livelihood there that it was not long before the habitants reverted, under temptation, to the preagricultural, hunting state after giving a moment's prophecy of the stirring life that was some day to make it the garden of the new world, the busiest spot in the busy world.

There are glimpses here and there of gayety and halcyon days that give brightness to the story so full of tragedy. There was in the very heart of the valley (near the site of St. Louis, where a great world's fair was held a few years ago), Fort Chartres, mentioned above, "the centre of life and fashion in the West" as well as "a bulwark against Spain and a barrier to England."[1] But in time the Indians, stirred by the English rivalry, swarmed as well as mosquitoes about the place, and there were battles, the echoes of which are still heard, we are told, in the regions south of St. Louis even in our days. A young French officer, the Chevalier d'Artaguette, captured by the Chickasaws, was burned at the stake. He and his kin were loved by all the French and the song they used to sing of him is kept in a negro melody whose "oft-repeated chorus" ran:

> "In the days of D'Artaguette,
>   Hé! Ho! Hé!
> It was the good old time.
> The world was led straight with a switch,
>   Hé! Ho! Hé!

[1] See Edward G. Mason, "Old Fort Chartres," in his "Chapters from Illinois History," 1901.

Then there were no negroes, no ribbons,
    No diamonds
    For the vulgar.
    Hé! Ho! Hé!"

And here even in this remote place premonitions of
the great and imminent struggle with the English are
ominously heard. We hear the governor-general of
Canada, the Marquis de la Galissonnière, asking the
home government in France not to leave the little
colony of Illinois to perish—not for its own sake, but
"else Canada and Louisiana would fall apart"; still
urging, moreover, the value for fabrics of the wool of
buffaloes, which roam the prairies in innumerable multitudes, the readiness of the earth for the plough, and
the availability of the buffalo as a domestic animal.
"If caught and attached to a plough," says the governor, who spoke truthfully but with little knowledge
of this wild animal, "it would move it at a speed superior
to that of the domestic ox." I do not know how appealing this harnessing of the original motive power of
the prairie to the uses of agriculture was, and it is not
of importance now. The buffalo has long since gone.
Even the ox and the Norman horse, so long in use
there, have been largely supplanted by that mysterious
force, electricity, which Franklin was discovering on
the other side of the Alleghany Mountains at the very
time that this suggestion was being made to the minister of Louis XV. It is known, however, that the
king took thought of the little Illinois colony, for the
fort of wood was transformed under the direction of
Chevalier de Macarty into a fortress of stone and
garrisoned by nearly a regiment of French troops. A
million crowns it cost the king, but this could not have

distressed his Majesty, engaged in "throwing dice with piles of Louis d'or before him" and princes about him.

This was in the early fifties, and the fort was hardly transformed before the rifles of George Washington's men were heard from the eastern barriers disputing the claim of the French to the Ohio country. Jumonville, who was slain among the rocks of the Laurel Mountains, in the Alleghanies (killed in the opening skirmish of the final struggle), had a young brother, Neyon de Villiers, a captain in Chevalier de Macarty's garrison at Fort Chartres; and eastward he hastened, up the Ohio, to avenge his brother's death. "M. de Wachenston" (as the name appears in French despatches) was driven back, and so the "Old French War" in America began.

It was from this mid-continent fortress and its fertile environs that help in arms and rations went to the support of that final struggle along the mountains and lakes, even as far as La Salle's old Fort Niagara, where the valiant Aubry, at the head of his Illinois expedition, fell covered with wounds and many of his men were killed or taken prisoners. That was about all that one in the interior of the valley heard of the battles of the Seven Years' War out upon its edges.

What gives peculiar interest in this fortress to us to-day is that it was for a little time the only place in North America where the flag of the French was flying. All New France had been ceded by the treaty of Paris in 1763, but the little garrison of forty men still held Fort Chartres. Pontiac and other friendly Indians intercepted all approaching English forces till, in 1765 (two years after the treaty of Paris and the cession of Canada and all the valley east of the Mississippi),

St. Ange, the commander, announced to Pontiac, friendly to the end, that all was over, that "Onontio, their great French father," could no longer help his red children, that he was beyond the sea and could not hear, and that he, Pontiac, must make peace with the English.   Then it was that the forty-second High-landers, the "Black Watch," were permitted to enter the fort and to put the red cross of St. George in place of the fleur-de-lis.   And so it was at Fort Chartres that the mighty struggle ended and that the titular life of the great empire of France in the new world actually went out.

The river, seemingly sentient, and still French, as I have said, soon swept away the site of the village outside the fort; and when the English had begun to look upon this as their permanent headquarters in the northwest—this fort, which Captain Pittman had re-ported to be the best-built fort in America—the still hostile river rose one night, and with its "resistless flood" tore away a bastion and a part of the river wall, then moved its channel away, and left the fort a mile inland.

The magazine still stands, or did a little time ago when I visited the site and found it nearly hidden by the trees, bushes, and weeds—all that is visibly left of the old French domain—and not far away, hidden at the foot of a hill, lies, as I have said, the village of Prairie du Rocher, "a little piece of old France transplanted to the Mississippi" a century and a half ago and forgotten.

It was on Champlain's cliff and beneath Cartier's Mount Royal that the unequal contest for the pos-session of America ended, where it began—a contest whose story, as Parkman says, in a sense demeaning his own great contribution, "would have been a history, if faults of constitution and the bigotry and folly of rulers had not dwarfed it to an episode." But if it was an episode to the New Englander, or even to Frenchmen at the distance in time at which I write, it rises to the importance of history out in that region of America, where a century of unexampled fortitude needs rather an epic poet than a historian to give it its place in the world's consciousness.

Indeed, historians of the United States to-day, as well as statesmen of that time, are in substantial agreement in this: That the presence of the French on all the colonial borders compelled a confederation of the varying interests of the several English colonies, kept them penned in between the mountains and the sea until there had been developed some degree of solidarity, some ability to act together; and then by the sudden, if compulsory, withdrawal of the pressure not only allowed their expansion but relieved them of all need of help from England and so of dependence upon her.

"We have caught them at last," said Louis XV's minister, Choiseul, speaking of the treaty of Paris in 1763.[1] Burke[2] prophesied that the removal of France from North America would precipitate, as it did, the division of the British Empire. And Richard Henry Greene, the great English historian, dates the foundation of the great independent republic of the west (the United States) from the triumph of Wolfe on the Heights of Abraham.

[1] Bancroft, "History of the United States," 4 : 460.
[2] William Burke, "Remarks on the Letter Addressed to Two Great Men."

It is interesting testimony in support of this fear of the eventual loss of all the colonies in such a cession, or such an acceptance, that the English commissioners debated long whether it might be more profitable to retain the little island of Guadeloupe instead of all New France. And it would appear that except for the advice of Benjamin Franklin this substitution would probably have been made.

France, then, having borne the brunt of conflict with nature and the natives in that valley, having revealed the riches of that valley to the world, having consecrated its entire length and breadth by high valor and sacrifice, having possessed that valley practically to the very eve of the birth of the nation that now occupies it, and having helped by substantial aid the struggling colonies to their independence, deserves (not through her monarchs or ministers chiefly, but through the new-world pioneers, who gave illustration of the spirit and stuff of Frenchmen) a lasting and a large share of credit for the establishment of the republic which has its most vigorous life in that valley.

New France has passed and New England, too, but in their stead the new republic, recruited from all nations under heaven, ties their lost dominions into a power which is immensely greater than the sum of the two could have been, greater than it could have been in the hands of either alone.

There was for a little time a dream of the revival of New France out beyond the Mississippi, for there was a vast part of that valley that did not pass to England in 1763. The great territory between the Mississippi and the mountains, whose "snow-encumbered" peaks the Vérendrye brothers had so longingly looked upon, was abandoned to Spain, or rather thrust upon Spain, already claiming it. France wanted to give it to England in order that Florida might be saved to Spain, her ally, but England did not hesitate as she did in making choice between the eastern half of the valley and Guadeloupe. She declined. So with an apparent magnanimity, which is greatly to be discounted when we come to know how worthless even the people of the United States, years later, considered this trans-Mississippi country, France, "secretly tired of her colony," finally induced Spain to accept it. The Spanish monarch, as if making the best of a bad bargain, took it with many excuses for his seemingly poor judgment.

But though Louis's minister, Choiseul, chuckled outwardly over the embarrassment to England of his compulsory cession of Canada, New France, Illinois, and Louisiana (instead of Guadeloupe) and made a show of magnanimity in thrusting the other half of the Mississippi upon Spain, and though Turgot's simile between colonies and ripe fruit was often repeated for justification and consolation, the loss of these possessions was undoubtedly keenly felt and the dream of their recovery cherished; at any rate, the recovery of that part which lay beyond the Mississippi.

But that possession had become more precious to the sovereign of Spain, who refused the proffers that France was able to make in the next thirty years. The dream of repossession became fonder to the French republic. Talleyrand, who had spent a year in travel in the United States, urged the acquisition not merely for France's own sake but to curb the ambitions of the Americans, "whose conduct ever since the moment of their independence is enough to prove this truth: the Americans are devoured by pride, ambition, and cupidity."

"There are," he said, "no other means of putting an end to the ambition of the Americans than that of shutting them up within the limits which nature seems to have traced for them; but Spain is not in a condition to do this great work alone. She cannot, therefore, hasten too quickly to engage the aid of a preponderating power, yielding to it a small part of her immense domains in order to preserve the rest."

"Let the court of Madrid cede these districts to France and from that moment the power of America is bounded by the limit which it may suit the interests and the tranquillity of France and Spain to assign her. The French Republic . . . will be a wall of brass forever impenetrable to the combined efforts of England and America."[1]

If in Napoleon's mind the dream was as sinister, as regards the United States, it was not so for long. It contemplated at first the occupation of Santo Domingo, the quelling of the insurrection there, then the seizure of Louisiana, already promised to France by Spain, then the acquisition of Florida, the conversion of the Gulf of Mexico into a French lake, and ultimately the extension of the province of Louisiana to the Alleghanies and, perhaps, even to the old borders of New France along the Great Lakes and the St. Lawrence. But plague and slaughter met his armies in Santo Domingo in the first step toward the realization of his vast design, and the vision, in the shifting light of events in Europe and on the shores of America as well, soon

[1] Quoted in Henry Adams's "History of the United States," I : 357.

assumed other shape and color and at last disappeared entirely, supplanted by the vision of a strengthened American republic that would come to be a rival of England. This was what came (in his own language) instead of his dream of a New France beyond the Mississippi, beyond the American republic:

"I know the full value of Louisiana, and I have been desirous of repairing the fault of the French negotiator who abandoned it in 1763. A few lines of a treaty have restored it to me, and I have scarcely recovered it when I must expect to lose it. But if it escapes from me, it shall one day cost dearer to those who oblige me to strip myself of it than to those to whom I wish to deliver it. The English have successfully taken from France, Canada, Cape Breton, Newfoundland, Nova Scotia, and the richest portions of Asia. They are engaged in exciting troubles in St. Domingo. They shall not have the Mississippi which they covet. Louisiana is nothing in comparison with their conquests in all parts of the globe, and yet the jealousy they feel at the restoration of this colony to the sovereignty of France acquaints me with their wish to take possession of it, and it is thus that they will begin the war. . . . I think of ceding it to the United States. I can scarcely say that I cede it to them, for it is not yet in our possession. If, however, I leave the least time to our enemies, I shall only transmit an empty title to those republicans whose friendship I seek. They only ask of me one town in Louisiana, but I already consider the colony as entirely lost, and it appears to me that in the hands of this growing power, it will be more useful to the policy and even to the commerce of France than if I should attempt to keep it."[1]

[1] Marbois, "History of Louisiana," pp. 263–264.

The United States Commissioner came one day to Paris to purchase New Orleans, and he went back to America with a deed to more than 800,000 square miles of the region which La Salle had claimed for Louis XIV by virtue of the commission which he carried in his bosom from the Rue de la Truanderie more than a century before:

"The First Consul of the French Republic, desiring to give to the United States a strong proof of friendship, doth hereby cede to the said United States, in the name of the French Republic, forever and in full sovereignty, the said territory, with all its rights and appurtenances, as fully and in the same manner as they might have been acquired by the French Republic."[1]

The dream faded into something undefined but greater, relieving Napoleon and France of immediate dangers and promising more to humanity, we must agree, than a colony administered at that distance and separated from a young, growing nation merely by a shifting river that must inevitably have made trouble instead of preventing it.

Whatever may be said of Napoleon's motives or compulsions in this matter or of his service to mankind in others, he has been "useful to the universe," not in preventing England from ruling in that valley and so dominating America, but in making it possible for the United States to undertake the greatest task ever given into the hands of a republic, and at the same time enabling it to keep the good-will of that people who might (if the other dream had been realized) have

[1] Treaty of Purchase between the United States and the French Republic, Art. I.

become the worst of her enemies. It was Napoleon, whatever his motive, Napoleon in the name of the French people, who gave the United States the possibility of becoming a world-power.

CHAPTER VII

THE PEOPLING OF THE WILDERNESS

LET us remind ourselves again, before the hordes of frontiersmen and settlers come over the mountains and up the lakes and down the rivers, erasing most of the tangible memories of the intermontane, primeval western wilderness, that France evoked it from the unknown.

A circle drawn round the Louvre with the radius of two kilometres, enclosed the little patch of earth from which were evoked these millions of acres of untouched forests and millions of acres of virgin plain and prairie, seamed and watered by a hundred thousand streams, washed by a chain of the mightiest inland fresh-water oceans, and guarded by two ranges of mountains. Within that narrow circle, four kilometres in diameter, stood Cartier dreaming of Asia, asking for permission to explore the mysterious square gulf, the St. Lawrence, and again presenting to the king the dusky captive Donnacona; within that circle was the street, Rue aux Ours, whose meat shops Lescarbot in Acadia remembered as the place of good food and doubtless of excited talk concerning the unexplored New France, whose hardships and pleasures he afterward tasted; within that circle Champlain walked, as in a dream, we are told, impatient as a lion in a cage, longing to be again upon the wilderness path, westward of Quebec, toward the unknown; within that circle the priest Olier, of St. Germain-des-Prés, had his vision that led to the founding of Montreal, whose consecration was celebrated also within that same circumference at the Cathedral of Notre Dame; within that circle La Salle lodged in Rue de la Truanderie, awaiting his fateful commission that should give him leave to make real his dream of a wilderness empire; not a stone's throw away from the Rue de la Truanderie ran the street having its beginning or end in Rue aux Ours, Rue Quincampoix, in which the thousands jostled and fought from morning till night for the purchase of stock in that same wilderness empire; and it was finally within that same circle that the wilderness dream, seen for a moment again by Napoleon, grew into the vision of a republic—a republic that might be found, as Napoleon said, "too powerful for Europe in two or three centuries," but in whose bosom dissensions, as he prophesied, could be looked for in the future. A wilderness, with a radius of nearly a thousand kilometres, was evoked from the envisioning, praying, adventuring, and enduring of a few Frenchmen, led by fewer Frenchmen, who stood sooner or later all within the narrow circle that sweeps around the Sorbonne, but four kilometres in diameter.

I walked, in the afternoon of the last day of the old year 1910, entirely around the old city of Paris by way of its fortifications, in a circle three kilometres longer of radius, within a few hours encompassing a ground, rich in what it yields to-day in fruits of art, literature, and science—of indefatigable, intellectual industry and imagination—but richer than its inhabitants know in what has grown upon the billion acres which it has lifted out of the ocean,[1] and given as a soil where civilization could gather its forces from all peoples and begin afresh on the problems of the individual and society.

It is a new view of Paris, I know. No historian of the United States has, so far as I am aware, presented it. Yet I think it is not a distorted vision which enabled me, looking in from the old fortifications, to see Paris not merely as the capital of art and of a great modern language and literature, as those who live there see her, nor as the centre of gayety and frivolity, as so many of my own countrymen see her, but as the parent of fruitful wildernesses, as a patron of pioneers, as the divinity of the verges, as the godmother of a frontier democracy.

It is to be remembered, too, let me say again, that, while England held control of one half of the Mississippi Valley for twenty years after 1763, and Spain of the other half for twenty more, the occupation was hardly more than nominal. Indeed, the English king, George III, in 1763 forbade colonization—as Louis XIV at one time had wished to prevent it—beyond the Alleghany Mountains without his special permission, and, moreover, it was hardly more than ten years after the titular transfer to England that the colonists declared themselves independent. As for the Spanish sovereign, delaying five years in sending a representative to take over the government of his unprofitable half of the wilderness, he had no need to make a decree forbidding settlement. There were no eager settlers.

What virtually happened, therefore, was that the

---

[1] For it will be remembered that to geographers before Cartier this Mississippi Valley was but a sea, even as ages before it actually was.

pioneers of France gave the valley not to England, not to Spain, not even to the American-English colonists, but to the pioneers of the young republic, who, whatever their origin, were without European nationality.

It may be said with approximate accuracy that, while the British flag supplanted the French for a little on a few scattered forts on the east side of the Mississippi and the Spanish flag floated for a little while on the other side of the river, the heart of America really knew in turn, first, only the old Americans, the Indians; second, the French pioneers; and third, the new Americans.

The valley heard, as I have said, hardly a sound of the Seven Years' War, the "Old French War" as Parkman called it. Only on its border was there the slightest bloodshed. All it knew was that the fleur-de-lis flags no longer waved along its rivers and that after a few years men came with axes and ploughs through the passes in the mountains carrying an emblem that had never grown in European fields—a new flag among national banners. They were bearing, to be sure, a constitution and institutions strange to France, but only less strange to England, and perhaps no less strange to other nations of Europe.

I emphasize this because our great debt to English antecedents has obscured the fact that the great physical heritage between the mountains, consecrated of Gallic spirit, came, in effect, directly from the hands that won its first title, the French, into the hands of American settlers, at the moment when a "separate and individual people" were "springing into national life."

This territory was distinct from that of the British

colonies up to the very time of the American Revolution.   And when the Revolution was over and independence was won, by the aid of France let it be remembered, the only settlements within the valley
were three little clusters of French gathered about the
forts once French, then for a few years nominally
English, and then American: two thousand inhabitants
at Detroit and four thousand at Vincennes, on the
Wabash, and in the hamlets along the Mississippi above
the Ohio.

How little the life of those settlements was disturbed is intimated by what occurred in one of the
Illinois villages—that about Fort Chartres.   The ven-
erable and beloved commander, Louis St. Ange de
Belle Rive, had upon the first formal surrender ascended the Mississippi River and crossed to the Spanish territory, where the foundations of the city of St.
Louis were being laid, but the British officer in command at Fort Chartres dying suddenly, and there being
no one competent to succeed him, St. Ange returned
to his old post, restored order, and remained there
until another British officer could reach the fort.   The
habitants were accustomed "to obey, without question, the orders of their superiors. . . . (They) yielded
a passive obedience to the new rulers. . . . They remained the owners, the tillers of the soil."[1]   And one
of the last acts of the Continental Congress and the
first of the new Congress, under the Constitution, was
to provide for an enumeration of these French settlers
and for the allotment to them of lands in this valley
where they had been the sole owners.

Many of the French habitants were not of pure

[1] Roosevelt, "Winning of the West," 1 : 38, Alleghany edition.

blood. The French seldom took women with them
into the wilderness. They were traders, trappers, and
soldiers. They married Indian wives, untrammelled,
as President Roosevelt says, "by the queer pride
which makes a man of English stock unwilling to make
a red-skinned woman his wife, though anxious enough
to make her his concubine."[1]

They were under ordinary circumstances good-
humored, kindly men, "always polite"[2]—in "agreeable
contrast" to most frontiersmen—religious, yet fond of
merrymaking, of music and dancing; and while, as
time went on, they came to borrow traits of their red
neighbors and even to forget the years and months
(reckoning time, as the Indians did, from the flood of
the river or the ripening of strawberries), still they
kept many valuable and amiable qualities, to be merged
eventually in the new life that soon swept over their
beautiful little villages. Of the coming of a strange,
new, strenuous life, a stray English or American fur
trader gave them occasional presentment, as it were,
the spray of the swelling, restless sea of human spirits,
beating against the mountain barriers and flung far
inland.

In the early part of the eighteenth century an
English governor of the colony of Virginia, Alexander
Spotswood, had led a band of horsemen known afterward as his "Knights of the Golden Horseshoe," with
great hilarity, "stimulated by abundance of wine,
champagne, rum," and other liquors, over the Blue
Ridge Mountains, a part of the Alleghany Range, to
the Shenandoah. He had talked menacingly of the

---

[1] Roosevelt, "Winning of the West," 1 : 41.
[2] "Winning of the West," 1 : 45.

French who held the valley beyond, had encouraged
the extension of English settlements to break the line
of French possessions, and had formed a short-lived
Virginia-Indian company to protect the frontier against
French and Indian incursions.   This expedition was a
visible challenge.   With his merry company he buried
a record of his "farthest west" journey in one of the
bottles emptied en route and then went back to tide-
water.   That was the end of his adventure; little or
nothing came of his "flourish" except the extension of
the Virginia frontier to the Blue Ridge Mountains.

Only traders and trappers ventured farther or even
so far during the next three or four decades, and they
were a "set of abandoned wretches," or so a later
governor characterized them, though Parkman mentions some exceptions, and I wish to believe there
were more, since one of them, I find, carried my own
name far into that country on his trading and hunting
expeditions among and with the Indians.

Searching, a few years ago, the files of a paper published early in the nineteenth century on the edge of
this wilderness, which was already calling itself the
Western World—a paper, one of the first of the myriad
white leaves into which the falling forests have been
converted and scattered thick enough to cover every
square foot of the valley—I happened upon this record, surprised as if a bit of the transmontane sea
spray had touched my own face on the Mississippi:
"That delightful country" (Kentucky), it ran, "from
time immemorial had been the resort of wild beasts and
of men only less savage, when in the year 1767 it was
visited by John Finley and a few wandering white men
from the British colony of North Carolina, allured by

the love of hunting and the desire of barter with the Indians. The distance of this country from populous parts of the colonies, almost continuous wars, and the claims of the French had prevented all attempts at exploration."

I seize upon this partly because, having succeeded to the name of this hunter and trader, who entered the valley just as St. Ange was yielding Fort Chartres to the English and crossing the Mississippi, I am able to show that my own ancestral sympathies while dwelling on the frontiers were not with the French. But I quote it chiefly because he was a typical forerunner, a first frontiersman.

Like the coureur de bois Nicolas Perrot, of exactly a century before, he was only the dawn of the light— the light of another day, which was beginning to appear in the valley. For it was he who led Daniel Boone to the first exploring and settling of that wilderness south of the Ohio, which, to quote further from the paper called the *Western World*,[1] had a soil "more fat and fertile than Egypt"—and was the place where "Pan, if he ever existed, held dominion unmolested of Ceres or Lucinia."

Such was the almost soundless beginning of what soon developed into a mighty "processional," its rumblings of wagons and shoutings of drivers on land and blowing of conches on the rivers increasing, accompanied by the sound of rushing waters, the cry of frightened birds, and the thunders of crashing trees. First came this silent hunter and fur trader, almost as stealthy as the Indian in his movements; then the

---

[1] *Western World*, published at Frankfort, Ky., 1806-8, by John Wood and Joseph M. Street.

pale, gaunt, slow-moving, half hunter, half farmer, too indolent to disturb the wilderness from which he got a meagre living, planting his meagre crops among the girdled trees of withered foliage, which he did not take the trouble to cut down; then the backwoodsman, sallow as his immediate predecessor from the shade of the forest, who with his axe made a little clearing, built a "shack," turned his cattle into the grass that had grown for centuries untouched, and let his pigs feed on the acorns; then the more robust agriculturist who aggressively pushed back the shadows of the forest, planted the wilderness with seeds of a magic learned in the valleys of Europe and Asia, put up the fences of individualistic struggle, and built his log cabin, the wilderness castle, the birthplace of the new American; then the speculator and promoter (the hunter and explorer of the urban occupation); and finally in their wake the builders of mills and factories and cities—drab, smoky, vainglorious, ill-smelling, bad-architectured centres of economic activity, fringed with unoccupied, unimproved, naked areas, plotted and held for increment, earned only by risk and privation.

This processional, "this gradual and continuous progress of the European race toward the Rocky Mountains," says the vivid pen of De Tocqueville, "has the solemnity of a providential event. It is like a deluge of men, rising unabatedly and driven daily onward by the hand of God."[1]

The story of this anabasis has been told in hundreds and thousands of fragments—the anabasis that has had no katabasis—the literal going up of a people, as

[1] "Democracy in America," ed. Gilman, 1 : 512.

we shall see, from primitive husbandry and handicraft and a neighborly individualism, to another level, of machine labor, of more comfortable living, and of socialized aspiration.

De Quincey has gathered into an immortal story the dramatic details of an exodus that had its beginning and end just at the time when these half huntsmen, half traders were creeping down from the farther ridges of the Alleghanies into the wilderness, where the little French settlements were clinging like clusters of ripened grapes to a great vine—the story of the flight of the Kalmuck Tartars from the banks of the Volga, across the steppes of Europe and the deserts of Asia to the frontiers of China—the story of the journey of over a half million semi-barbarians, half of whom perished by the way from cold or heat, from starvation or thirst, or from the sabres and cannon of the savage hosts pursuing them by day and night through the endless stretches—the story of the translation of these nomad herdsmen on the steppes of Russia through "infinite misery" into stable agriculturists beneath the great wall of China.

If the myriad details of this new-world migration could be summarized with like genius, we should have a drama to put beside the exodus of Israel from Egypt and their conquest of Canaan—a drama, less picturesque and highly colored than that of the flight of the Tartars—their Oriental costumes, their fierce horses, their camels and tents, showing, unhidden of tree against the snowy or sandy desert—but infinitely more consequential in the history of the human race.

The Indians, hostile to this horde that built cabins upon their hunting-grounds and devoured their forests,

were to the wilderness migrants, driven, not of the
hand of man but, as De Tocqueville says, "of the hand
of God" made manifest in some human instinct, some
desire of freedom, some hatred of convention, some
hope of power or possession, what the Kirghese and
Bashkirs and Russians were to those Asiatic migrants,
pursuing them day and night like fiends for thousands
of miles. And the myriad sufferings of the American
migrants from hunger and thirst, from the freezing
cold and the blasting, blistering, wilting heat, from
the fevers of the new-broken lands, from the ravages
of locust and grasshopper, and chinch-bug and drought,
from isolation from human friendships, from want of
gentle nursing—even De Quincey's improvident travellers did not endure more, nor the children of Israel,
to whose thirst the smitten rock yielded water, to whose
hunger the heavens ministered with manna and the
earth with quail, whose pursuing enemies were drowned
in the sea that closed over their pathway, and whose
confronting enemies in the land they entered to possess
were overcome by the aid of unseen armies that were
heard marching in the tops of the mulberry-trees, or
were seen by friendly vision assembling their chariots
in the skies above.

Here across the Mississippi Valley is an exodus accomplished not of a single night, as these two of which
I have just spoken, but extended through a hundred
years of home leavings and love privations. Here is
an anabasis of a century of privations, titanic labors,
frontier battles, endured countless times, till these
migrants of Europe and of the new-world seaboard,
became, as children of the wilderness, a new people,
with qualities so distinctive as to lead the highest

authority[1] on the history of that valley to characterize the west not as a geographic division of the United States, but as a "form of society" with its own peculiar flowering, developed, not as Parkman's magnificent fleur-de-lis,[2] by cross-fertilization, nor by grafting, but simply by the planting or sowing of Old World seeds on new and free land, where the mountains kept off the pollen of alien spirit, where the puritanical winds of the New England coast were somewhat tempered by the warmer winds from the south, where the waters had some iron in them, but, most of all, where the soil was practically as free as when it came from the hands of the glaciers and the streams.

It is this distinctiveness of development, due to the mountains' challenge to every man's spirit as he passed, to the isolation which compelled him to work out his own salvation, and to the constant struggle, largely single-handed, with frontier forces—as well as the uniqueness of background—that gave the west a character which identifies it to discerning minds quite as much as its geographic boundaries. It is this fact which makes the French pioneering preface to a civilization different from anything that has developed elsewhere in the United States, and not only different in the past but now the dominant force in American education, politics, and industry.

What that civilization would have been without the adventurous French preface we can but vainly surmise. What it is with that background, that preface, is indeed the "foremost chapter in the files of time." As

[1] Frederick J. Turner, "The Significance of the Mississippi Valley in American History," in Proceedings of the Mississippi Valley Historical Association (1909-10), 3 : 159-184.

[2] See Epilogue.

Ambassador James Bryce has said: "What Europe is
to Asia, what England is to the rest of Europe, what
America is to England, that the western States are
to the Atlantic States."[1] The French may dispute
the implied claim of the second of these comparisons,
but even they will have a satisfaction in admitting that
their particular part of the United States is to the rest,
which was not touched by their priests and explorers,
what "Europe is to Asia." And here is my particular
justification for asking the imaginations of the people
of France to occupy and hold that to which the preface has given them the best of titles.

Meanwhile, that migration, heralded, as we have
seen, just before the Revolution, by huntsmen and
traders, meagre by reason of Indian hostility and the
need of soldiers on the Atlantic side of the mountains
till independence had been won, became appreciable
at the end of the century and grew to an inundating
stream after the War of 1812 had made the Mississippi
secure to the new republic beyond all question.

"Old America," said an observing English traveller
in 1817, "seems to be breaking up and moving westward. We are seldom out of sight, as we travel on this
grand track (the national turnpike through Pennsylvania) towards the Ohio, of family groups behind and
before us. . . . A small waggon so light that you
might almost carry it, yet strong enough to bear a
good load of bedding and utensils and provisions and
a swarm of young citizens, and to sustain marvellous
shocks in its passage over these rocky heights with
two small horses and sometimes a cow or two, comprises
their all; excepting a little store of hard earned cash

[1] "American Commonwealth," 1913 ed., 2 : 892.

for the land-office of the district; where they may obtain a title for as many acres as they possess half dollars, being one-fourth of the purchase money. The waggon has a tilt, or cover, made of a sheet, or perhaps a blanket. The family are seen before, behind, or within the vehicle, according to the road or the weather, or perhaps the spirits of the party. . . . A cart and single horse, frequently affords the means of transfer, sometimes a horse and pack saddle. Often the back of the poor pilgrim bears all his effects, and his wife follows, bare footed, bending under the hopes of the family."[1] This is a detail of the exodus through the most northern mountain pass.

Farther south the procession moved in heavy wagons drawn by four or six horses. "Family groups, crowding the roads and fords, marching toward the sunset," at right angles to the courses of the migratory birds, not mindful as they of seasons, "were typical of the overland migration" across Tennessee and Kentucky. The poorer classes travelled on foot, as at the north, but drew after them carts with all their household effects.[2]

Still farther south "the same type of occupation was to be seen; the poorer classes of southern emigrants cut out their clearings along the rivers that flowed to the gulf and to the lower Mississippi,"[3] and later still farther west into what is now Texas.

The squatters whom I saw in my walk around the city of Paris, inhabiting what was the military zone with their portable houses, or in their dilapidated shacks, had better shelter than they who first invaded

---

[1] Morris Birkbeck, "Notes on a Tour in America, 1817," pp. 34, 35.
[2] F. J. Turner, "Rise of the New West," p. 80.
[3] F. J. Turner, "Rise of the New West," p. 90.

the zone beyond the mountain walls that were the natural western fortifications of the Atlantic colonies.

But though many of those western wilderness immigrants were "poor pilgrims" and for a time squatters (as the immediately extramural population of Paris), they were recruited from the sturdiest stock on the Atlantic side of the fortifications. Some went, to be sure, who had failed in the old place, but were ready to make new hazard; some wanted greater freedom than the more highly socialized and conventionalized life within the fortifications would permit; some longed for adventure; some sought a fortune or competency perhaps impossible in the old settlements; some had only the inherited promptings of the nomad savage in them, and kept ever moving on, making their nameless graves out in the gloom of the forest or upon the silent plains.

It was indeed a motley procession, the by-product of the more or less conservative, sometimes politically or religiously intolerant, aristocratic tide-water settlements. Yet do not make the mistake of thinking that it was slag or refuse humanity, such as camps in the narrow zone around the gates of Paris. It is rather like an industrial by-product that has needed some slight change or adaptation to make it more valuable to society than the original product upon which the manufacturers had kept their attention fixed—or, at any rate, to make the margin of profit in the whole industry greater. Out of once discarded, seemingly valueless matter have come our coal-tar products: saccharine many times sweeter than sugar, colors unknown to the old dyers, perfumes as fragrant as those distilled from flowers, medicines potent to allay fevers.

Up in the woods of Canada last summer I found a chemist trying to do with the wood waste what Remsen and Perkin and others have done with coal waste, and I cannot resist the suggestion of my metaphor that there in the forest valleys beyond the Alleghanies the elements and conditions were found to convert this Atlantic by-product, unpromising outwardly, into the substance of a new and precious civilization.

This overmountain procession came chiefly up the watercourses of the south and middle States. Prior to 1830 the mass of pioneer colonists in most of the Mississippi Valley had been contributed by the up-country of the south. The dominant strain in those earlier comers, as President Roosevelt reminds us, was Scotch-Irish, a "race doubly-twisted in the making, flung from island to island and toughened by exile"—a race of frontiersmen than whom a "better never appeared"—a race which was as "steel welded into the iron of an axe." They form the kernel of the "distinctively and intensely American stock who were the pioneers of the axe and the rifle, succeeding the French pioneers of the sword and the bateaux."

What I have just said of them, these Scotch-Irish, is in quotation, for as I have already intimated, my own ancestry is of that double-twisting; and since the time when my first American ancestor settled as the first permanent minister beyond the mountains, following the paths of the French priests in their missions and became a member of a presbytery extending from the mountains to the setting sun, until my last collateral ancestor living among the Indians helped survey the range lines of new States and finally marked the boundaries of the last farms in the passes of the Rockies, that ancestry has followed the frontier westward from where Céloron planted the emblems of French possession along the Ohio to where Chevalier la Vérendrye looked upon the snowy and impassable peaks of the Rockies.

The immigrants to America of that stock had, many of them, at once on reaching the new land found the foot-hills of mountains, chiefly in Pennsylvania. Here they settled, gradually pushing their way southward in the troughs of the mountain streams and making finally a "broad belt from north to south, a shield of sinewy men thrust in between the people of the seaboard and the red warriors of the wilderness," the same men who declared for American independence in North Carolina before any others, even before the men of Massachusetts. With this stock there went over the mountain men of other origins, of course, English, French Huguenots, Germans, Hollanders, Swedes; but the Scotch-Irish were the core of the new life, which in "iron surroundings" became strongly homogeneous— "yet different from the rest of the world—even the world of America, and infinitely more the world of Europe."

In the north the great rivers lay across the tedious paths that ran with the lines of latitude. And so it was partly for physiographic reasons that the first far-stretching expansions of the New England settlements were not toward this great western wilderness but northward along the narrower valleys. It was not until the migration had filled the meagre limits and capacities of these smaller valleys and had carried school-houses and churches and town halls well up granite hillsides, that the western exodus came, to leave those hillside homes and institutional shelters as shells found far from a receding sea, empty or habited by a new species of immigrant.[1] Farms were abandoned for the fertile fields of the far west, from which wheat can be imported for less than the cost of raising it on the sterile hills and in the short-summered valleys. New England had once claimed a fraction of the great west, as, indeed, had most of the other seaboard colonies. But these claims were surrendered to the general government, as we shall see later, "for the common good," and so her migrants had none other than that instinct which follows lines of latitude to keep them practically within the zone of her relinquished claims. Over into New York, New Jersey, and Pennsylvania her children overflowed till a map of these States in 1820, colored to show the origin and character of their various communities, made practically all of western New York, a part of New Jersey and the northern third of Pennsylvania, an expanded New England. Meanwhile the hardiest joined the transmontane migration, and in the decade after the opening of the Erie Canal (1830–40) the whole northern edge of the valley takes color of New England conquest.

So the first peopling was a mingling of the children of the first strugglers with a raw savage continent; men already schooled in adversity, already acquainted with some of the frontier problems—civilization's most highly individualized, least socialized material, the wheat of the new world's first winnowing.

What is particularly to be observed is that men of

[1] In one of those far northern valleys which I know best there was a school, before the exodus, of some seventy pupils, gathered from the farmers' families of the neighborhood. Now there are not a half-dozen pupils, and they are carried to a neighboring district.

the north and the south, as far apart as Carolina and Massachusetts, came together beyond the mountains in the united building of commonwealths; for over those mountains the rivers all ran toward the Mississippi, which tied the interests of all together.

There was no north-and-south line then. The men of the valley were all westerners, "men of the western world"; not yet very strong as nationalists, that is, as men of the United States. "Men of the western waters" they also called themselves, for they shunned the uplands and kept near the streams by which or along which they had come into the wilderness and from which they drank. Men of the axe they were, too, in that first occupancy, never venturing far from the trees that gave them both roof and fuel. It was later, as we have seen, that the men of the plough came where the men of the axe had cleared the way.

It is interesting to notice that when these builders of new States came to devise symbols for their official seals, many of them took the plough, that implement which we know was carried in the first Aryan migration into the plains of Europe, but some of them put a rising sun on the horizon of their shields—the sign of the consciousness of a new day.

The foundation, then, of the new societies was laid in what might be called a concrete of character and lineage—heterogeneous, but all of the neo-American period and not of the paleo-European. Here came the ancestors of Abraham Lincoln, among the axemen from the South, and here the ancestors of General Grant, among the builders of towns, from New England, both born in cabins. And these instances are but suggestive of the conglomerate that was to be as practicable for building purposes (the co-efficient of spirit being once determined) as any homogeneous, age-old rock used in the structure of nations. It became "homogeneous" not as bricks or stones built into a wall by mortar or cement but as concrete, eternal as the hills, needing not to be chiselled and split but only to be moulded and "set" at just the right moment. If this gives any suggestion of want of permanence, of liability of cracking, then the figure is not fortunate. I mean only to suggest, by still another metaphor, that out of the myriad rugged individualities, idiosyncrasies, and independences a new rock has been formed.

How distinctly western this first migration was you may know from the fact that there was frequent talk of secession from the Union by the seaboard commonwealths in the early post-revolutionary days. There were even, as we have seen, hopes and fears that a Franco-American republic might grow out of that solidarity and independent spirit that were ready to forsake the government on the eastern side of the mountains, which seemed to be heedless of western needs. This tells us, who are conscious of the national spirit which is now stronger, perhaps, in that valley than in any other part of the Union, how strong the western, the anti-nationalistic, spirit must have been then.

But that was before the coming of the east-and-west canal and the east-and-west railroads, which virtually upheaved a new watershed and changed the whole physiographic, social, and economic relationships of the west. The old French river Colbert, the Eternal River, was virtually cut into two great rivers, one of which was to empty into the gulf (just as it did in

La Salle's day and in Iberville's day), while the other was to run through the valley of the Great Lakes, down through the valley of the hostile Iroquois, into the harbor of New York. This is not observable on the topographical maps simply because of our unimaginative definition of a watershed. A watershed is changed, according to that definition, only by an actual elevation or depression of the surface of the earth, whereas a railroad or canal that bridges ravines and tunnels or climbs elevations, or a freight rate that diverts traffic into a new course, as suddenly raises or lowers and as certainly removes watersheds as if mountains were miraculously lifted and carried into the midst of the sea.

So there came to be not only two rivers but two valleys, the one of the lake and prairie plainsmen and the other of the gulf plainsmen. The steam shuttles flying east and west by land and water wove a pattern in the former different from the latter but on the same warp. Two widely unlike industrial and social systems gradually developed, and they, in turn, struggling for the mastery of lands beyond the Mississippi, divided the nearer west—once a homogeneous state of mind—into two wests and all but disrupted the Union.

Then the direct European immigration began, millions coming from single states of Europe, sifting into the neo-American settlements, but for the most part passing on, in mighty armies, to possess whole tracts farther west, along and beyond the Mississippi. In some parts of the northwest to-day the parents of three men out of four were born in Europe—in Scandinavia, in Germany, in Russia, in Italy.

So France, keeping near her those whom she loves best, her own children, has yet seen her Nouvelle

France draw to it the children of all other nations. As from Hagar exiled in the wilderness has a new race sprung—has the wilderness been peopled.

In my boyhood the last division of that great exodus, largely made up of migrants from the eastern half of the valley, was still passing westward. One of the banners which some of the wagons covered with canvas ("prairie-schooners," as they were called) used to fly was "Pike's Peak or Bust," an Americanism indicating the intention of the pilgrims to reach the mountain at the western terminus of the great valley or die in the attempt. Occasionally one came back with the inglorious substitute legend upon his wagon, "Busted"—a laconic intimation of failure. But this was the exception. The west kept, till it had made them her own, most of those who ventured their all for a home in the wilderness.

There were "two great commemorative monuments that arose to mark the depth and permanence of the awe" which possessed all who shared the calamities or witnessed the results of the Tartar migration. One was a "Romanang"—a "national commemoration, with music rich and solemn," of all the souls who departed to the rest of Paradise from the "afflictions of the desert"—and the "other, more durable and more commensurate to the scale of the calamity and to the grandeur of the national exodus," "mighty columns of granite and brass," where the exodus had ended in the shadow of the Chinese wall. The inscription on these columns reads:

By the Will of God,
Here, upon the Brink of these Deserts,
Which from this Point begin and stretch away

Pathless, treeless, waterless,
For thousands of miles, and along the margins of many
mighty Nations,
Rested from their labors and from great afflictions,
Under the shadow of the Chinese Wall,
And by the favor of Kien Long, God's Lieutenant upon
Earth,
The ancient Children of the Wilderness—the Turgote
Tartars—
Flying before the wrath of the Grecian Czar,
Wandering Sheep who had strayed away from the Celestial
Empire in the year 1616,
But are now mercifully gathered again, after infinite sorrow,
Into the fold of their forgiving Shepherd.
Hallowed be the spot forever,
and
Hallowed be the day—September 8, 1771 !
Amen.

There have been many expositions of the fruits of
the Mississippi Valley's agriculture and manufacture
and mining and thinking and teaching and preaching
and ministering, but there has been no general commemoration with "music rich and solemn" of those who
endured the "afflictions of the wilderness," though the
last of the pioneers will soon have departed to his rest,
for fourteen years ago it was officially declared that
there was no longer a frontier.   But mighty columns
not of man's rearing stand upon the farther edge of
that western valley, columns of rock rich with gold
and silver and every other precious metal, surmounted,
some of them the year through, with capitals of snow
and lacking only the legend:

Here upon the Brink of the Plains
Which stretched away pathless, treeless, boundless,

Ended their century-long exodus
The New Children of the Wilderness,
Driven by the Hand of God
Westward and ever Westward
Till they have at last entered
Into the full Heritage of those
Who, first of Pioneers,
Traced the rivers and lakes of this Valley
Between the eternal mountains.

CHAPTER VIII

THE PARCELLING OF THE DOMAIN

THE domain of Louis XIV in the midst of America (between the Great Lakes and the gulf, the Alleghanies and the Rockies) embraced over seven hundred and fifty million acres. One-half of it, roughly, was covered with giant forests inhabited by fur-bearing animals with opulence upon their backs. One-half was covered with vegetation, varying from the luxuriant prairie grass to the sage-brush of the shadeless plains, plains roamed by beasts clothed with valuable robes. Two-thirds of this domain was arable, with only the irrigation of the clouds, and all of it was destined some day to be cultivated, the clouds having the assistance of man-made irrigation or dry farming.

The portion east of the Mississippi (about three hundred million acres) was at one time estimated to be worth not more, politically and physically, than the island of Guadeloupe—an island represented by a pin-head on an ordinary map—producing forty thousand tons of sugar and about two million pounds each of coffee and cocoa.

Even the people of the Atlantic States were accused by westerners as late as 1786 of threatening secession and of being as ignorant of the trans-Alleghany country as Great Britain had been of America, and as inconsiderate. The western half, urged by the minister of Louis XV upon Spain after sixty or seventy millions of francs had been spent fruitlessly upon it by France, recovered by Napoleon and sold to the United States for one-fourth of the amount that was expended a century later for the celebration of the purchase, was regarded at the time of the purchase, even by many seacoast Americans, as useless, except as it secured control of the mouth of the Mississippi. An important New York paper said editorially:

". . . As to the unbounded region west of the Mississippi, it is, with the exception of a very few settlements of Spaniards and Frenchmen bordering on the banks of the river, a wilderness through which wander numerous tribes of Indians. And when we consider the present extent of the United States, and that not one-sixteenth part of its territory is yet under occupation, the advantage of the acquisition, as it relates to actual settlement, appears too distant and remote to strike the mind of a sober politician with much force. This, therefore, can only rest in speculation for many years, if not centuries to come, and consequently will not perhaps be allowed very great weight in the account by the majority of readers. But it may be added, that should our own citizens, more enterprizing than wise, become desirous of settling this country, and emigrate thither, it must not only be attended with all the injuries of a too widely dispersed population, but, by adding to the great weight of the western part of our territory, must hasten the dismemberment of a large portion of our country, or a dissolution of the government. On the whole, we think it may with candor be said, that whether the possession at this time of any territory west of the river Mississippi will be advantageous, is at best extremely problematical. For ourselves, we are very much inclined to the opinion that, after all, it is the Island of N. Orleans by which the command of a free navigation of the Mississippi is secured, that gives to this interesting cession its greatest value, and will render it in every view of immense benefit to our country. By this cession we hereafter shall hold within our own grasp, what we have heretofore enjoyed only by the uncertain tenure of a treaty, which might be broken at the pleasure of another, and (governed as we now are) with perfect impunity. Provided therefore we have not purchased it too dear, there is all the reason for exultation which the friends of the administration display, and which all Americans may be allowed to feel."[1]

I quote this to show how far from appreciating France's generosity the easterners, and especially the anti-Jeffersonian Federalists in America, were at that time. Other and less conscientious newspapers put the prodigality of Jefferson's commissioners more graphically:

"Fifteen millions of dollars! they would exclaim. The sale of a wilderness has not usually commanded a price so high. Ferdinand Gorges received but twelve hundred and fifty pounds sterling for the Province of Maine. William Penn gave for the wilderness that now bears his name but a trifle over five thousand pounds. Fifteen millions of dollars! A breath will suffice to pronounce the words. A few strokes of the pen will express the sum on paper. But not one man in a thousand has any conception of the magni-

[1] *New York Herald*, July 6, 1803.

tude of the amount. Weigh it and there will be four hundred and thirty-three tons of solid silver. Load it into wagons, and there will be eight hundred and sixty-six of them. Place the wagons in a line, giving two rods to each, and they will cover a distance of five and one-third miles. Hire a laborer to shovel it into the carts, and, though he load sixteen each day, he will not finish the work in two months. Stack it up dollar on dollar, and supposing nine to make an inch, the pile will be more than three miles high. It would load twenty-five sloops; it would pay an army of twenty-five thousand men forty shillings a week each for twenty-five years; it would, divided among the population of the country, give three dollars for each man, woman, and child. . . . Invest the principal as school fund, and the interest will support, forever, eighteen hundred free schools, all owning fifty scholars, and five hundred dollars to each school."[1]

Napoleon had, indeed, made a good bargain for France, selling a wilderness, which at best he could not well have kept long, for a price which all the specie currency in the poor young republic would not be adequate to meet.

It was of this domain (a part of the claim of La Salle for Louis XIV in 1682, divided between England and Spain in 1763, made one again in 1803 by the will of Napoleon, under the control of the United States, added to by the purchase of Florida from Spain and the acquisition of Texas, filling all the Great Valley)— it was of this valley that, as late as the early fifties, a member of Congress (afterward to become vice-president of the United States, then President), Andrew Johnson, although an earnest advocate of a liberal

[1] McMaster, "History of the People of the United States," 2 : 630.

land policy, predicted that it would take "seven hundred years to dispose of the public lands at the rate we have been disposing of them."[1]   Seven hundred years—as long as from the founding of Charlemagne's new empire of the west to the discovery of the coasts of a still newer empire of the west.

But in two hundred years from the day that La Salle so miserably perished on the plains of Texas, in exactly one hundred years from the time when, under the epoch-making "Ordinance of the Northwest" (as it has been called), the parcelling of the land began, and in less than half a century from the year when Andrew Johnson's seven-hundred-year prophecy began to run, practically the entire domain had been surveyed and sold or given by the nation to private or municipal or corporate possession.   It was the 24th of July, 1687, that La Salle died; it was July 27, 1787, that the first great sale of a fragment of the domain was made; and it was in 1887, approximately, that all the humanly available domain was occupied by at least two persons to a square mile; for in 1890 it was officially declared by the government of the United States that it had no frontier.   Not that the land was all sold, but all that was immediately valuable.

As soon as the War of Independence was over, and even during the struggle, the territories of several of the Atlantic States (or colonies) expanded to the Mississippi.   There was a quadrilateral, trans-Alleghany Massachusetts, as indifferent to natural boundaries as a "state of mind" (which Massachusetts has often been defined to be), respectful only of imaginary lines of latitude and the Mississippi River, the Spanish border.   Little Connecticut multiplied its latitude by

[1] Speech on the Homestead bill, April 29, 1852.

degrees of longitude till it reached in a thin but rich slice from Pennsylvania also to the Mississippi. Virginia disputed these mountain-to-river claims of her New England sisters, but held unquestioned still larger territories to the north and south—and so on from the sources of the river to Florida, South Carolina even claiming a strip a few miles wide and four hundred long. There was almost a duplication of the Atlantic front on the Mississippi River. These statements will not interest those who can have no particular acquaintance with the personalities of those several commonwealths, quite as marked as are those of Normandy and Brittany; but even without this knowledge it is possible to appreciate the magnanimity and the wisdom which prompted those States, many with large and rich claims, to surrender all to the central government, the Continental Congress, for the benefit of all the States, landful and landless alike.[1]

[1] LANDS CEDED BY THE STATES TO THE UNITED STATES

NORTHWEST OF THE OHIO RIVER	SQUARE MILES
Ohio	39,964
Indiana	33,809
Illinois	55,414
Michigan	56,451
Wisconsin	53,924
Minnesota, east of the Mississippi River	26,000
	265,562

or 169,959,680 acres.

Virginia claimed this entire region.
New York claimed an indefinite amount.
Connecticut claimed about 25,600,000 acres and ceded all but 3,300,000.
Massachusetts claimed about 34,560,000 acres.

SOUTH OF KENTUCKY

South Carolina ceded about 3,136,000 acres.
North Carolina ceded (nominally) 29,184,000 acres.
Georgia ceded 56,689,920 acres.
—Payson J. Treat, "The National Land System, 1785-1820."

So it was that even before the National Government was organized under a federal constitution in 1789, the land beyond the western boundaries of the several colonies, out as far as the Mississippi, was held for the good of all. And later the same policy followed the expansion to the Rockies and beyond. Can one imagine a greater or more fateful task than confronted this young, inexperienced republic—to have the disposal of a billion acres of timber lands, grazing lands, farm lands, ore lands, oil lands, coal lands, arid lands, and swamp lands for the good not only of the first comers and of those then living in the Atlantic States but also of the millions that should inhabit all that country in future generations as well—for the good of all of all time?

This one-time bed of the Paleozoic sea between Archæan shores, raised in time above the ocean and enriched of the mountains that through millions of years were gradually to be worn down by the natural forces of the valley, and finally, as we have seen, opened by the French as a new-created world to be peopled by the old world, then overflowing its brim, became all of it in the space of a single lifetime the property of a few million human beings, their heirs, and assigns forever. The "men of always"[1] had actually come and were to divide and distribute among themselves the stores of millions of years as if reserved for them from the foundation of the world.

When Deucalion and Pyrrha went forth to repeople the world after a flood, they were told by the oracle to cast over their shoulders the bones of their mother.

[1] The Iroquois, according to Châteaubriand, called themselves Ongoueonoue, the "men of always," signifying that they were a race eternal, immortal, not to fade away.—"Travels in America," 2 : 93.

These they rightly interpreted, according to the myth, to be the stones of the earth, and so the valleys of the ancient world became populous. Peopling *per se* was not, however, the object or the first object of the act under which the government, after the manner of Deucalion, went across this new-world valley, casting in stoneless areas clods of earth and tufts of virgin sod before it and behind it. It was not people that the government wanted. Indeed, it was afraid of people. What it desired, the "common good," was the immediate payment of the debt incurred in the War of Independence, and the only resource was land. The land that the French had discovered, whose nominal transfer to England Choiseul had said he had made to destroy England's power in America, was now to meet a portion at least of the expense of the brave struggle for the winning of independence. France's practically untouched wilderness was now to supplement the succor of French ships and arms and sympathy in the firm founding of the new nation. The acres that France under other fortunes might have divided among her own descendants, children of the west, she gave to a happier destiny than La Salle could have desired in his wildest dreams as he traversed the streams that watered those first-parcelled fields.

So, incidentally, the French pioneers before the fact and the first settlers of the west after the fact had their part, witting or unwitting, willing or unwilling, written or unwritten, along with George Rogers Clark and his men, who seized the British forts in that territory during the Revolution (and thus gave standing to the claim for its transfer), and along with the men of the Atlantic colonies who sacrificed their fortunes

and their lives—these all had their part in the inauguration of this experiment in self-government. There
was no higher, more far-reaching "common good"
than this to which acres prepared from Paleozoic days
and consecrated of unselfish adventure could be devoted.

I cannot find anywhere in our history an appreciation of this particular contribution to the foundation
of free institutions in America. But it is one that
should be recorded and remembered along with the
more tangible contributions. Every perilous journey
of the French across that territory for which France
got not a franc, every purchase which Scotch-Irish or
New England or other settlers went out to conquer,
was a march or a skirmish in the War of Independence,
for all was turned to the confirming of the fruits of victory of the American Revolution.

Those who have written of the land policy which
prescribed the conditions of sale have divided its history roughly into two periods: the first, from 1783 to
1840, in which the fiscal considerations of the general
government were dominant; and the second, from 1840
to the present time, when the social conditions, either
within the territory itself or in the nation at large,
were given first consideration.

The statistical story of the first period, under that
accurate classification, would be about as interesting
as a bulletin of real-estate transactions in Chicago
would be to a professor of paleontology in the Sorbonne. It is only when those sales are considered tel-
eologically (as the philosophers would say) that they
can seem absorbingly vital to others than economists
or to the fortunate heirs of some of the purchasers.

I am aware (let me say parenthetically) that customs duties might have a somewhat like interpretation under a higher imaginative power; but this possibility does not lessen to me the singularly spiritual character of this series of transactions—of land sales, or transmutations of lands, on the one hand, into the maintenance of the fabric of a government by the people, and, on the other, into the ruggedest, hardiest species of men and women the world has known in its new hemisphere.

Land-offices, as I have seen them described in the newspapers of the early part of the nineteenth century, gave no outward suggestion of being places of miracles —sacred places. They were noisy, dirty, ephemeral tabernacles of canvas or of boards in the wilderness, carried westward till the day of permanent temples should come. But like the Ark of the Covenant in the history of Israel, they blessed those in whose fields they rested on the way, even as the field and household of Obed-edom the Gittite were blessed by the presence of the ark on its way up to Jerusalem in the days of David.

The initial policy of the government was to sell in as great tracts as possible (the very reverse of the present conserving, anti-monopolistic policy, as we shall see). The first sale (1787) was of nearly a million acres, for which an average of two-thirds of a dollar per acre in securities worth nine or ten cents was received. This sale, whatever may be said for it as a part of a fiscal policy, was significant not only in opening up a great tract (one thousand three hundred square miles) but in the fact that the purchase and holding were conditioned by certain provisions of a precious ordinance—the last of importance of the old Continental Congress—only less important than the Constitution, which it preceded by two years—the "basis of law and politics" in the northwest.

It, moreover, gave precedent for a policy of territorial control by the central government that has been effective even to the present time. Daniel Webster said of it: "I doubt whether any single law of any lawgiver, ancient or modern, has produced effects of more distinct, marked, and lasting character."[1] It forbade slavery and had in this provision an important influence on the history of the valley. But there was another far-reaching and a positive provision which must be of special interest to the people of France even to-day. Its preamble lies in this memorable passage: "Religion, morality, and knowledge being necessary to good government and the happiness of mankind, schools and the means of education shall forever be encouraged." As to the specific means of encouraging religion, morality, and knowledge, and so, ultimately, of promoting good government and the happiness of mankind, it was proposed by the representative of the Ohio Company, which stood ready to purchase a million acres, that the government should give support both to education and religion, as was done in New England, and as follows: one lot in each township (that is, a section one mile square in every tract six miles square) to be reserved for the common schools, another for the support of the ministry, and four whole townships, in the whole tract, for the maintenance of a university. Congress thought this too liberal, but finally, under

[1] First Speech on Foot's Resolution in "Writings and Speeches of Daniel Webster," national edition, 5 : 263.

the stress of need of revenue which the high-minded, reverend lobbyist, Reverend Menasseh Cutler, was prepared through his company to furnish, acceded, with a reduction only of the proposed appropriation to the university. The provision specifically was: "Lot number sixteen to be given perpetually by Congress to the maintenance of schools, and lot number twenty-nine to the purpose of religion in the said townships; two townships near the center and of good land to be also given by Congress for the support of a literary institution, to be applied to the intended object by the legislature of the State."

A second great tract was sold the same year under similar conditions. This was the last occasion on which provision for the support of religion was made by the national Congress, and what came of this particular grant I have not followed beyond the statement below.[1]

But the "section-sixteen" allotment for the aid of public schools continued as a feature of all future grants within the Northwest Territory, and also in all the new States of the southwestern and trans-Mississippi territory erected prior to 1850, from which time forward two sections in each township (sixteen and thirty-six) were granted for school purposes, besides specific grants for higher education amounting to over a million acres.

A recent student[2] of this subject has traced this policy of public aid to education back through New

[1] In 1828 Ohio petitioned for permission to sell the lands reserved for religious purposes, and in 1833 this was granted. The proceeds of the sales were to be invested and used for the support of religion, under the direction of the legislature within the townships in which the reserves were located. —Payson J. Treat, "The National Land System, 1785–1820."

[2] Joseph Shafer, "The Origin of the System of Land Grants for Education." Bulletin of the University of Wisconsin, No. 63. History Series, Vol. I, No. 1, August, 1902.

England, where colonies, in grants to companies or townships, made specific stipulations and reservations for the support of schools and the ministry and where townships voluntarily often made like disposition of surplus wild lands; and through New England to England of the sixteenth and seventeenth centuries, where, the monasteries and other religious foundations being destroyed and the schools depending upon them perishing, schools were endowed by the kings, sometimes out of sequestered church lands, or were established by towns and counties, in addition to those chartered under private patronage, so strong was the new educational movement of the time.

In the Mississippi Valley, then, or the greater part of it—whatever the historical origin of the provisions may be—from one-thirty-sixth to one-eighteenth of the public land has been set apart to the education of generation after generation till the end of the republic —or as Americans would be disposed to put it in synonymous phrase, "till the end of time."

Acres vary in size, one of our eminent horticulturists has reminded us, measured in terms of productivity. And the gifts to the various townships have been by no means of the same size, measured in terms of revenue for school purposes. "Number sixteen" may sometimes have fallen in shallow soil or on stony ground and "thirty-six" in swamp or alkali land. The lottery of nature is as hard-hearted as the lotteries of human devising; but the general provision has put an obligation upon the other thirty-five or thirty-four sections in every township that I suppose is seldom evaded. The child's acres are practically never, I suspect, less valuable than the richest and largest of those in the township about it, for the reason that the difference is made good by the local taxpayer. The child's acre is, as a rule, then, as large as the largest, the most productive acre. And roughly there are fifty thousand of those little plots in that domain—fifty thousand sections a mile square, thirty-two million acres reserved from the beginning of time, theoretically at least, to the end of time. As a matter of fact, they are not to be distinguished objectively from other acres now; they are to be distinguished only subjectively, that is, as one thinks of what is grown year by year in the schools, to which their proceeds, if not their products, are given.

I quoted above an estimate made in 1803 of what might have been done with the fifteen million dollars, paid to the French for Louisiana. One alternative suggested was the permanent endowment of eighteen hundred free schools, allowing five hundred dollars a year per school and accommodating ninety thousand pupils. The public-school allotment for that part of the valley alone is fifteen million acres. Even at two dollars an acre (a very low estimate), the endowment is twice the total amount paid for Louisiana—and I am estimating this school acreage at but one thirty-sixth instead of one-eighteenth of the total acreage. Therefore, France may, in a sense, be said to have given these acres to the support of the "children of always" —since these plots alone have probably yielded many times the purchase price of the entire territory.

To be sure, these white plots, as I would have them marked on a map of the valley, have in many States been sold and occupied as the other plots, with only this distinction, that the proceeds are inviolably set apart to this sacred use, as certain parts of animals were, under Mosaic law, reserved for public sacrifice. In one trans-Mississippi State, Iowa, for example, of a total grant of 1,013,614.21 acres[1] (less what the boundary rivers, the Mississippi and the Missouri, had carried away in their voracious encroachments, and plus what other natural agents had added), only 200 acres remained unsold in 1911.

As we view the policy from the year 1903 and from the midst of a populous valley, in which land values have risen from one dollar and twenty-five cents per acre to a hundred or two hundred dollars in most fertile farm tracts, and to thousands in urban centres, we can but regret that these lands themselves had not been held inviolate, and can but wish that only their rentals had been devoted to the high uses to which the nation and State had consecrated these lands. This policy would have put in the heart of every township a common field whose rental would have grown with the development of the country. It would have furnished fruitful data for comparison between two systems of land tenure. And it would have kept ever visibly, tangibly before the people their heritage and their obligation. As it is, one has to use the greatest imagination in translating the figures in a State treasurer's or county supervisor's report, back into the little plots that gathered into the soil of their acres the noblest purposes that ever animated a nation—these spots where one generation made its unselfish prayer and sacrifice for the next.

That the purpose still exists, despite the passing of

[1] Iowa, 1,013,614.21 acres from section 16 and 535,473.76 acres by congressional grant in 1841.

the tangible symbol, and that the prayer is still made in
every township of that territory, where even a few children live, is evidenced by the fact that every two
miles north and south, east and west of settled region
there stands a schoolhouse. I shall speak later of this
wide-spread provision, not only for universal elementary
education but also for secondary and higher education, ordained of the people and for the people, to be
paid for by the people out of their common treasury.
But attention must here be called, in passing, to the
fact that the parcelling of the domain of Louis XIV
in the new world fixed irrevocably the public school
in the national consciousness and purpose and made it
the foundation of a purely democratic social system
and the nourisher of a more highly efficient democratic
political system.

On the Atlantic side of the mountains there was
bitter controversy between those who held that education was necessary for the preservation of free institutions and those who held that free education increased
taxation unduly; between those who desired and those
who regretted the breaking down of social barriers
which both claimed would ensue as a result of such
education; between those who regarded education as
a natural right and those who considered taxation for
such a purpose a violation of the rights of the individual; between those who saw in it a panacea for
poverty and distress and those who urged that it
would not benefit the masses; and, finally, between
those of one sect and race and those of another.   But
in the trans-Alleghany country north of the Ohio, and
in all the territory west of the Mississippi (practically
coterminous, let me again remind you, with that region
where the French were pioneers within the present

bounds of the United States) there was practically no dissension, though the provision was meagre at the start. The public school had no more of the atmosphere or character of a charity, a "pauper" school than the highway provided for out of the same grant, where rich and poor met in absolute equality of right and opportunity. It became the pride of a people, the expression of the people's ideal, the corner-stone of the people's hope. I suppose that three-fourths of the children of the territory whose ranges have been surveyed by the magic chains forged of this first great parcelling ordinance have had the tuition of the public schools—future Presidents of the United States, justices, railroad and university presidents, farmers, artisans, artists, and poets alike.

So while it was desire for revenue that prompted the early sales of the public domain in the Mississippi Valley, the nation got in return not only means to help pay its Revolution debt, but, incidentally, settlements of highly individualistic, self-dependent, and interdependent pioneers, gathered about one highly paternalistic or maternalistic institution—the public school. The credit for this has gone to New England and New York, but the "white acres" came of the territory and the riches of Nouvelle France.

You will not wish to follow in detail the ministrations of the priests of the land-offices and the surveys of the men of the magic chains, for it is a long and tedious story that would fill thousands of pages, and in the end only obscure the real significance of the movement. Here is a summary of allotments made up to 1904 of all the public domain, that of the Mississippi Valley being somewhat more than half.[1]

[1] See Report of the Public Lands Commission, Washington, 1905.

		ACRES
Private land claims, donations etc. (the first of the latter being made to the early French settlers)..............................		33,400,000
Wagon-road, canal, and river improvement grants (provision for the narrow strips of common that intersect each other at every mile of the settled parts of the valley)......		9,700,000
Railroad grants for the subsidizing of the private building of railways chiefly up and down and across the valley.....................		117,600,000
Swamp-land grants (being tracts of wet or overflowed lands given to the various States for reclamation)...........................		65,700,000
School grants to States (those which we have been considering).......................		69,000,000
Other grants to States (largely for educational purposes)...............................		20,600,000
Military and naval land warrants.............		61,000,000
Scrip issued for various purposes (chiefly in view of service to the government).........		9,300,000
Allotment to individual Indians...............		15,100,000
Mineral lands (under special entries).........		1,700,000
Homestead entries (that is, by settlers taking claims under homestead acts of which I shall speak later)............................		96,500,000
Timber-culture entries (final).................		9,700,000
Timber and stone entries.....................		7,600,000
Cash entries, including entries under the preemption and other acts...................		276,600,000
Reservoir rights of way......................		300,000
Forest reserves (tracts of forest land permanently reserved from sale)......................		57,900,000
For national reclaiming purposes............		39,911,000
Reserved for public purposes (public buildings, forts, etc.)..............................		6,700,000
Indian reservations.........................		73,000,000
Entries pending.............................		39,500,000
Unappropriated public land..................		841,872,377
Total *(including Alaska)*..............		1,852,683,377

By June 30, 1912, homestead entries had increased
to 127,800,000 acres; timber and stone entries to
13,060,000 acres; forest reserves to 187,400,000 acres,
and there was left 682,984,762 acres, more than half
of which was in Alaska; that is, of the billion and
a half of acres, exclusive of Alaska, over a billion have
been sold to private uses, granted in aid of private
enterprises, used for public improvements, appro-
priated forever to public uses, or given to the support
of education.

The controlling motive at the start, I repeat, was
revenue. But gradually the people, seeing great
tracts of land held unimproved for speculation, seeing
the domain of free land narrowing while the pressure
of want was beginning to make itself felt east of the
mountains, as in Europe, and feeling concerned, as
some men of vision did, at the passing of the world's
great opportunity for the practical realization of man's
natural right to the land without disturbing the system in force in older settled communities, the people
strove to effect the subordination of revenue to the
social good of the frontier and the country at large.
By the middle of the century this many-motived feeling had expression in a party platform; that "the
public lands—belong to the people and should not be
sold to individuals nor granted to corporations, but
should be held as a sacred trust for the benefit of the
people and should be granted in limited quantities,
free of cost, to landless settlers."[1]

It was ten years before this doctrine became em-
bodied in law over the signature of Abraham Lincoln,
but the agitation for its enactment had been active for

[1] Free-Soil Democratic Platform, 1852, p. 12.

thirty years, beginning with the cry of a poor printer in New York City,[1] taught of French doctrine, who in season and out kept asserting the equal right of man to land. It was as a voice in the wilderness proclaiming a plan of salvation to the already congested areas on the seashore and, incidentally, a means of making the wilderness blossom. He was not then a disciple of Fourier (as many of his associates were and he himself had been originally), threatening vested privileges of rights; he did not preach a communistic division of property; he was an individualistic idealist and saw in the opening of this wild, unoccupied land, not to speculators or to alien purchasers, but to actual settlers permitted to pre-empt in quarter-sections (one hundred and sixty acres) and forbidden to alienate it, a means of social regeneration that would not disturb the titles to property already granted to individuals by the State, and yet would bless all the propertyless, for there was enough free land for every landless man who wanted it, and would be for decades if not for centuries beyond their lives, or so he thought.[2]

A German economist has expressed the view that it was only this movement, so inaugurated, that prevented America from going into socialism. One of our foremost economists in America, in discussing this very subject, begins with these observations:

"The French are a nation of philosophers. Starting with the theory of the rights of man, they build up a logical system, then a revolution, and the theory goes into practice. Next a coup d'état and an emperor.

[1] George Henry Evans.
[2] See J. R. Commons, "Documentary History of American Industrial Society," VII : 287–349.

"The English are a nation without too much philosophy or logic. They piece out their constitution at the spot where it becomes tight. . . . They are practical . . . unlogical.

"The Americans are French in their logic and English in their use of logic. They announce the universal rights of man and then enact into law enough to augment the rights of property."

The homestead law owed its origin to the doctrine of natural rights, whose transcendental glory faded often into the light of common day during the discussions but still enhaloes a very practical and matter-of-fact statute. Economic reasons, both of eastern and western motive, were gathered under the banner of its idealism, till finally it came to be an ensign not only of free soil for the landless but of free soil for the slaves. The "homestead" movement put an end to slavery, even if within a half century it has exhausted in its generosity the nation's domain of arable land. The voice in the wilderness cried for a legalized natural right that would not disturb vested rights, for an individualism based on private property given without cost, for equality by a limitation of that property to one hundred and sixty acres, and finally for the inalienability from sale or mortgage of that little plot of earth. Thirty years later the natural right to unoccupied land was recognized, individualistic society was strengthened by the great increase in the number of property holders, and inalienability was recognized by the States; but the failure to reserve the free lands to such actual settlers alone and to limit the amount of the holding left the way open for railroad grants, which alone have in two generations exceeded the homestead entries, and for the amassing of great stretches by a few.

The logic of France, speaking through the voice of that leader and other men such as Horace Greeley, led the later exodus as certainly as her pioneers opened the way for the first American settlers. And though the logic was applied in English fashion, yet it had a notable part in making, as I have just said, the free soil of the Mississippi Valley contribute to the freeing of a whole people in slavery, inside and outside of the valley. That logic learned in France would doubtless have accomplished a conclusion needing less patching and opportunistic repair if the immediate interests of those of the frontiers, those who wanted immediate settlement and development, had not disturbed one of the premises. At any rate, a great and perhaps the last opportunity to carry such doctrines to their conclusions without overturning all social and industrial institutions has gone by. A half-billion acres of inalienable farms, all of the same size, trespassing upon no ancient rights, interspersed with the white blocks held for the education of the children of that free soil, might have furnished an example for all time to be followed or shunned—if, indeed, all acres had been born of the primeval sea and glaciers not only free but equal in size. As it was, some acres were born large and some small, some fruitful and some barren, some with gold in their mouths and some with only the taste of alkali; and only an infinite wisdom could have adjusted them to the unequal capacities of that army of land lackers who declared themselves free and equal, and who, with free-soil banners, advanced to the territory where the squatters became sovereigns and homesteads became castles.

President Andrew Johnson (who as a congressman, in 1852, made the seven-hundred-year prophecy) estimated that a homestead (of one hundred and sixty acres) would increase every homesteader's purchasing ability by one hundred dollars a year; and if (he argued) the government enacted a 30-per-cent duty it would be reimbursed in seven years in the amount of two hundred and ten dollars, or ten dollars more than the cost of the homestead. By such reckoning he reached the conclusion that the homesteaders would defray the expenses of the government for a period of four thousand three hundred and ninety-two years —each homesteader of the nine millions contributing indirectly twenty-four thousand four hundred dollars in seven hundred years and all of them two hundred and nineteen billion six hundred million dollars—a scheme as ingenious, says one, as Fourier's "scheme to pay off the national debt of France with a setting hen."[1]

There are approximately nine million homes (or homes, tenements, and flats) in that domain to-day, and it is quite easily demonstrable that they not only contribute to the support of government, directly and indirectly, far more than the seemingly fantastic estimates of Andrew Johnson suggested but also give to the world a surplus of product undreamed of even in 1850. It is hardly likely that any system of parcelling would have more rapidly developed this vast domain. There is a question as to whether some more logical, conserving, long-viewed policy might not have been devised for the "common good" of the generations

[1] Speech on the bill to encourage agriculture, July 25, 1850. Speeches on the homestead bill, April 29, 1852, and May 20, 1858.

that are yet to occupy that valley with the generation that is there and the three or four generations that have already gone. It is that "common good" that is now engaging the thought of our foremost economists, natural scientists, and public men. Of that I shall speak later.

Here we celebrate merely the fact that there are fifty or sixty million geographical descendants of France living in the midst of the valley at the mouth of whose river La Salle took immediate possession for Louis XIV, but prophetic possession for all the peoples that might in any time find dwelling there.

CHAPTER IX

IN THE TRAILS OF THE COUREURS DE BOIS

"IT is a mistake," said one of the statesmen of the Mississippi Valley, Senator Thomas H. Benton, "to suppose that none but men of science lay off a road. There is a class of topographical engineers older than the schools and more unerring than the mathematicians. They are the wild animals—buffalo, elk, deer, antelope, bears—which traverse the forest not by compass but by an instinct which leads them always the right way—to the lowest passes in the mountains, the shallowest fords in the rivers, the richest pastures in the forests, the best salt springs, and the shortest practicable lines between remote points. They travel thousands of miles, have their annual migrations backwards and forwards, and never miss the best and shortest route. These are the first engineers to lay out a road in a new country; the Indians follow them, and hence a buffalo road becomes a warpath. The first white hunters follow the same trails in pursuing their game; and after that the buffalo road becomes the wagon road of the white man, and finally the macadamized road or railroad of the scientific man."[1]

A hunter of wild sheep in the Rocky Mountains following their trails wonders if they were made a

[1] Speech on a bill for the construction of a highway to the Pacific, December 16, 1850.

year, five, or ten years ago, and is told by the scientist
at his side that they may have been sixteen thousand
years old, so long have these first engineers been at
work.   In some places of Europe, I am told, their fellow engineers, longer in the practice of their profession,
have actually worn paths in the rocks by their cush-
ioned feet.

It is a mistake, therefore, we are reminded, to suppose that the forests and plains of the Mississippi
Valley were trackless.   They were coursed by many
paths.   If you have by chance read Châteaubriand's
"Atala," you will have a rather different notion of the
American forests, especially of the Mississippi Valley.
"On the western side of the Mississippi," he wrote,
"the waves of verdure on the limitless plains (savannas)
appear as they recede to rise gradually into the azure
sky"; but on the eastern half of the valley, "trees of
every form, of every color, and of every perfume
throng and grow together, stretching up into the air
to heights that weary the eye to follow.   Wild vines
. . . intertwine each other at the feet of these trees,
escalade their trunks and creep along to the extremity
of their branches, stretching from the maple to the
tulip-tree, from the tulip-tree to the hollyhock, and
thus forming thousands of grottos, arches and porticos.
Often, in their wanderings from tree to tree, these
creepers cross the arm of a river, over which they throw
a bridge of flowers. . . . A multitude of animals spread
about life and enchantment.   From the extremities of
the avenues may be seen bears, intoxicated with the
grape, staggering upon the branches of the elm-trees;
caribous bathe in the lake; black squirrels play among
the thick foliage; mocking-birds, and Virginian pigeons

not bigger than sparrows, fly down upon the turf, reddened with strawberries; green parrots with yellow heads, purple woodpeckers, cardinals red as fire, clamber up to the very tops of the cypress-trees; humming-birds sparkle upon the jessamine of the Floridas; and bird-catching serpents hiss while suspended to the domes of the woods, where they swing about like creepers themselves. . . . All here . . . is sound and motion. . . . When a breeze happens to animate these solitudes, to swing these floating bodies, to confound these masses of white, blue, green, and pink, to mix all the colors and to combine all the murmurs, there issue such sounds from the depths of the forests, and such things pass before the eyes, that I should in vain endeavor to describe them to those who have never visited these primitive fields of nature." And when René and Atala were escaping through those forests they "advanced with difficulty under a vault of smilax, amidst vines, indigo-plants, bean-trees, and creeping-ivy that entangled our feet like nets. . . . Bell serpents were hissing in every direction, and wolves, bears, carcajous and young tigers, come to hide themselves in these retreats, made them resound with their roarings."[1]

A trackless, howling wilderness, indeed, if we are to accept this as an accurate description of scenes which, as I have intimated, it is now suspected that Châteaubriand's imagination visited, unaccompanied of his body. But a recent indigenous writer on the valley and its roads—having in mind, to be sure, the forests a little farther north than those in which Atala and René wandered—assures us that they were neither

---

[1] Châteaubriand, "Atala," trans. Harry, pp. 2, 3, 19.

"pathless" nor "howling." He writes that in 1775 (eighteen years before the first white settlement in the State of Ohio) there were probably as many paths within the bounds of that State on which a man could travel on horseback at the rate of five miles an hour as there are railways in that State to-day. And the buffalo paths were—some of them, at any rate—roads so wide that several wagons might have been driven abreast on them—as wide as the double-track railroads. So the Indian farther west had his highways prepared for him by the instincts of these primitive engineers that knew nothing of trigonometry or the sextant or the places of the stars.[1]

Nor did these first makers of roads howl or bellow their way over them. On this same authority (Hulbert) I am able to assure you that the forest paths were noiseless "traces," as they were originally called, in the midst of silences disturbed only by the wind and the falling waters. Wolves did sometimes howl in the forests or out upon the plains, but it was only in hunger and in accentuation of the usual silence. Neither they nor the bears growled or howled, except when they came into collision with each other, or starvation.

And there were not even birds to give cheer to the gloom of these black forests, whose tree tops were knitted together by vines, but had no undergrowth, since the sun could not reach the ground. "The birds of the forest came only with the white man." There were parrots in Kentucky, and there were in Ohio pigeons and birds of prey, eagles and buzzards, but the birds we know to-day and the bees were later immigrants from lands that remembered Aristophanes or

[1] Hulbert, "Historic Highways," vol. I, pt. II.

the hills of Hymettus, or that knew Shelley's skylark or Keats's nightingale or Rostand's tamer fowls or Maeterlinck's bees.

Even if we allow to the forests Châteaubriand's color in summer and the clamor in times of terror— color and clamor which only a keen eye and ear would have seen and heard—we cannot longer think of them as pathless, if inhabited by those ancient pathmakers, the buffalo, deer, sheep. And, naturally, when the Indian came, dependent as he was upon wild game, he followed these paths or traces made and frequented by the beasts—the ways to food, to water, to salt, to other habitats with the changing seasons. The buffalo roads and the deer trails became his vocational trails —the streets of his livelihood. And as his enemy was likely to find him by following these traces, they became not only the paths of peace but the paths of war. When the red man trespassed upon the peaceful trails of his enemy, he was, in an American idiom, "on the war-path."

Then in time the European trader went in friendly search of the Indian by these same paths, and they became the avenues of petty commerce. As street venders in Paris, so these forest traders or runners went up and down these sheltered paths, as dark in summer as the narrowest streets, only they went silently, though they were often heard as distinctly in the breaking of twigs or in their muffled tread by the alert ears of the Indians as the musical voices of these venders are heard in the city. And the places where these traders put down their cheap trinkets before their dusky patrons grew into trading-posts, prophetic of future cities and towns.

Such were the paths by which the runners of the woods, the French coureurs de bois, first emerged—after following the watercourses—upon the western forest glades and the edges of the prairies and astonished the aboriginal human owners of those wild highways that had known only the soft feet of the wolf and fox and bear, the hoofs of the buffalo and deer, and the bare feet or the moccasins of the Indians (the "silent shoes," as I have seen such footgear advertised in Boulevard St. Germain).

It has been said by a chemist of some repute that man came, in his evolution, out of the sea; that he has in his veins certain elements—potassium, calcium, magnesium, sodium—in the same ratio in which they appeared in the water of the Pre-Cambrian ocean. Whether this be true or not, one stage of human development carries marks of the forest, and from that period "having nothing but forest knowledge, forest dreams, forest fancies, forest faith," as an American writer has said, man emerges upon the plains of history.

So, though the French civilization still smells and sounds of the sea, and followed the streams that kept its first men in touch with it, it had finally, in its pioneering, to take to the trails and the forests. And these runners of the woods were the amphibious ambassadors from this kingdom of the sea to the kingdom of the land. They were, as Étienne Brûlé of Champlain's time, the pioneers of pioneers who, often in unrecorded advance of priest and explorer, pushed their adventurous traffic in French guns and hatchets, French beads and cloth, French tobacco and brandy, till they knew and were known to the aboriginal habitants, "from where the stunted Esquimaux burrowed in their snow caves to where the Comanches scoured the plains of the south with their banditti cavalry."

They were a lawless lot whom this mission, not only between water and land but also between civilization and barbarism, "spoiled for civilization." But they must not be judged too harshly in their vibrations between the two standards of life which they bridged, making periodical confession to charitable priests in one, of the sins committed in the other, which, unforgiven, might have driven them entirely away from the church and into perdition.

The names of most of these coureurs de bois are forgotten by history (which is rather particular about the character of those whom it remembers—other than those in kingly or other high places). But they who have followed immediately in the trails of these men of the verges have written these names, or some of them, in places where they are more widely read than if cherished by history even. Étienne Brûlé—who, as interpreter, led Le Caron out upon the first western mission—after following trails and waters for hundreds of miles back of the English settlements, where the timid colonists had not dared to venture, suffered the martyrdom of fire, and is remembered in a tempestuous stream in the west and perhaps in an Indian tribe. The name of Jean Nicolet of Cherbourg (the ambassador to the Winnebagoes, from the record of whose picturesque advent in the "Jesuit Relations" the annals of the west really began) has been given to a path now grown into one of the most populous streets along the whole course of the Mississippi River—in Minneapolis.

And Du Lhut, the cousin of Tonty, a native of Lyons —a man of "persistent hardihood, not surpassed perhaps even by La Salle," says Parkman, "continually in the forest, in the Indian towns, or in the remote wilderness outposts planted by himself, exploring, trading, fighting, ruling lawless savages, and whites scarcely less ungovernable,"[1] and crossing the ocean for interviews with the colonial minister, "amid the splendid vanities of Versailles"—he is remembered for all time in that city, built up against the far shores of Lake Superior, bearing his name, Duluth, the city that has taken the place of London in the list of the world's great harbors. Macaulay's vision of the New Zealander standing amid the ruins of London and overlooking the mastless Thames seems to have some realization in the succeeding of a city, founded in the path of a wood runner, out on the borders of civilization, to one of London's distinctions among the cities of the world.

"This class of men is not extinct," said Parkman twenty or thirty years ago; "in the cheerless wilds beyond the northern lakes, or among the solitudes of the distant west they may still be found, unchanged in life and character since the day when Louis the Great claimed sovereignty over the desert empire."

But their mission, if any survive till now, is past. The paths, surveyed of the beasts and opened by these pioneers to the feet of priests, explorers, and traders, have let in the influences that in time destroyed all these forest lovers braved the solitude for. The trace has become the railroad, and the smell of the gasolene motor is even on the once wild Oregon trail;

---

[1] Parkman, "La Salle," p. 274.

for, in general, it has been said of the forest part of
the valley, "where there is a railway to-day there was
a path a century and a quarter ago" (and that means
longer ago); and it may be added that where there was
a French trading-post, or fort, or portage, there is a
city to-day, not because of the attraction of the populations of those places for the prospecting railroad, but
because of their natural highway advantage, learned
even by the buffaloes. Not all paths have evolved
into railroads, but the railroads have followed practically all of these natural paths—paths of the coureurs
de bois, instinctively searching for mountain passes,
the low portages from valley to valley, the shortest
ways and the easiest grades.

One of America's greatest railroad presidents has
noted this significant difference between the railroads
of Europe and those of America, or at any rate of the
Mississippi Valley. In Europe they "took the place
of the pack-animal, the stage-coach, the goods-van that
crowded all the highways between populous centers,"
whereas in the Mississippi Valley and beyond they
succeeded the pioneer and pathfinder. The railroad
outran the settler and "beckoned him on," just as the
coureur de bois outran the slower-going migrant and
beckoned him on to ever new frontiers. The buffalo,
the coureur de bois, the engineer in turn. The railroad, the more modern coureur de bois and coureur
de planche, has not served the new-world society
merely as a connecting-link between communities already developed. It has been the "creator of cities."[1]

Out on those prairies beyond the forests I have seen
this general statement of Mr. Hill's illustrated. Down

[1] James J. Hill, "Highways of Progress," pp. 235, 236.

from Lake Michigan the first railroad crept toward
the Mississippi along the Des Plaines and then the
Illinois, where La Salle had seen from his canoe great
herds of buffalo "trampling by in ponderous columns
or filing in long lines morning, noon, and night." That
railroad was a path, not to any particular city but to
the water, a path from water to water, a long portage
from the lake to the Mississippi and back again.

One day, within my memory, a new path was marked
by stakes that led away from that river, off across the
prairie, to an uninhabited place which the first engineers had not known—a place of fire, the fields of
coal, of which the practical Joliet had found signs on
his memorable journey. And so one and another
road crossed that prairie (on which I can even now
clearly see the first engine standing in the prairie-
grass), making toward the places of fire, of wood, of
grain, of meat, of gold, of iron, of lead, till the whole
prairie was a network of these paths—and now the
"transportation machine" (as Mr. Hill calls it) has
grown to two hundred and fifty-four thousand seven
hundred and thirty-two miles (in 1911), or about 40
per cent of the world mileage, of which one hundred
and forty thousand miles are within the Mississippi
Valley, carrying with them wherever they go the
telegraph and telephone wires, building villages, towns,
and cities—still bringing the fashions of Paris, as did
Perrot, in the paths of the buffalo.

When the surveyors crossed that prairie, treeless
except for the woods along the Aramoni River (just
back of the Rock St. Louis) and along the Illinois
River at the other edge, the wild animals and the Indians had disappeared westward, the prairie ground

was broken and planted in patches; fences had begun
to appear on the silent stretches; houses stood four
to a section, with a one-room schoolhouse every two
miles and churches at long intervals. After the
construction train ploughed its slow way across that
same prairie, in the trail staked by the surveyors, a
place was marked for a village; the farmers upon whose
land it promised to trespass wanted each to give it the
name of his wife, his queen, as La Salle of his king;
but one day a workman, representing the unsentimental
corporation, without ceremony nailed a strip of board
to a post, with the name "Aramoni," let us say, painted
upon it. Wooden buildings, stores, elevators, blacksmith, harness, and shoemaker shops, and the dwellings of those who did the work of the little town,
gathered about; in time some of the pioneer settlers
leaving their farms to the care of children or tenants
moved into the town; the primitive stores were rebuilt
in brick; houses of pretentious architecture crowded
out of the best sites the first dwellings; and in twenty
or thirty years it had become a village of several hundred people: retired farmers or their widows, men of
the younger generation living on the income of their
farms without more than nominal occupation, and
those who buy the produce and minister to the wants
of this little community. Most of the villagers and
most of the farmers in all the country about have the
telephone in their houses and can talk as much as they
please with their neighbors at a very small yearly
charge. They also keep track of the grain and stock
markets by telephone, have their daily metropolitan
paper, a county paper, monthly magazines (of which
they are the best readers), perhaps a piano or an organ,

more likely, now, a phonograph, which reproduces, if they choose, what is heard in Paris or in concerts or the grand opera; reproductions of pieces of statuary or paintings in the Louvre; and either a fast driving horse or an automobile. They are often within easy reach of a city by train, and the wives or daughters know the fashions of Paris and begin to follow the modes as quickly as local talent can make the adaptations and transformations.

Aramoni is not an imaginary much less a Utopian village. There are thousands of "Aramonis" where the railroads have gone, drawing all the physical conveniences and social conventions after them, where once coureurs de bois followed the buffaloes.

Mr. Hill, whom I have just quoted above, has said: "Next after the Christian religion and the public school the railroad has been the largest single contributing factor to the welfare and happiness of the people of that valley."[1]

The first great service of the railroads to the republic, as such, was to make it possible that the people of a territory three thousand miles wide, crossed by two mountain ranges, should be bound into one republic. The waters to the east of the Alleghanies ran toward the Atlantic, the waters west of the Rockies ran toward the Pacific, and the waters between the mountains ran to the Gulf of Mexico. If the great east-and-west railroads had not been built and some of the waters of the Lakes had not been made to run down the Mohawk Valley into the Hudson it is more than probable that there would have been a secession of the men who called themselves the "men of the

[1] James J. Hill, "Highways of Progress," pp. 236, 237.

western waters," a secession of the west from the
east, rather than of the south from the north. If the
men of this valley had continued men of the "western waters" there would probably have been at least
three republics in North America and perhaps as
many as in South America.

When Josiah Quincy, a famous son of Massachusetts, said for the men of the east in the halls of Congress, "You have no authority to throw the rights
and liberties and property of this people into hotch-
pot with the wild men on the Missouri, nor with the
mixed though more respectable race of Anglo-Hispano-
Gallo-Americans, who bask on the sands in the mouth
of the Mississippi," he was visualizing the men whose
interests followed the rivers to another tide-water
than that of Boston and New York harbors. The
railroads made a real prophecy of his fear that these
men of the western rivers would some day be "man-
aging the concerns of a seaboard fifteen hundred miles
from their residences, and having a preponderance in
the councils," into which, as he contended, "they should
never have been admitted."[1]

He was thinking and speaking rather of the south-
west than of the northwest, but it was the east-and-
west lines of railroad that prevented the vital interest
of that northern valley from flowing with the water
along parallels of longitude to where the gulf currents would catch its commerce, instead of over the
mountains along the sterner parallels of latitude and in
straighter course to Europe.

The force of gravity, the temptation of the tropics,

[1] Speech on the bill to admit Orleans Territory into the Union. Annals of
Congress, 11th Cong., 3d Sess., 1810-11, pp. 524-542.

the indifference of the east, the freedom from eastern and puritanical restraints, were all on the side of a "republic of the western waters" and against that larger, continent-wide nationalism which now has its most ardent support in that valley through which the iron shuttles fly from sea to sea, weaving the waters as strands of color into a unified pattern of sublimer import.

It looks now as if the north-and-south lines were to be strengthened the world over, as the occupied and exploited north temperate zone reaches north toward the frigid zone, now grown warmer by the very opening of the lands to the sun and the long burning of coal, and south toward the tropics, now made more habitable by the new knowledge of tropical medicine, and even across the tropics to the sister temperate zone of the southern hemisphere.[1] In the Mississippi Valley, the gulf ports, fed of river and railroad, are increasingly busy, partly, to be sure, because they look toward the east-and-west path through Panama, but partly, too, because they lie between the two temperate zones, which must inevitably be brought nearer to each other. We cannot imagine two permanently dissociated or distantly associated temperate civilizations on this globe, which is becoming smaller every day.

It was inevitable, perhaps, and happily inevitable, that the east-and-west lines should be well established before the temperate zone should venture into tropic lotus-lands again, and perhaps it was inevitable that

[1] I have been told by one who has been studying conditions in the great northwest fields of Canada that it is now possible to grow crops there that could not have been grown before the country was opened and cultivated to the south of them, so much longer have the frosts been delayed in the autumn.

the west should eventually, even without the help of steam and steel, attach itself to the east—even by streams of water.

Washington had hardly put off his uniform, after the peace of 1783, when he was planning for a western trip, and his diary on the third day of that trip of six hundred and eighty miles shows that his one object was to obtain information of the nearest and best communication between the eastern and the western waters. One of the kings of France said, when his grandson was made king of Spain, "There are no longer any Pyrenees," and Washington, when he saw the new republic forming, said, in effect, "There must be no Alleghanies." He expected a canal to erase the mountains, but the railroad accomplished this gigantic task with but slight aid of water.

And as the railroad tied the Mississippi Valley to the Atlantic coast, so in time, aided of a government that had every reason to be grateful, it reached across the uninhabited plains, over the Rocky Mountains, which even the western statesmen said were the divinely appointed barriers, and across the desert beyond to the Pacific slope and tied it to a capital which is now nearer to San Francisco than once it was to Boston. A man from Missouri is speaker of the house in which Josiah Quincy spoke his provincial fears. A man from the mouth of the Mississippi, the highest authority in America on the French code, was but a little time ago appointed as the chief justice of the Supreme Court of the United States by a President who was born on the banks of the Ohio; that is, the highest office in each of the three independent branches of government (the executive, the legislative, and the judicial) have at one time been filled by men of the western waters. I am anticipating a fact that belongs to a later theme, but there is no single fact that can better illustrate the political service of the paths over which we are to-day travelling.

On the economic consequences we need not now dwell. They have had too frequent and sufficiently conspicuous illustration in every foreign mind that knows anything whatever of that valley to make it necessary to insist in this cursory view upon their great contribution to physical comfort. It is, however, begun to be felt that in the rapid development and exploitation of the resources of that valley (made possible only by the railroads) the future has not been enough in our minds. It was said a few years ago that there was not money enough in the world to lay track to take the traffic that the Mississippi Basin offered. The valley wanted to get everything to market in one generation, indifferent to the fate of those who should come after—the passes through the mountains being choked by cars carrying to the coasts crops from increasing acreage of declining productivity or the products of swiftly disappearing forests or the output of mines that must soon be exhausted.

Perhaps the railroads are not to be blamed for this decrease in productivity—a passing phase of our agricultural life, as recent crop reports show. They are very loudly blamed that they do not carry these products fast enough or cheaply enough, though, according to a recent authority, their rates are less on the average than the cost of the French water traffic.

Nevertheless, their wheels alone have made possible that phenomenal draining of the riches of the land to the coasts and other shores, assisting the waters that carry a half-billion tons of soil into the gulf every year. Perhaps this hurried, panting development has been for the good of all time, but until recently there has been little or no thought of that "all time" (as we observed in the policies of land parcelling).

Practically the whole western country has tied itself to a wheel, and so whatever its happiness and welfare may be, come of or with the wheel. This territory is capable of self-support; it has still its independent spirit, bred of the pioneer who lived before the day of wheels; it is responsive to appeals that stop its restless movement—as the wheel of Ixion when Orpheus played; but none the less is it an eager, restless, unquiet life, driven as a wheel, driven by the same hand that urged it into the valley.

No one asks—or few ask—if the wheel brings good or ill. The only concern is that it shall run as quickly and safely as is humanly and mechanically possible and shall not discriminate between one shipper and another, one community and another, one consumer and another. That is the railroad problem. The wheel has removed watersheds at pleasure, created cities and fortunes by its presence or its taking thought. But under the new policy of the government it is not likely that there will ever again be such ruthless disturbance of nature, or such wild, profuse creation. Democracy, beginning in that valley, is seeking now a perfect impersonal transportation machine.

But such a machine will drain quite as effectively the country districts. The census returns for 1910 show, for example, that in one prosperous agricultural State, Missouri, just west of the Mississippi, while the

State as a whole showed an increase of 187,000 in ten years, there was a net decrease of 84,000 in the rural districts. A partial explanation of the latter statistic is the moving on of farmers to still newer lands; another, the decline in the size of families; but it is attributable chiefly to the first statistic, the drift to the city—and to this the wheels contribute more than any other influence, carrying, as they do, the glamour or the opportunity of the city life daily before the eyes of the country boy.

To be sure, these same wheels are lessening, to some extent, the congestion of the great centres of population, and lightening their shadows by extending them —spreading them—but none the less are the shadows spreading faster from the coming of the country to the city than of the suburbanizing of the city.

This movement is not peculiar to the Mississippi Valley, but it is more rapid there, perhaps, than in any other great area.

Let me give you an illustration of that demigrating influence. Two years ago I invited several leaders of great transportation and educational interests in New York to meet one of their number who, beginning life as a telegraph operator out beyond the Mississippi, was at the head of one of the two greatest railroads in the east. Of the guests, one, the president of another important railroad, was once a farm boy, then a freight brakeman in that same western State; another, the president of one of the longest railroads, was the son of a stone-mason out in that valley; another, the head of the Interborough system of New York, also a prairie-born boy; another, president of the greatest southern railroad, was born at the mouth of the Mississippi;

and still another, one of the wealthiest men in the world, was at one time a messenger boy and telegraph operator just over the mountains on the site of Fort Duquesne.   Only one man of the company of nearly twenty men, assembled without thought of origin, had been born in New York.   All had come from the country or from across the water, and most of them from the great Mississippi Valley.   I speak of this while discussing the railroad, because it is their paths through the valley of the French that have made this phenomenon possible.

I have spoken of what the wheel has done in making the permanence of one republic of such an area a possibility.   Nothing save a loose, heterogeneous confederation could have been practicable without its unifying service.   It is only fair to those who made such gloomy prophecies in the early days to say that they had no intimation of what steam was destined to do.   When Robert Fulton, the inventor of the steamboat, early in the nineteenth century, on a journey back from the west in a stage-coach, said that some day steam would drive wagons faster than they were going in the coach, his fellow passengers thought him a dreamer—a visionary.   But it was only a man of such dreams or visions who in those days could have seen the possibility which has to-day been realized through the railroad.

I have spoken of the part which the steam wheel has had in the rapid development and the exploitation of that great valley which, except for its pioneering in wild places, might have been seven hundred years, as Andrew Johnson predicted, in filling up, or at least two or three centuries.

I have intimated its influence in promoting migra-

tion cityward—a movement as wide as European civilization—but intensified there, where the inhabitants
have not been tied through generations of inheritance
or historic associations to particular fields, where primo-
geniture has no observance, and where the traditions
are of the wilderness and the visions are ever of a
promised land beyond. The city is on every boy's
horizon. Its glow is in every prairie sky at twilight.

When a boy on those silent plains I had my Horace
and my Euripides in the field. The unattainable
eternal cities lent their charm and glory to the valley
whose childhood horizon I had not crossed. But now
no country boy thinks of the ancient or the mediæval.
It is the nearer city and civilization that impress the
imagination. The valedictorian of a class, graduat-
ing as I entered college, told me a few months ago
that he was building a trolley-line in Rome, and that,
after all, Falernian wine, of which we who had never
tasted wine out in that vineless region thought as some
drink of the gods, was very bitter.

I have hinted at what the wheel has done, in what it
carries, to make all look alike and think alike and act
alike, but there is one supreme service that must have
mention. In that country when travel was slow we
had a representative government. But while we still
have the same form, the wheel has made possible, and
so necessary, a more democratic government. When a
representative was weeks in reaching the capital he
acted on his own responsibility in larger measure than
now, when his constituency can reach him every morning. The valley is reached every day, just as the
people in a pure democracy were reached by the ancient stentor. The people are reserving to themselves

more and more of the function of their one-time representatives, in such measures as the referendum and initiative intimate, and are trying to secure more accurate representation in such systems as the direct primary and proportional representation suggest; but these all are possible only through the aid of the wheel and of what it has brought. If the improvement of democracy is to come through more democracy, as some think, then the railroad is an essential agent of political progress as well as of economic exploitation and social homogeneity. I am not discussing this thesis but simply showing how dependent upon this physical agent is the machinery of democracy.

Moreover, mobility is almost an essential quality of the spirit of democracy, the free way to the farthest horizons, the open road to the highest position and service. When the atom becomes practically fixed by its environment, reposeful and stable, stratification sets in. We may or we may not have then something better.

It may seem to you a far cry from those rough, lawless coureurs de bois to the mobile but orderly people of that valley to-day. But after an experience of a few summers ago the distance does not seem so great.

Here is a journal of three days:

In the morning of an August day I was gathering some last data from the library of one of the greatest, though one of the newest, universities in the world —a two-hours' journey from where the coureur de bois Jean Nicolet, in robe of damask, first looked over the edge of the basin. (Not many years ago I sat there in an assembly of learned men gathered from the ends of the earth and arrayed in academic robes.) In the afternoon I walked over that first and most famous of the French portages, but not content with that, I walked on into the night along the Wisconsin, that I might see the river as the explorers saw it. However, at midnight I took a palace car, with such conveniences as even Louis the Great did not have at Versailles, and woke well up the Mississippi. I spent the day at another great State university and at dusk set off by the actual trails of the French coureurs de bois (only by wheels instead of on foot), first through the woods and along rivers, above Green Bay to the "Soo," then above Lake Huron and the Nipissing and down the Ottawa River, where I saw the second day break, and then on past La Salle's seigniory of St. Sulpice, around Cartier's mountain into Montreal, and thence to the Rock of Quebec.

It is a common, unimaginative metaphor in the United States to call the engine which leads the mighty trains across the country the iron horse; but it is deserving of a nobler figure. It is the iron coureur de bois, still leading Europe into America, and America into a newer America.

CHAPTER X

IN THE WAKE OF THE "GRIFFIN"

IN the lower St. Lawrence Valley, among the French Canadians, where France is best remembered and where the shut-in life is not disturbed by current events or changing conventions or evanescent fashions, I am told there are traces in their language of the sea life of their ancestors on the coasts of Brittany and Normandy. When, for example, a neighbor approaches a farmhouse on horseback he is asked not to "alight" or to "dismount" but to "disembark," and he is invited not to "tie" his horse but to "moor" it. It is as if they were still crying ever in their unconscious memories, "Thalassa, Thalassa"; as if the very shells of speech still carried the roar of the ocean which they who hold them to their ears have never seen.

If the language of the upper valley of the St. Lawrence and of the valley of the Mississippi remembered as distinctly its origin we should everywhere hear the plash of the oar in all the hospitality of their settlements. But all such traces have disappeared, or all but disappeared, in the Mississippi Valley. The only one that comes to me now, as possibly of the old French days, is one which is preserved in an adage not at all French but quite characteristic of the independent life that has occupied the banks of all the rivers:

"Paddle your own canoe." Yet even in the space of one or two generations of agricultural life that, too, is disappearing, supplanted by a synonymous phrase, borrowed of fields that have entirely forgotten the primitive days, when men travelled only by water and lived near the streams: "Hoe your own row."

The first sound of the overmountain migration of which I spoke above was of the stealthy step of the hunter, yet back of that for a century was the scarcely audible plash of the paddle and the answering swirl of the water. But as in overmountain migration the noisy wheel soon followed the foot, so in the other the noiseless sail followed the swishing paddle.

The city of Paris bears a sailing ship upon her shield, though she sits a hundred miles or more from the sea. Whatever the significance of that symbol has been to the people of France, it has a peculiar appropriateness (probably never realized before) in the fact that the iron, cordage, and anchors for the first vessel which sailed upon the inland waters of the new world were carried out from France to the first shipyard, beyond the mountains, in the midst of the forest, above the mighty Falls of Niagara.

Jason of Thessaly, sailing for the Golden Fleece in Colchis, and braving the fiery breath of the dragon, did not undertake a more perilous or more difficult labor than he who bore from the banks of the Seine the equipment of a vessel in which to bring back to France, as he hoped, the fleece of the forest and the plain.

We are accustomed to call those who crossed the plains and the Rocky Mountains for the gold-fields of California nearly two centuries later (in 1849) the

Argonautæ; but the first American Argonauts went from France, and they built their *Argo* on what is now Lake Erie, on the edge of the Field of the Bulls, near a place, grown into a beautiful city, which now bears the very name of the wild bull, the "buffalo," and within sound of the roaring of the dragon that had frightened all earlier explorers. So accurately do the details of the story of Jason's adventure become realities to-day! Champlain and others had heard only at a distance the thunder of the great cataract that was some day to become not only as docile as the dragon under Jason's taming but as useful as a million harnessed bulls.

La Salle gathered his ship-carpenters and his ship furniture between his journeys to Rouen (the place of his birth) and elsewhere for the means of purchase. But before the winter had come in Normandy his messengers were out amid the snows and naked forests of Canadian winters in continuance of that voyage toward the western Colchis.

In the autumn of 1678 a Franciscan friar, Hennepin, set out with two canoemen, the first solitary figures of the expedition—a gray priest from the gray Rock of Quebec, in a birch canoe, carrying with him the "furniture of a portable altar"—a priest who professed a zeal for souls, but who admitted a passion for travel and a burning desire to visit strange lands. He relates of himself that, being sent from a convent in Artois to Calais at the season of herring fishing, he made friends of the sailors and never tired of their stories. "Often," he says, "I hid myself behind tavern doors while the sailors were telling of their voyages. The tobacco smoke made me very sick at

the stomach, but nevertheless I listened attentively.
. . . I could have passed whole days and nights in
this way without eating."[1]

Along the way up the St. Lawrence he stopped to
minister to the habitants—too few and too poor to
support a priest—saying mass, exhorting, and baptizing. Early in November he arrived at the mission of
Fort Frontenac, which he had two or three years before helped to establish in the wilds. Soon La Salle's
lieutenants, La Motte and Tonty, appeared with most
of the men, and while some were despatched in canoes
to Lake Michigan to gather the buffalo-hides and
beaver-skins against the coming of the ship, whose
keel had not yet been laid, the rest (La Motte, Hennepin, and sixteen men) embarked for the Niagara River,
by which the upper lakes empty into Lake Ontario
and the St. Lawrence. After a tempestuous voyage
up and across the lake they reached this river, whose
torrent fury, gathered of "four inland oceans," stopped
even the canoes. Then, led of the priest, they toiled
up the cliffs called the "Three Mountains," because, I
suppose, of the three terraces. (Having climbed up
the face of the cliffs in winter, with a heavy camera
for my portable altar, and having broken the great
icicles formed by the trickling stream over one of the
terraces, in order to make my way across a narrow
ledge to the top of the precipice, I am able to know
what the journey must have meant to those first
European travellers.) Once upon the upper plateau,
they marched through the wintry forest and at length,
in "solitude unprofaned as yet by the pettiness of

[1] Parkman, "La Salle," p. 133. Hennepin, "A New Discovery of a
Large Country in America," ed. Thwaites, 1 : 30.

man," they beheld the "imperial cataract"—the "thunder of water," as the Indians called it—or, as Hennepin described it, that "vast and prodigious cadence of water which falls down after a surprising and most astonishing manner, insomuch that the universe does not afford its parallel, those of Italy and Switzerland being but sorry patterns." To this priest, Hennepin, we owe the first description and picture of Niagara,[1] probably now more familiar to the world than any other natural feature of this continent. He has somewhat magnified the height of these falls, making it five hundred feet in the edition of 1683, and raising it to six hundred in 1697; but they are impressive enough to acquit him of intentional falsification and powerful enough to run virtually all the manufacturing plants in the United States, if they could be gathered within its easy reach.

As it is, less than 9 per cent of the water that overflows from the four upper Great Lakes into the lower lake, once known as Lake Frontenac and now as Ontario, is diverted for utilitarian purposes; it supplies the Americans and the Canadians almost equally between the two shores five hundred thousand horse-

[1] "Four leagues from Lake Frontenac there is an incredible Cataract or Waterfall, which has no equal. The Niagara river near this place is only the eighth of a league wide, but it is very deep in places, and so rapid above the great fall that it hurries down all the animals which try to cross it, without a single one being able to withstand its current. They plunge down a height of more than five hundred feet, and its fall is composed of two sheets of water and a cascade, with an island sloping down. In the middle these waters foam and boil in a fearful manner.

"They thunder continually, and when the wind blows in a southerly direction the noise which they make is heard for more than fifteen leagues. Four leagues from this cataract, or fall, the Niagara river rushes with extraordinary rapidity especially for two leagues into Lake Frontenac."—Hennepin, "Description of Louisiana," pp. 71-73.

power.[1] What the conversion of the strength of this
Titan (for ages entirely wasted and for a century after
Hennepin only a scenic wonder) means, or may mean,
to industry in the future is intimated in some statistics,
furnished by a recent writer on the Great Lakes, showing the relative cost per month of a certain unit of
power in a number of representative American cities.[2]

Boston	$937.50
Philadelphia	839.25
New York	699.37
Chicago	629.43
Cleveland	559.50
Pittsburgh	419.62
Buffalo	184.91
Niagara Falls	144.17

These figures are more significant as one contem-
plates the diminishing supply of coal in coming centuries, if not decades. According to the estimate of a
reliable authority the available and accessible coal sup-

[1] "Under a treaty between the United States and the British Government only about 25 per cent of the theoretical horsepower of Niagara Falls
can be developed. The estimate of the minimum amount of power that
can be developed on the Niagara River above and including the Falls is
5,800,000 h.p., and the assumed maximum is 6,500,000 h.p. The treaty,
therefore, limits present possible minimum development on both sides of
the Falls to 1,450,000 h.p. Under the treaty only five-fourteenths of the
power made available thereby belongs to the United States, its share being
reduced by the diversion of water from Lake Michigan into the Drainage
Canal at Chicago. There is thus left at Niagara Falls only about 518,000
h.p. that can at present be developed on the American side." About one-
half of this total is now developed.—United States Commissioner of Corporations. Report on water-power development in the United States. 1912.

[2] "Assuming the maximum power used to be one hundred horse-power,
the number of working hours a day to be ten, and the 'load factor,' or
average power actually used, to be seventy-five per cent of the total one
hundred, the cost per month in the cities named is as [above]."—Curwood,
"The Great Lakes," p. 135.

ply of the United States will be exhausted at the present rate of exploitation by the year 2027, and the entire supply by the year 2050.

Such statistics intimate the advantage possessed, perhaps beyond any other site in America, by the strip of shore on which La Salle's men, from the banks of the Seine, and Hennepin, the priest from Calais, that December night in 1678 encamped, building their bivouac fires amid the snows, three miles above the falls—and so opening to the view of the world a natural source of power and wealth more valuable than extensive coal-fields or rich mines of gold or silver.

It was but a great waterfall to La Salle and Tonty and Hennepin—an impeding, noisy, hostile object. And to the half-mutinous, quarrelsome workmen (French, Flemings, Italians) it was a demon, no doubt, whose very breath froze their beards into icicles. It was, in reality, potentially the most beneficent single, incarnate force bounded by any one horizon of sky, in that new world, developed by the tipping of the continent a little to the eastward after the upper lakes had been formed and the consequent emptying of their waters into the St. Lawrence instead of the Gulf of Mexico.

In January, 1679, a file of burdened men, some thirty in number, toiling slowly on their way over the snowy plains and "through the gloomy forests of spruce and naked oak trees," the priest accompanying with his altar lashed to his back, reached a favorable spot beside calm water several miles above the cataract: the site is identified as situate a little way above the mouth of Cayuga Creek, just outside the village of La Salle, in the State of New York. There is a stone erected by the local historical society to mark the spot. When I saw the bronze tablet the inscription was almost illegible, covered, as it was, with ice and the snow that was at that very hour falling upon it.

There, began the felling and hewing of trees that were to touch the farther shores of Michigan. The supplies brought out from Paris had been lost by the wreck of La Salle's smaller vessel on the way up Ontario, but enough was saved, or brought by La Salle on his return from Fort Frontenac, to give this sixty-ton vessel full equipment, for in the spring she was launched. The "friar pronounced his blessing on her; the assembled company sang *Te Deum;* cannon were fired; and French and Indians . . . shouted and yelped in chorus as she glided into Niagara." She carried five cannon and on her prow was carved such a "portentous monster" as doubtless is to be found among the grotesques of Notre Dame—a griffin (that is, a beast with the body of a lion and the head, beak, and pinions of a bird), in honor of the armorial bearings of Count Frontenac.

Through spring and half the summer the vessel lay moored beyond reach of the Indians but near enough so that Hennepin "could preach on Sundays from the deck to the men encamped along the bank." When La Salle, who had been obliged by disasters to go back to Fort Frontenac during the building of the ship, again appeared above the falls in midsummer, the *Griffin* was warped up into the placid lake, and on the 7th of August anchor was lifted and the fateful voyage was begun.

There was (as when the *Argo*, the "first bold vessel,

dared the seas") no Orpheus standing "high on the stern" and "raising his entrancing strain." Nor did a throng of proud Thessalians or of "transported demigods" stand round to cheer them off. The naked Indians, their hands over their mouths in wonderment or shouting, "Gannorom! Gannorom!" alone saw the great boat move out over the waters without oar or paddle or towing rope. For music there was only the *Te Deum* again, sung by raw, unpractised voices, such as one might hear among the boatmen of the Seine. It was not such music, at any rate, as that of Orpheus, to make plain men grow "heroes at the sound." Doubtless no one felt himself a hero. The only intimation of any consciousness of a high mission comes from Hennepin, who, when the *Griffin*, some days later, was ploughing peacefully through the straits that led to the Mer Douce—"verdant prairies, dotted with groves and bordered with lofty forests" on either side, "herds of deer and flocks of swans and wild turkeys" within sight, and the "bulwarks plentifully hung with game"—wrote: "Those who will one day have the happiness to possess this fertile and pleasant strait, will be very much obliged to those who have shown them the way."

"Very much obliged"? No, Hennepin! Of the hundreds of thousands who now pass through or across those straits every year, or of those thousands who possess its shores, not a hundred, I venture to say, remember "those who showed the way"! They have even forgotten "that the first European voice that Niagara ever heard was French"! Ste. Claire!—the name you gave to the beautiful strait beyond the "Symplegades" of your voyage, in gratitude and in

honor of the day on which your company reached it—
has become masculine in tribute to an American general. If your later praying to that patron of seamen,
St. Anthony of Padua, had not availed to save you
from the peril of the storm and you had gone to death
in unsalted water, you could hardly have been more
completely forgotten. One has spoken now and then
lightly of the vow made by your commander, La Salle,
to build a grateful chapel to St. Anthony if your lives
were saved during that storm, forgetting that so long
as the Mississippi runs to the sea there will be a chapel
to St. Anthony (St. Anthony's Falls) in which gratitude will be continually chanted through ages for the
preservation of the ship and its crew to find haven in
quiet waters behind Point St. Ignace.

It was there, at St. Ignace that we have seen La
Salle, in scarlet, kneeling before the altar, where Marquette's bones were doubtless by that time gathered
by his devoted savage followers, and it was thence that
they passed on to an island in Green Bay, the goal of
their journey.

From that far port the first cargo carried of sails
was sent out, bound for the shore on which the *Griffin's*
timbers had been hewn. That it never reached harbor
of that calm shelter, or any other, we know; but that
loss, once the path was traced in the waters, is hardly
of consequence save as it helped further to illustrate
the indomitable spirit of La Salle and his companions.

What good came to Thessaly or Greece of the yellow
peltry that Jason brought back is not even kept in
myth or fable. The mere adventure was the all.
They did not even think of its worth. The goatskin
was valueless except as a proof or token, and the

boat *Argo*, though the greatest ship known to the
early myths of Greece, and though dedicated, we are
told, to Neptune at the end of the voyage, became the
pioneer of no such mighty fleet as did the *Griffin*. The
list of the Greek ships and commanders in the Iliad
offers but a pygmy analogy. And if you were to go to
Buffalo to-day, near the site of that first shipyard (a
little farther away from the falls), you would know that
the successors of La Salle in new *Griffins* had actually
brought back the golden fleece—the priceless fleece,
the fleece of the plains if not of the forests. Day after
day its gold is hung against the sky as the grain is
lifted from the ships into elevators which can store at
one time twenty-three million bushels of wheat.

The coasts of the lakes up which the *Griffin* led the
oarless way are three thousand three hundred and
eighty-five miles in length, or, including those of the
lower lake, Frontenac, which was also first touched of
French keels, over four thousand miles. The statistics
of the traffic which has grown in the furrow of that
wind-drawn plough would be fatiguing if they did not
carry you to heights of a wider and more exhilarating
view.

We have occupied and apportioned the billion acres
of French domain among sixty million people. Here
is an added domain in which no landmarks can be set
—which belongs to all men.

These are a few graphic facts gathered from recent
reports and books about the Great Lakes:[1]

Nearly as many people live in States that have

[1] Edward Channing and M. F. Lansing, "The Story of the Great Lakes."
Macmillan, New York, 1909. James O. Curwood, "The Great Lakes."
Putnam, New York, 1909. James C. Mills, "Our Inland Seas." McClurg,
Chicago, 1910.

ports upon those shores as in France to-day—between thirty-five and forty millions.

The lakes have a tonnage equal to one-third of the total tonnage of North America.[1]

They have made possible a saving in cost of transportation (and so of production) of several hundred million dollars in a single year.[2]

Only ninety million dollars have been spent by the government for their improvement in the whole history of their occupation, above Niagara Falls,[3] while France in that time has spent for harbors and waterways alone seven hundred and fifty million dollars.[4] They have been privately developed.

Six times as much freight passes over these lakes as through the Suez Canal in a year.[5]

Three thousand five hundred vessels and more than twenty-five thousand men are required to move the hundred million tons of freight which every year would fill a train encircling the globe.[6]

If one were to stand on the shore of that "charming strait," between Erie and Huron, the Detroit River (which Hennepin so covetously describes, wishing to make settlement there, until La Salle reminded him of his "professed passion for exploring a new country"), one would now see a vessel passing one way or the

---

[1] Curwood, "The Great Lakes," p. 4. "In 1913 the total tonnage of the Great Lakes was 2,940,000 tons, of the United States 7,887,000 tons."—Report United States Commission of Navigation.

[2] Curwood, "The Great Lakes," p. 4.

[3] Curwood, "The Great Lakes," p. 9.

[4] "Four hundred and fifty million dollars of this total has been for the improvement and maintenance of the waterways."—Report of National Waterways Commission, p. 507.

[5] Curwood, "The Great Lakes," p. 6.

[6] Curwood, "The Great Lakes," pp. 25, 26, and Report of United States Commission of Navigation, 1913.

other every twelve minutes, on the average, day and night during the eight months of open navigation.

Nor are they small sailing vessels of a few tons' burden, but great sailless, steam-propelled hulks, carrying from five to ten thousand tons.

So it is no fleet of graceful galleons—half bird, half lion, as the *Griffin* was—that have followed in her wake up what Hennepin called "the vast and unknown seas of which even the savages knew not the end." They have, in the evolution of nautical zoology, lost beak, wings, and feathers, and now like a shoal of wet lions, tawny and black, their powerful heads and long steel backs just visible above the blue water, they course the western Mediterranean from spring to winter.[1]

The ships of the lion brood are, some of them, five or six hundred feet in length, and carry eleven thousand tons of cargo. I have seen the skeleton of one of these iron-boned beasts, and I have been told that eight hundred thousand rivets go into its creation. And upon hearing this I could not but hear the deafening clamor caused by La Salle's driving the first nail or bolt, Father Hennepin declining the honor because of the "modesty of [his] religious profession."

As to the cargoes that these ships bring back, the story is even more marvellous. First in quantity is

---

[1] It is an intruding and probably whimsical, but fascinating, thought that the wings of the griffin have become evolved into the air-ships which first began successfully to fly, in America, near the shores of the lake on which the *Griffin* itself was hatched. The Wright brothers were born near one of those lakes. It is not a far-fetched or labored thought which pictures that simple, rough-made galleon—very like the model of the ship on the shield of Paris—as leading two broods across the valley above the Falls, one of lions that cannot fly and one of sea-birds, hydroplanes, whose paths are the air, but whose resting-places are the calm water; the brood of the sea and the brood of the sky, hatched from one nest at the water's edge.

iron ore, forty-seven million four hundred and thirty-five thousand seven hundred and seventy-one tons in 1912[1] from the shores of Superior, where Joliet had made search for copper mines, where Father Allouez —in the midst of reports of baptisms and masses— tells of nuggets and rocks of the precious metal, and where has grown up in a few years the "second greatest freight-shipping port on earth"—a port that bears the name of that famous French coureur de bois, Du Lhut. Forty-seven millions of tons, and there are still a billion and a half in sight on those shores, which have already given to the ships hundreds of millions of their dark treasure.

After the ore, lumber, one billion one hundred and sixty-five million feet[2] in one year (1911); a waning amount from the vanishing forests that once completely encircled these lakes. Alexander Pope, whose "Ode on St. Cecilia's Day" I have quoted (and would there were a Homer, Pope, or Kipling to sing this true legend), speaks of *Argo* seeing "her kindred trees descend from Pelion to the Main"—from the mountain to the sea, where Jason's boat was launched. So, with the departure of the *Griffin* from her Green Bay Island, might a prophetic poet have seen her masts beckoning all the kindred trees to the water, in which one hundred and sixty billion feet of pine have descended from the forests of Michigan alone,[3] and that is but one of the circling States.   And there is this singular fact to be added, that nearly a third of the annual cargo goes to the "Tonawandas,"[4] the "greatest lumber towns"

[1] "Mineral Industry," 21 : 455.
[2] Monthly Summary of Internal Commerce of the United States, December, 1911.
[3] Curwood, "The Great Lakes," p. 57.
[4] Curwood, "The Great Lakes," p. 54.

in the world that have grown up practically on the very site of the shipyard at the mouth of Cayuga Creek, a little way above the falls.

And after the ore and lumber, grain—the fleece of the fields, immensely more valuable than that of the forests; one hundred and fifty million bushels in one year and eleven million barrels of flour—a fortnight's bread supply for the entire world.[1]

And after ore and lumber and grain, fuel and other bulky necessities of life.

The casual relation between the pioneer building and journey of the *Griffin* and these statistics cannot, of course, be established, but what no inspired human prophecy could have divined, or even the wildest dreaming of La Salle have imagined, is as sequential as the history that has been made to trace all new-world development in the wake of the caravels of Columbus. The storms of nature and the jealousies in human breasts thwarted La Salle's immediate ambitions, but what has come into that northern valley has followed closely in the path of his purposes, the path traced by his ship built of the trees of Niagara and furnished by the chandleries of Paris.

The mystery of the vanishing of this pioneer vessel only enhances the glory of its venture and service—as its loss but gave new foil to the hardihood of La Salle and Tonty. We can imagine the golden-brown skins scattered over the blue waters as the bits of the body of the son of the king of Colchis strewn by Medea to detain the pursuers of the Argonauts. It was the first sacrifice to the valley for the fleece. In the depths of these Lakes or on their shores were buried the bones of

[1] Curwood, "The Great Lakes," p. 49.

these French mariners who, first of Europeans, trusted themselves to sails and west winds on those uncharted seas.

But this is not the all of the tragic story. The *Griffin* carried in her the prophecies of other than lake vessels. She had in her hold on that fateful trip the cordage and iron for the pioneer of the river ships. So when she went down she spoke to the waters that engulfed her the two dreams of her builder and commander: one dream the navigation of the lakes and the other the coursing of the western rivers.

The Spanish council which decreed long ago that "if it had pleased God that . . . rivers should have been navigable, He would not have wanted human assistance to make them such" would be horrified by the sacrilege that has been committed and is being contemplated by the followers of the men of the *Griffin*.

They have made a canal around the Falls (which Hennepin first saw breathing a cloud of mist over the great abyss)—a canal that, supplemented by other canals along the St. Lawrence River, allows vessels of fourteen-foot draught to go from Lake Erie to Montreal and so on to the sea. If this achievement were put into the poetry of legend it would show the outwitting of the dragon.

They have deepened the straits where the *Griffin* had to wait for favorable breezes and soundings to pass from Erie to Huron—the Symplegades (clashing rocks) of the new-world voyage.

They have made canals on either side of the Sault Ste. Marie—the rapids of the St. Mary's River, by the side of which St. Lusson took formal possession of all that northern empire and Father Allouez made his extraordinary address—canals through which sixty-two million tons passed in 1910 toward the east and south.

They have made and deepened harbors all the way around the shores till ships two hundred times the size of the *Griffin* can ride in them.

Yet this is not all. The symbols of La Salle's vision revived in the lakes memories of the days when their waters ran through the Mississippi Valley to the gulf —the very course which La Salle's unborn *Griffin* was to take.

When the continent tilted a little to the east and in the tilting poured the water of the upper lakes over the Niagara edge into the St. Lawrence, that same tilting stopped the overflow down into the Mississippi and the Gulf of Mexico at the other end of the lakes. But so slight was the tilting that the water still sweeps over, in places, when the lakes are high, and sometimes even carries light boats across.

Of late engineers have, in effect, been undoing with levels and scoops and dredges what nature did in a mighty upheaval. They are practically tipping the bowls back the other way and so making currents to run down the old channel toward the gulf through the valleys of the Des Plaines and the Illinois to the Mississippi.

And so that dream which the dying *Griffin* spoke to the lake, and the lake to the rivers in the time of flood —when intercommunication was possible—is to be realized, except that steam or electricity will take the place of winds, and screws of sails.[1]

Meanwhile a great battle of the lakes is waging— a battle of levels, it might better be called, between

[1] Herbert Quick, "American Inland Waterways," New York, 1909.

those, on the one side, who wish to maintain the grandeur of Niagara much as it was when Hennepin first pictured it, and with them those who for utilitarian reasons do not wish its thunderous volume diminished, except, perhaps, for their local uses, and those also who fear disaster to their harbors and canals all around the lakes, deepened at great expense, if water is led away toward the Mississippi; and, on the other side, the public health of millions at the western end of the lakes and the commercial hopes of other millions in the Mississippi Valley waiting for the *Griffins* of the lakes to come with more generous prices for their produce and bring to their doors what the rest of the world has now to send to them by the more expensive railroad.

Some day, perhaps, the great upper lake, Superior, will be made a reservoir where enough water will be impounded in wet seasons for a steady and more generous supply during the dry seasons; in which event there will be water enough to keep Niagara in perennial beauty and power, to fill all the present and prospective harbors and canals to their desired depths and float even larger fleets of *Griffins*, and, at the same time, have enough left to make the Mississippi, as the Frenchman who first saw it visualized it, and as President Roosevelt, two centuries later, expressed it, "a loop of the sea."[1]

But another amicable battle is on—a battle of the eastern levels—between the men of the old French valley to the north (*i. e.*, the St. Lawrence) and the men of the old Iroquois valleys to the south, of the Mohawk and the Hudson. In 1830 a canal was built

[1] Herbert Quick, "American Inland Waterways," New York, 1909.

by the latter from above the Falls to the navigable
Hudson, and with high ceremony a cask of the water
of Lake Erie was emptied into New York harbor as
symbol of the wedding of lake and ocean.   Then
Canada built her Welland Canal around Niagara and
made canals along the St. Lawrence and channels in
the St. Lawrence past the Lachine Rapids to Montreal, and even made the way from there to the sea
deeper that the growing ocean vessels might come to
old Hochelaga.   Now New York has begun deepening
the old and almost useless Erie Canal from seven and
nine feet to twelve feet, and to take barges one hundred
and fifty feet long and twenty-five feet beam, with a
draught of ten feet, and Canada is contemplating still
deeper channels that will let the ocean steamers into
every port of the Great Lakes.   She is even thinking
of a canal that will follow the path of Champlain, up
the Ottawa and across the old portage to Lake Nipissing and thence by the French River into Lake Huron;
and of an alternative course by another of Champlain's
paths, from Ontario across to Huron by way of Lake
Simcoe and the Trent River, in either route avoiding
Niagara altogether, paths that would shorten the water
distance by hundreds of miles and bring Europe almost
as near to the shores where Le Caron ministered to the
Hurons as to New York City.

It is a rivalry between the old Champlain paths
and the La Salle paths, with just an intimation from
those who look far into the future that a new water
path still farther north—of which Radisson gave some
premonition—may carry the wheat of the far northwest from Winnipeg beyond Superior and beyond the
courses of the Mississippi up to Hudson Bay and

across the ocean to European ports, brought a thousand miles nearer.

This is but the merest intimation of the prophetic service of the water pioneers. And when the prophecy of these pioneers, as interpreted in terms of steam and locks and dams unknown to them, is fulfilled, it is not beyond thinking that a captain of a seagoing vessel of ten or twenty thousand tons from Havre or Cherbourg may some day be calling in deep voice (as last summer in a room on the twenty-ninth floor of a Chicago "sky-scraper" I heard a local descendant of the *Griffin* screeching) for the lifting of the bridges that will open the way to the Mississippi, the heart of America.

CHAPTER XI

WESTERN CITIES THAT HAVE SPRUNG FROM FRENCH FORTS

IT is a strange and varied crop that has grown from the leaden plates with French inscriptions, planted by St. Lusson, La Salle, and Céloron by lakes and rivers in that western country. The mythical story of the sowing of Cadmus in the Bœotian field is again rather tame by comparison with a true relation of what has actually occurred within the memory of a few generations in a valley as wild when Céloron traversed the course of La Belle Rivière (the name given by the French to the Ohio, which was known to the Indians as the "River of the Whitecaps") with his little fleet only a century and a half ago as was Bœotia when Cadmus set out from Phœnicia in search of his sister, Europa (that is, Europe), back beyond the memory of history.

It was a bourgeoning, most miraculous, in those spots of the west, a new Europa, where soldiers sprang up immediately upon the sowing, like the sproutings of Cadmus' dragon's teeth, to fight one another and to build strongholds that should some day be cities, even as Cadmea, the fortress of the "Spartoi," became the city of Thebes.

So, in this sowing, did France become the mother of western cities, of Pittsburgh and Buffalo, of Erie, of St. Louis, of Detroit and New Orleans, of Peoria and

St. Joseph, and still other cities whose names have never been heard by the people of France—even as Phœnicia, in the wanderings of her adventurous son, Cadmus, became the mother of Thebes and the god-mother of Greek culture and of European literature. Palamedes and Simonides added some letters to the alphabet brought, according to tradition, by Cadmus to Greece, and Cadmus suffered the doom of those who sow dragon's teeth, as France has suffered, but still is his name kept in the memory of every school child; and so should be remembered those who planted the lead plates and sowed the teeth that sprang into the "Spartoi" of a new civilization.

Of the sowing of St. Lusson at the "Soo" and La Salle at New Orleans we have spoken. Long later (1749), the first of whom we have record after La Salle, another French sower went forth to sow along the rivers close to the foot of the Alleghany Mountains —Céloron de Bienville, Chevalier de St. Louis.' It is of his sowing that the main cities have sprung, for he planted a plate of "repossession" at the entrance of every important branch of the Ohio and fastened upon trees sheets of "white iron" bearing the arms of France. Chief among them is Pittsburgh, which stands on the carboniferous site of Fort Duquesne like the prow of a vessel headed westward, a place which Céloron is believed to have had in mind when he wrote in his journal, "the finest place on La Belle Rivière"—what was then a wedge of wild black land lodged between two converging streams that drained all the slope of the northern Alleghanies being now the foundation of the world's capital of a sterner metal than lead— scarred with fires and smothered with smoke from

many furnaces, two of which alone, it has been estimated by some one, have poured forth enough molten
iron in the last thirty years to cover with steel plates
an inch thick a road fifty feet wide stretching from
the Alleghany edge of the valley not merely to the
mouth of the Ohio but on to the other mountain border, where all dreams of a way to the western sea
were ended.

And this highway of plates across the empire of New
France gives but suggestion of the meagerest fraction
of the fruitage of the planting of the leaden plates or
the grafting of the arms of France upon the trees along
the Ohio—forty pounds of iron, it has been estimated
by one graphic statistician, for every man, woman,
and child on the globe to-day,[1] and I do not know how
much tin.   And, in a sense, all from a small box or
crate of plates made of lead—six, eight, or more in
number, eleven inches long, seven inches wide, and one
eighth of an inch thick, and engraved with an inscription—one of which was found not long ago, by some
lads, protruding from the bank of one of the tributary
rivers!   The inscription ran (in translation):

"Year 1749, in the reign of Louis XV., King of
France, We, Céloron, commanding the detachment
sent by the Marquis De la Galissonière, Commander
General of New France, to restore tranquillity in certain villages of these cantons, have buried this plate
at [here is inserted the name of the tributary at its
confluence with the Ohio] this [date] as a token of
renewal of possession heretofore taken of the aforesaid
river, Ohio, of all streams that fall into it, and all

[1] H. N. Casson.   United States produces thirty million tons annually,
Pennsylvania eleven and a quarter million.   "Mineral Resources," 1912.

lands on both sides to the sources of the aforesaid streams, as the preceding Kings of France enjoyed it, or ought to have enjoyed it, and which they have upheld by force of arms and by treaties, notably by those of Ryswick, Utrecht, and Aix la Chapelle."

And with these plates (to be buried at the confluences of the important rivers along the way) were carried sheets of tin—of white iron—on which the arms of France had been stamped, to be nailed to trees above the places of the plates.

"As the Kings of France enjoyed it, or ought to have enjoyed it"—what a blight of regret was in the very seed that in its flower of to-day makes one wish for some delicate beauty or subtle fragrance that is not there, because the Kings of France did not let France enjoy it.

One can but pause here again, as I have paused many, many times in the preparation of these chapters, to ask what would have been the result if France had but chosen as Portia's successful suitor in Shakespeare's "Merchant of Venice" when he was confronted with the caskets of gold, silver, and lead—had but chosen "to owe and hazard all for lead," instead of deciding as did the Prince of Morocco, the other suitor, that "a golden mind stoops not to shows of dross"—if France had hazarded all for the holding and settling of those regions whose worth was symbolized in those unpromising pieces of lead planted in the fertile soil of Louisiana, Michigan, and Ohio along the watercourses, rather than in the caskets of gold and silver sought among the mountains—if Louis XV, throwing dice at Versailles in the valley of the Seine, as Parkman describes him, with his piles of louis d'or before him, and the princes and princesses, dukes and duchesses and courtiers about him, had but followed the advice of Marquis de la Galissonnière, the humpbacked governor-general of Canada, who furnished Céloron with his leaden seeds and appointed the place of the sowing—if Louis XV had but answered his Canadian governor's prayer and sent French peasants where the plates were buried, or had even let those who wanted to flee to that valley, as they would have fled by tens of thousands, preferring the hardships and privations of the pioneer to the galleys, the dungeons, or the gallows—then "Versailles" in that valley of the Ohio would not be merely what it is, a ward or township in a city that bears the name of a British statesman.

"Or, if soldiers had been sent!" Parkman, approaching the great valley in imagination with Céloron, from the north, exclaims, "the most momentous and far-reaching question ever brought to issue on this continent was: 'Shall France remain here or shall she not?' If by diplomacy or war she had preserved but the half or less than half of her American possessions, then a barrier would have been set to the spread of the English-speaking races, there would have been no Revolutionary War and, for a long time at least, no independence."[1] (Which but emphasizes what I have said as to the part, the negative part as well as the positive, France conspicuously and unconsciously played in the making of a new nation.)

If "the French soldiers left dead on inglorious continental battle-fields could," as Parkman says, "have saved Canada, and perhaps made good her claim to

[1] Parkman, "Montcalm and Wolfe," p. 5.

the vast territories of the West,"[1] could they after all
have done more for the world than those who, in effect,
sacrificed their lives on glorious western battle-fields
for the United States?

A little way back I spoke of the first expedition
looking toward that valley from the Atlantic side of
the Alleghanies—the expedition of the "Knights of
the Golden Horseshoe"—and of its vain threats. In
1748 a company of still wider horizon was formed in
Virginia, George Washington's father being a member of it. It was known as the Ohio Land Company
and derived its transmontane rights through George
II from John Cabot, an Italian under English commission, who may have set foot nearly two centuries
before somewhere on the coast of North America below Labrador, and from a very expansive interpretation of a treaty with the Indians at Lancaster, Pa., in
1744, the trans-Alleghany Indians protesting, however,
not less firmly than the French, that the lands purchased by the English under that treaty extended no
farther toward the sunset than the laurel hills on the
western edge of the Alleghanies.

News of this Virginia corporate enterprise was
willingly carried, it is surmised, by jealous Pennsyl-
vanians and hostile French, till it reached Montreal,
and so it was that Céloron was despatched with his
little company to bury "Monuments of the Renewal
of Possession" by France.

It was a significant and rather solemn, but most
picturesque, processional that this chevalier of St.
Louis led from Montreal through one thousand two
hundred leagues of journey by water and land to the

[1] Parkman, "Montcalm and Wolfe," p. 41.

mouth of the Miami River and back. There are no
hilarious songs in this prelude such as were heard
from the crests of the Blue Ridge when Spotswood's
horsemen came up from the other side. It has to me
the atmosphere and movement of some Greek tragedy,
though one writer likens it to mediæval mummery.
Perhaps it is only a knowledge of its import and the
end that makes it sombre and grave despite the beautiful setting to this prelude which one may read to-day
in the French archives. So full of portent and color
it is that I wonder no one has woven its incidents,
slight as they are, into French literature or into that
of America.

"I left Lachine on the 15th of June," begins Céloron's
journal,[1] now in the Département de la Marine, in
Paris, "with a detachment formed of a captain, eight
subaltern officers, six cadets, an armorer, twenty men
of the troops, one hundred and eighty Canadians, and
nearly thirty savages—equal number of Iroquois and
Abenakes." They filled twenty-three canoes in a procession that was halted by shipwreck, by heat, by lack
of rain and by too much rain, by difficult portages, and
damage to the canoes.

Over a part of their first portage from Lake Erie
I walked one night years ago through a drenching rain,
such as they endured in the seven days in which they
were carrying their canoes and baggage up those steep
hills through the then dense forest of beech, oak, and
elm, to the waters of Lake Chautauqua, where now
many thousands gather every summer, from children
to white-haired men and women, to study history,
language, sciences, cooking, sewing, etc., and to attend
conferences daily.

[1] Margry, 6 : 666.

But the expedition then was often stopped by savages who ran away to avoid the excessive speech-making and lecturing of these old-world orators, conférenciers; and the ears and eyes of the auditors who did not run away were opened by strings of wampum, though they were often too little moved by the love of their father Onontio and his concern lest the English should make themselves masters and the Indians their victims.

There is in a Paris library a map of this expedition made by the hand of Père Bonnecamps, who signs himself "Jesuitte Mathematiciant." He kept a diary[1], also preserved in Paris, in which there has crept some of the sombreness of that narrow, dark valley (now filled with oil-derricks) surrounded by mountains sometimes so high as to let them see the sun only from nine or ten o'clock in the morning till two or three in the afternoon. And across the mountains one may hear even to-day the despairful, yet appealing, voice of Céloron, speaking for the great Onontio: "My children," he says, "since I have been at war with the English I have learned that that nation has seduced you; and, not content with corrupting your hearts, they have profited by my absence from the country to invade the land which does not belong to them and which is mine. . . . I will give you the aid you should expect from a good father. . . . I will furnish you traders in abundance if you wish them. I will send here officers if that please you—to give you good spirit, so that you will only work in good affairs. . . . Follow

[1] Translation in "Jesuit Relations," ed. Thwaites, vol. 69. "Account of the voyage on the Beautiful River made in 1749 under the direction of Monsieur de Céloron."

my advice. Then the sky will always be beautiful and clear over your villages."[1]

"My father," said the spokesman for the savages at another council, "we pray you have pity on us; we are young men who cannot reply as the old men could; what you have said to us has opened our eyes [received gifts], given us spirit, we see that you only work with good affairs. . . . [The great Onontio in Paris is playing all the while in Paris with the louis d'or.] Examine, my father, the situation in which we are. If thou makest the English to retire, who give us necessaries, and especially the smith who mends our guns and hatchets, we would be without help and exposed to die of hunger and of misery in the Belle Rivière. Have pity on us, my father, thou canst not at present give us our necessaries. Leave us at least for this winter, or at least till we go hunting, the smith and some one who can help us. We promise thee that in the spring the English will retire."[2]

And so the expedition passed on from river to river, from tribe to tribe, planting plates and making appeals to the savages, down the Ohio to the Miami, up the Miami, stopping at the village of a chief known as La Demoiselle, thence by portage to the French settlement on the Maumee, and so back to Lake Erie. Then came the fort builders in their wake, and so the "Spartoi," the soldiers, almost literally sprang from the earth of the sowing of the plates.

At one place (the place where the Loups prayed for a smith) they found a young Englishman with a few dozen workmen building a stockade, but they sent him back beyond the mountains over which he

[1] Margry, 6 : 677.　　　　[2] Margry, 6 : 683.

had come and built upon its site Fort Duquesne—
the defense of the mountain gate to the great valley—
here with a few hundred men on the edge of a hostile
wilderness to make beginning of that mighty struggle
which was to end, as we know, on the river by which
Cartier and Champlain had made their way into the
continent.

It is a fact, remarkable to us now, that the first
to bring a challenge from behind the mountains to
that brave and isolate garrison sitting in Fort Duquesne
at the junction of the water paths, was Washington
("Sir Washington," as one chronicler has written it),
not Washington the American but Washington the
English subject, major in the colonial militia, envoy
of an English governor of Virginia, Dinwiddie, who,
having acquired a controlling interest in the Ohio
Company, became especially active in planning to seat
a hundred families on that transmontane estate of a
half-million acres and so to win title to it.

"So complicated [were] the political interests of [that]
time that a shot fired in America [was] the signal for
setting all Europe together by the ears," wrote Voltaire,[1] and "it was not a cannon-shot" that gave the
signal but, as Parkman said, "a volley from the hunting pieces of a few backwoodsmen, commanded by a
Virginia youth, George Washington."[2]

We must stop for a moment to look at this lithe
young English colonist, twenty-one years of age,
standing on the nearest edge of the French explorations and claims and the farthest verge of English ad-

[1] Voltaire, "The French in America" in his "Short Studies in English
and American Subjects," p. 249.
[2] Parkman, "Montcalm and Wolfe," 1 : 3.

venture, on the watershed twenty miles from Lake
Erie, and requesting, in the name of Governor Dinwiddie and of the shade of John Cabot, the peaceable
departure of those French pioneers and soldiers, who,
as the letter which the young colonel bore stated, were
"erecting fortresses and making settlements upon the
the river [Ohio] so notoriously known to be the property of the Crown of Great Britain."

The edge of the Great Lakes' basin is only a little
way, at the place where he stood, from the watershed of the Mississippi River. A little farther up the
shore, where Céloron made portage, it is only six or
eight miles across, and here it is but a little more, and
the "height of land" is hardly noticeable. The French
built a fort on a promontory in the lake—a promontory almost an island—Presque Isle; and there, where
the waters begin to run the other way, that is, toward
the gulf, they built still another which they called
Le Bœuf, an easier portage than the Chautauqua.
From the former fort the city of Erie, a grimy, busy
manufacturing city, has grown. The latter has produced only a village, on whose weed-grown outskirts
the ruins of a fort still look out upon the meadow
where the little stream called "French Creek" starts,
first toward France, in its two-thousand-mile journey
to the gulf that lies in the other direction.

For twenty miles I followed the stream one day to
where it became a part of Céloron's river—in imagination calling the French back to its banks again, but
finding them slow to come, for that part of the valley
seemed not particularly attractive. It is a little farther
down the lake that the vineyards fill all the shore from
the lake to the watershed. And in that very country

I have often wondered at the miracle which raised from one bit of ground the corn and the pumpkin, and from another the vine and filled its fruit with wine.

The one-eyed veteran, Legardeur de St. Pierre, the commander of Fort Le Bœuf, asked Washington, in rich diplomatic sarcasm, to descend to the particularization of facts, and the lithe figure disappeared behind the snows of the mountains only to come again across the mountains in the springtime with sterner questioning. There was then no talk of Cabot or La Salle, of Indian purchase or crown property. Jumonville may have come out from Duquesne for peaceable speech, but Washington misunderstood or would not listen. A flash of flint fire, a fresh bit of lead planted in the hill of laurel, a splash of blood on the rock, and the war for the west was begun.

What actually happened out on the slope of that hill will never be accurately known; but, though Washington was only twenty-two years old then, "full of military ardor" and "vehement," he could not have been guilty of wilful firing on men of peaceful intent.

It doubtless seemed but an insignificant skirmish when Washington attacked Jumonville near Pittsburgh, and it is now remembered by only a line or two in our histories and the little cairn of stones "far up among the mountain fogs near the headwaters of the Youghiogheny River," which marks the grave of Jumonville.

Washington, the major of colonial militia in the Alleghany Mountains, the scout of a land company, has been entirely forgotten in Washington, the father of a nation; but Jumonville, the French ensign with no land-scrip, fighting certainly as unselfishly and with as high purpose, is not forgotten in any later achievement. That skirmish ended all for him. But let it be remembered even now that he was a representative of France standing almost alone, at the confluence of all the waters for hundreds of miles on the other slope of the Alleghanies, in defense of what other men of France had won by their hardihood.

I heard a great audience at the Academy applaud the brave endurance of French priests and soldiers in Asia. Some day I hope these unrenowned men who sacrificed as much for France in America will be as notably remembered. There is a short street in Pittsburgh that bears Jumonville's name—a short street that runs from the river into a larger street with the name of one of his seven brothers, De Villiers, Coulon de Villiers, who hastened from Montreal, while another brother hastened from the Illinois to avenge his death.

But the cairn on the hillside has grown to no high monument. Mr. Hulbert, who has written with filial pen of the valley, says that occasionally a traveller repairs a rough wooden cross made of boards or tree branches and planted among the rocks of the cairn.[1] But on a recent visit to the grave out in that lonesome ravine, I found that a permanent tablet had been placed there instead of this fragile cross.

I must leave to your unrefreshed memories the exploits of Beaujeu and Braddock, of Contrecœur and Forbes, blow up Fort Duquesne of the past, and come into the city of to-day, for I wish to put against this background this mighty city where it is often difficult to see because of the smoke.

The French, as we are well aware, came to their

[1] A. B. Hulbert, "The Ohio River," pp. 44, 45.

forts by water. Quebec, Frontenac, Niagara, Presque
Isle, the Rock St. Louis, St. Joseph, Chartres, and
many others stood by river or lake. But the going
was often slow. Céloron (whose name is often spelled
Céleron but would seem not to deserve that spelling)
was fifty-three days in making his water journey from
Montreal to the site of Pittsburgh. But a Céloron of
to-day may see the light of the Bartholdi statue in
New York harbor at ten o'clock by night and yet pass
Braddock's field in the morning (before the time that
Bonnecamp said the sun came up in the narrow valley
of the Belle Rivière), and have breakfast at the Duquesne Club in time for a city day's work. It was
about as far from Paris to Marseilles in 1750 as it is
to-day from Paris to Pittsburgh.

Pittsburgh is the front door of the valley of La
Salle, as we now know the valley, and the most important door; for the tonnage that enters and leaves
it by rail and water (177,071,238 tons in 1912 for the
Pittsburgh district) exceeds the tonnage of the five other
greatest cities of the world [1] and is twice the combined
tonnage of both coasts of the United States to and
from foreign ports—which is probably due to the fact
that so much of its traffic is not in silks and furs
but in iron and coal. And the multitudes of human
beings that pass through it are comparable in number
with the migrant tonnage and inanimate cargoes; for
Pittsburgh is "the antithesis of a mediæval town";
"it is all motion;" "it is a flow, not a tank." The
mountains, once impenetrable barriers that had to be
gone about, have been levelled, and in the levelling

[1] R. B. Naylor, address before the Ohio Valley Historical Association
(quoted in Hulbert, "Ohio River," pp. 365-6).

the watersheds, as we have seen, have been shifted. One who sees that throng pass to-day back and forth, to and from the valley and the ocean, must know that there are no Alleghanies in our continental topography, as Washington saw and as Webster stated there could not be in our politics. If one makes the journey from the ocean in the night, one may hear, if one wakes, the puffing of two engines, as in the Jura Mountains, but there will be nothing else to tell him that the shaggy Alleghany Mountains have not been cast into the midst of the sea—nothing except the groaning of the wheels.

The Indians near Pittsburgh, I have said, prayed the messenger of Onontio that they might keep their English smith—and the prayer seems to have been abundantly answered, for Pittsburgh appears at first to be one vast smithy, so enveloped is it in the smoke of its own toil, so reddened are its great sky walls by its flaming forges, so filled is the air with the dust from the bellows, and so clangorous is the sound of its hammers. It is a city of Vulcans—a city whose industry makes academic discussions seem as the play of girls in a field of flowers. It is not primarily a market-place, this point of land, one of the places where the French and English traders used to barter guns, whiskey, and trinkets for furs. It is a making place—a pit between the hills, where the fires of creation are still burning.

Céloron and his sombre voyage had been in my mind all day, as I sat in a beautiful library of that city among books of the past; but in the evening, as Dante accompanied by Virgil, I descended circle by circle to the floor of the valley—with this difference,

that it was not to a place of torment but to the halls
of the swarth gods of creation, those great, dim,
shadowy sheds that stretch along the river's edge.
Into these, men of France, has your Fort Duquesne
grown—mile on mile of flame-belching buildings, with
a garrison as great as the population of all New France
in the day of Duquesne.

The new-world epic will find some of its color and
incident there—an epic in which we have already heard
the men of France nailing the sheets of "white iron"
against the trees of the valley of La Belle Rivière. And
as I saw the white-hot sheets of iron issuing from those
crunching rollers, driven by the power of seven thousand horses, I felt that the youth with the stamping
iron should have put a fleur-de-lis upon each with all
his other cabalistic markings, for who of us can know
that any metal would ever have flowed white from the
furnaces in that valley if the white-metal signs of
Louis XV had not first been carried into it?

In each of these halls there pass in orderly succes-
sion cars with varied cargoes; red ore from the far-
away hills beyond Superior, limestone fragments from
some near-by hill, and scrap of earlier burning. These,
one by one, are seized by a great arm of iron, thrust
out from a huge moving structure that looks like a
battering-ram and is operated by a young man about
whom the lightnings play as he moves; and, one by one,
they are cast into the furnaces that are heated to a
temperature of a thousand degrees or more. There
the red earth is freed of its "devils," as the great
ironmaster has named the sulphur and phosphorus—
freed of its devils as the red child was freed of his sins
by the touch of holy water from the fingers of Allouez

out in those very forests from which the red ore was dug—and comes forth purified, to be cast into flaming ingots, to be again heated and then crushed and moulded and sawed and pierced for the better service of man.

In the course of a few minutes one sees a few iron carloads of ore that was a month before lying in the earth beyond Superior transformed into a girder for a bridge, a steel rail, a bit of armor-plate, a beam for a sky-scraper—and all in utter human silence, with the calm pushing and pulling of a few levers, the accurate shovelling by a few hands, the deliberate testing by a few pairs of experienced eyes.

Here is the new Fort Duquesne that is holding the place of the confluence of the rivers and trails just beyond the Alleghanies, and this is the ammunition with which that begrimed but strong-faced garrison defends the valley to-day, supports the city on the environing hills and the convoluted plateau back of the point, spans streams the world around, builds the skeletons of new cities and protects the coasts of their country.

There are many others in that garrison, but these makers of steel are the core of that city, in which "the modern world," to use the words of one of our first economists, "achieves its grandest triumph and faces its gravest problem"[1]—the "mighty storm mountain of capital and labor."

I quote from this same economist a comprehensive paragraph descriptive of its riches: "Through hills which line these [confluent] rivers run enormous veins of bituminous coal. Located near the surface, the coal

---

[1] John R. Commons, in *Survey*, March 6, 1909, 21 : 1051.

is easily mined, and elevated above the rivers, much of
it comes down to Pittsburgh by gravity. There are
twenty-nine billion tons of it, good for steam, gas or
coke. Then there are vast stores of oil [seven million
five hundred thousand gallons annually] natural gas
[of which two hundred and fifty million feet are consumed daily], sand, shale, clay and stone, with which
to give Pittsburgh and the tributary country the lead
of the world in iron and steel, glass, electrical machinery, street-cars, tin plate, air-brakes and fire-
brick."[1]

And to all this natural bounty the national government has added that of the tariff and of millions
spent in river improvements, while Europe has contributed raw labor already fed to the strength of oxen
and often already developed to highest skill. It was a
young chemist trained in Europe who conducted me
through the mills, explaining all the processes in a
perfect idiomatic speech, though of broken accent.

The white-hot steel ingot swinging beneath a smoky
sky is a sign of the contribution of France through
Pittsburgh to civilization, not merely the material
but the human contribution. The ingot, a great
block of white-hot steel, is the sign of her labor, which
has assembled the scattered elements of the valley
and, in the fierce heat of natural and unfed fires, has
compounded them into a new metal that is something more than iron, more valuable than gold. But
it is only another sign, too, of forces that have assembled from all parts of the earth, men represented
in the varied cargoes that are poured by a seemingly

[1] J. R. Commons, "Wage Earners of Pittsburg," in *Survey*, March 6,
1909, 21 : 1051-64.

omnipotent hand into those furnaces—red-blooded men, and with them slag that has gone through the fires of older civilizations.

Here, let me say again, is being made a new metal; this no one can doubt. It is not merely a melting and a restamping of old coin with a new superscription, a new sovereignty—a composite face instead of a personal likeness—it is the making, as I have said in other illustrations and metaphors, of a new race.

If I had an instinct of human character, such as the intuitive sense of the fibre and tension of steel possessed by the man who watches the boiling in the furnaces and who, from time to time, puts aside his smoked glasses and looks at the texture of a typical bit of his metal, or who stands at the emptying of the furnace into the ladle and directs the addition of carbon or magnesium to bring his output to the right constituency, I could tell you what strains and stresses this new people would stand. As it is, I can only make a surmise, perhaps not more valuable than yours.

The makers of steel were concerned only to get the primacy in steel. Human character was of concern only as it made better steel and more of it. They took the red ore where they could get it richest in iron and cheapest, and they took red-blooded labor where they could get it strongest-sinewed, clearest-eyed, and cheapest. "There are no able-bodied men between the ages of sixteen and fifty years left in my native town," said a Servian workman in the mills. "They have all come to America. The agricultural districts and villages of the mid-eastern valleys of Europe are sending their strongest men and youths, nourished of good diet and in pure air, stolid and care-free, into that dim canyon—Servians, Croatians, Ruthenians, Lithuanians, Slovaks, with Italians, Poles, and Russian Jews."[1] It is from Slavs and mixed people of the old European midland, says one, "where the successive waves of broad-headed and fair-haired peoples gathered force and swept westward to become Celt and Saxon, and Swiss and Scandinavian and Teuton," the old European midland with its "racial and religious loves and hates seared deep, that the new immigration is coming to Pittsburgh to work out civilization under tense conditions"—not with that purpose, to be sure, but with that certain result. The conscious purposes have been expressed in the tangible ingots, the wages they have offered them in their hot hands, and the profits. The civilization has been incidental.

There is developing, however, an effort in the midst of this "dynamic individualism" to make both the new and the old immigration work out "civilization." This individualism was prodigal, profligate, at first. But it has learned thrift; it by and by came to burn its gas over and over; it made the purifying substances go on in a continued round of service; it became more mindful of human muscles and bones and eyes and ears; it took the latest advice of experts, but for steel's sake, not civilization's.

Mr. Carnegie, when a manufacturer there, found 90 per cent of pure iron in the refuse of his competitor, it is said. This he bought under long contract and worked over in his own mills. His neighbor's waste became a part of his fortune. And the result of that

---

[1] P. Roberts, "The New Pittsburg," in *Charities and the Commons,* January 2, 1909, 21 : 533. See also J. A. Fitch, "The Steel Workers," New York, 1910.

discernment and thrift is now furnishing an analogue for the conscious utilization of other waste—waste of native capacity of the steel-worker for happiness and usefulness.

Mr. Carnegie has indeed led the way in the establishment of libraries, art galleries, museums, institutes of training and research out of what were but waste if spent as some millionaires spend their profits. All these things upon the hills are by-products of the steel-mills down in the ravine. In every luminous ingot swung in the mills that were his, there is something toward the pension of a university professor out in Oregon, something for an artist in New York or Paris, something for an astronomer on the top of Mount Wilson, something for the teacher in the school upon the hill, something for every library established by his gift.

What is now making itself felt, however, is a desire to get the wage element in the ingot as thriftily, as efficiently, as nobly converted and used to the last ounce as is the profit element. There has been in the past a masterful individualism at work. Now there is a masterful aggressive humanism beginning to make itself felt, comparable in its spirit with the masterful venturing of the French explorers or the masterful faith of the French missionaries, that promises to constrain the city "to the saving and enhancing of individual and collective human power," even as the French missionaries tried to constrain the great fur-trading prospects of France to the saving of human souls.

The attempt to realize an urban paradise is becoming a conscious purpose as this extract made from a report made to a city-plan committee of a Pittsburgh commission will indicate:

"A third undeveloped asset in the Pittsburgh water-front is its value for recreation and as an element of civic comeliness and self-respect. One of the deplorable consequences of the short-sighted and wasteful commercialism of the later nineteenth century lay in its disregard of what might have been the æsthetic by-products of economic improvement; in the false impression spread abroad that economical and useful things were normally ugly; and in the vicious idea which followed, that beauty and the higher pleasures of civilized life were to be sought only in things otherwise useless. Thus the pursuit of beauty was confounded with extravagance.

"Among the most significant illustrations of the fallacy of such ideas are the comeliness and the incidental recreation value which attach to many of the commercial water fronts of European river ports, and it is along such lines that Pittsburgh still has opportunity for redeeming the sordid aspect of its business centre.

"Wherever in the world, as an incident of the highways and wharves along its river banks, a city has provided opportunity for the people to walk and sit under pleasant conditions, where they can watch the water and the life upon it, where they can enjoy the breadth of outlook and the sight of the open sky and the opposite bank and the reflections in the stream, the result has added to the comeliness of the city itself, the health and happiness of the people, and their loyalty and local pride. This has been true in the case of a bare paved promenade, running along like an elevated railroad over the sheds and tracks and derricks of a busy ocean port, as at Antwerp, in the case of a tree-shaded sidewalk along a commercial street with the river quays below it, as at Paris and Lyons and hundreds of lesser cities; and in the case of a broad embankment garden won from the mud banks by dredging and filling, as at London."

I had great difficulty in finding a bookstore in Pittsburgh. Some day that idealistic condition which makes the Seine so dear to thousands who know its every mood, and so dear both to the wise and the ignorant, may obtain on La Belle Rivière.

This is but one item of a planning for the future of this city which thinks not merely of its beautifying and of the pleasure of its people in their leisure, but of all conditions which affect the health, convenience, education, and general welfare of the whole district—that region once called the "black country," of which Pittsburgh was the "dingy capital"—one of the regions where the French were pioneers.

I have spoken of this as the "taking thought" of a democratic community. More accurately, a body of one hundred volunteer citizens, disposing themselves in fourteen different committees (including those on rapid transit, industrial accidents, city housing, and public hygiene), have undertaken all this labor of constructive planning at their own expense (based upon a series of investigations made by endowed researchers), but with the hope of creating a public opinion favorable to their plans, which look to the establishment by the democratic community of "such living and working conditions as may set a standard for other American industrial centres." [1]

---

[1] Olmsted, F. L., "Pittsburgh, Main Thoroughfares and the Down-Town District." Pittsburgh Civic Commission, 1910. *Survey*, February 4, 1911, 25: 740-4.

No such thorough and systematic study of existing city conditions has been made anywhere else in America. It is quite as scientific as the scholarly studies of buried cities, only immensely more complex and difficult. Knowing itself and possessed of an unconquerable spirit, it seems likely now that Pittsburgh will win back the beautiful site which Céloron remarked when he passed down La Belle Rivière—a site which even "Florence might covet"—and will make it a city that will deserve to keep always the other part of the name of the sower of the leaden plates—Bienville.

A pillar of cloud stands over the city by day and a pillar of fire by night. They have together shown the way out of the wilderness. It now remains to be seen whether the highest things of men's longing will have realization, in giving that "dynamic individualism" a social ideal with distinct, practicable working plans.

Pittsburgh stands on the edge of the valley of the new democracy. It has put its plates along every path. There is hardly a village of any size from the Alleghanies to the Rockies that it has not laid some claim to by its strips of steel. There is hardly a stream of any size that it has not claimed by a bridge. It has, indeed, the spirit of Céloron, in other body, still planting monuments of France's renewal of possession, wherever the steel rails and girders and plates from the Pittsburgh mills have been carried. And Pittsburgh is but one of the renewed cities which encompass the eastern half of the valley where once stretched the chain of French forts futile in defense but powerful in prophecy.

When we see the American city, even through the

eyes of Walt Whitman, that poet of democracy, it seems a desperate hope that is left her: "Are there, indeed, men here in the city," he asks, "worthy the name? Are there athletes? Are there perfect women to match the generous material luxuriance? Is there a pervading atmosphere of beautiful manners? Are there crops of fine youths and majestic old persons? Are there arts worthy freedom and a rich people? Is there a great moral and religious civilization—the only justification of a great material one? Confess that to severe eyes, using the moral microscope upon humanity, a sort of dry and flat Sahara appears, these cities crowded with petty grotesques, malformations, phantoms, playing meaningless antics. Confess that everywhere, in shop, street, church, theatre, barroom, official chair, are pervading flippancy and vulgarity, low cunning, infidelity—everywhere the youth puny, impudent, foppish, prematurely ripe—everywhere an abnormal libidinousness, unhealthy forms, male, female, painted, padded, dyed, chignon'd, muddy complexions, bad blood, the capacity for good motherhood decreasing or deceas'd, shallow notions of beauty, with a range of manners, or rather lack of manners (considering the advantages enjoy'd) probably the meanest to be seen in the world."[1]

But it is no such desperate hope that the cities we have seen spring from French fort and portage keep in their hearts. It is not even a confession that one would have to make to-day in the American cities which Whitman had in mind in his gloomy, foreboding vision. I have seen on the streets of one of the Whitman cities[2]

[1] "Democratic Vistas," in his "Complete Works," pp. 205, 206.
[2] New York City.

those same grotesques, malformations, and meaningless
antics, that flippancy and vulgarity and cunning, that
foppishness and premature ripeness, that painted, bad-
complexioned, bad-mannered, shallow-beautied humanity; but touching, as I have had opportunity to
touch, three of the great agencies of its aspirations—
its philanthropies, its literature, and its schools—I
know that no body of five million people, whether
huddled in tenements or scattered over plain and mountain and along rivers and seas, has with more serious
or sacrificing purpose aspired, though constantly disturbed in its prayers, its operations, by people of every
tongue, nearly a million strong, who are emptied at her
port every year from Europe and Asia, besides the
hundreds of thousands who come up from the country.
There are public schools, for example, in certain parts
of that city where there is not a child of American
parentage. There is one, in particular, which I visit
frequently and which I call the "oasis" in the desert
of humanity (Walt Whitman's Sahara), where two or
three thousand children are gathered, literally from
the plains of Russia, the valleys of Italy, and other
parts of Europe—for these were their ancestral homes,
though they come immediately from the swarming
streets and dimly lighted, ill-smelling tenements of
New York—and there, aspiring under the hopeful
teaching of the city, I have heard them, boys and girls
together, sing, with all the joy and cleanliness of
shepherd children, of a leading in green pastures and
by still waters.

But to come back to the cities in the valley of Nouvelle France, there is no note of else than hope there.
Mistakes, disappointments, crudities, infidelities?

Yes, but the mistakes, disappointments, crudities, failures of youth—youth of strong passions and love of play but of a masterful will that a generous nature has so much encouraged and aided as to obscure its limitations.

A few rods from the Carnegie Library and Museum of Art and Concert Hall in Pittsburgh is a baseball field, where a million people or more come in the course of the season to see trained men play an out-of-door game (and if it chanced that the President of the United States were visiting the city, he might be seen there accompanied by his secretary of state or the president of a great university). In Chicago I found the whole city, young and old, united in its interest in the results of the "game" of the day before or the prospects of the next. When games are played for the great championship pennant the city virtually takes a holiday.

But that is the spirit of youth in those overgrown, awkward cities that are only now beginning to be self-conscious and seriously purposeful in doing more than the things conventionally and for the most part selfishly done by cities generally. In the conjugation of their busy, noisy life they do not often use the past tense, never the past-perfect, and they have had for the most part little concern as to the future, except the rise in real-estate values and the retaining of markets. When in Pittsburgh I asked a prominent man, of French ancestry, why the people did not keep from the destroying hand of private enterprise the site of old Fort Duquesne (the fecund plot from which the great city had grown), and he said it was all they could do to keep the little blockhouse that remained of Fort Pitt, filling a space a few yards square. What claim has the past as against the needs of industry in the present? That was the attitude of that grimy individualism born in "barefoot square" or in "slab alley," in the land of smoke and flame and "rusty rivers."

And the future? Well, the voice of the French priest and of those ministers of his own and other faiths that have followed in his footsteps is still heard there crying of the world to come.

Several years ago on my way into that valley, on one of those fast trains that tie the east and west together, we came shrieking, thundering down the mountain slopes in the dusk of the day, past Jumonville's grave, past Braddock's field, past miles on miles of glowing coke-ovens, past acres upon acres of factories with their thousands of lighted windows, past flaming towers and chimneys into the midst of the modern babel, the tops of whose buildings were hidden in smoke, when suddenly, above the noise and clangor of whistles and wheels, I heard the rich, deep voice of a cathedral bell telling that the priest was still at the side of the explorer and trader and the iron coureur de bois.

It is not, however, of the celestial but of the terrestrial future that I am permitted to speak.

For, as I intimated, these young cities of the west, only a half-century old as cities—children by the side of Paris, London, Rome—are beginning seriously to take thought of the morrow, not simply of multiplying their numbers nor of sending their multitudes back to the country but of giving them prospect and promise of a better, more comfortable, more wholesome life, capable of a higher individual and collective

244 THE FRENCH IN THE HEART OF AMERICA

development within the city. For while cities have been preached against since the time when Jonah cried against Nineveh, and while cities have perished and have been buried, even as Nineveh, the generic city, the assembling of gregarious men, continues and increases.

The census returns for 1910 for the American cities show, so far as I noticed, scarcely a single loss of population in the last ten years[1] and a large gain for nearly every city of the middle west. It is prophesied that before long one-half of the people of the United States will be living in cities, and there is the more distant prospect that the urban population will be two-thirds of the whole.[2]

It is hopeless to try to turn that tide away from the cities except to suburban fields. So the great problem of that valley is to improve the cities, since from them are to be the issues of the new life, since they are, indeed, the hope of democracy.

I have thought it of significance that the envisioned place of ultimate celestial felicity—seen though it was by a man in the solitude of a cave in an island of the Mediterranean (the place which the civilized world has dimly hanging over it, whenever it looks away from its tasks and into the beyond)—is not a lotus-land, not an oasis of spring and palm, not a stretch of forest and mountain, not even a quiet place by a sea of jasper, but a place of many tenements—a city, a perfect city

[1] Cities with losses of population in the decade are Galveston, Texas: 37,389 in 1900, 36,981 in 1910; Chelsea, Mass.: 34,072 in 1900, 32,452 in 1910; St. Joseph, Mo.: 102,979 in 1900, 77,403 in 1910.

[2] In 1910 46.3 per cent resided in communities classed by the census as urban, and 55.1 per cent in cities and incorporated or unincorporated villages.

to be sure, let down ultimately from the skies, with walls of precious stones—and no zone for Kipling's "Tomlinsons" about it—with gates whose octroi officials keep out whatever makes an abomination or a lie, but which are open to the east and west, the north and south, that the kings of earth may bring their glory and honor into it—a city whose streets are clean and smooth—a city that has flowing through it a river of pure water, on whose banks grow trees whose leaves are for the healing of the nations.

The obvious thing to do, since, good or bad, the country is emptying its population into the cities, since we cannot go back through the gates of Eden into the garden paradise of Genesis, is to go toward the city of the Apocalypses, not, to be sure, as the Oriental mind of John saw it, paved and walled with precious stones and gold, but made as beautiful as the Occidental taste and architectural skill will permit, as comfortable as Occidental standards demand, and as sanitary as the mortal desire for immortality can with finite wisdom make it.

I was speaking some time ago of a painting I once saw, in illustration of the death of Eve, which represented her as on a journey in her haggard old age, accompanied by Cain (whose son built the first city in a wilderness), and as pausing in the journey on a height of ground, pointing toward a little cluster of trees in the distance, and saying to her son: "There was Paradise." But paradise is not to be realized by the masses of men in the return of man to the forests. The healing trees and the river are to be carried to the city.

CHAPTER XII

WESTERN TOWNS AND CITIES THAT HAVE SPRUNG FROM FRENCH PORTAGE PATHS

THE old French portage paths were also fruitful of cities on the edge of the Mississippi Valley, though the growth of these short paths was not—with one notable exception—as luxuriant as that from the earth enriched of human blood and bones about the old French forts.

These portages, or carrying paths, which differ from the trails of the wood runners in that they are but short interruptions of the water paths and were not designed or laid out, as a rule, by the wild engineers of the forests and prairies but by human feet, lie across the great highway along which, before the days of canals, one might have walked dry-shod from the Atlantic to the Pacific—between the basins of the St. Lawrence and the Atlantic, the Great Lakes and the Mississippi, the Pacific and the Arctic—a highway which has, however, been trodden by no one probably through its entire length, for in places it runs over inaccessible peaks of mountains and winds around the narrowest of ledges. But the paths across it—those connecting the streams that flow in opposite directions from the continental watersheds—are like isthmian paths between great oceans—great dry oceans with watercourses through them.

There were, to be sure, still other portage paths

than those across watersheds, and the most common were those that led around waterfalls or impassable rapids, such as Champlain and the Jesuits followed on their journeys up the Ottawa to the Nipissing. It was of such portages that Father Brébeuf wrote—portage paths passing almost continually by torrents, by precipices, and by places that were horrible in every way. In less than five days they made more than thirty-five portages, some of which were three leagues long. This means that on these occasions the traveller had to carry on his shoulders his canoe and all his baggage, with so little food that he was continually hungry and almost without strength and vigor.[1] Another priest tells of a portage occupying an entire day, during which he climbed mountains and pierced forests and carried, the while, his chapel and his little store of provisions.

Of whatever variety, however, these portage paths were frequently burying-grounds. Sometimes altars were erected beside them. They were often places of encampments, of assemblies, and more often of ambuscades. So it came about, too, that they were made the places of minor forts or gave occasion for forts farther on the way. In those precivilized Panama days, the neutrality of the isthmian paths could not be assured, and so they were fortified.

Céloron tells of the mending of boats at the end of his Chautauqua portages, and that statement, with other like incidents, has led one authority to picture the birches—those beautiful white and golden trees of the sombre northern woods that gave their cloaks to the travellers who asked and shivered till they grew

[1] "Jesuit Relations" (Thwaites), 8 : 75-77.

others—stripped of their bark where those paths came down to the streams. He has even imagined primitive carpenter shops and ovens and huts on these paths where the voyageurs must stop for repairs, food, and rest—the precursors of garage, road-house, and hotel.

But on maps in the Bibliothèque Nationale names of portage paths have been found which assure us that these difficult ways were not without charm to those early travellers, as they have been to many a wanderer since; for there was Portage des Roses, where the wild rose brightened the way; and Portage de la Musique, where the water sang constantly its song in the solitude. Then there were Portage de la Roche Fendue, Portage des Chênes, Portage des Perches, Portage Talon, and Portage des Récollets, named in memory of experiences of men whom the voyageurs wished to recall or to honor, just as the French give to their streets such names as "Rue des Fleurs," "Boulevard des Capucines."[1]

The portage paths that became in time most fruitful were generally short, well-cleared, and deep-furrowed by feet. On three of the most important and historic of these paths from the basin of the Great Lakes to that of the Mississippi I have walked with the memories of these precursors; in one place it was suggested that I should ride in a carriage, but I refused, feeling that these men must be worshipped on foot.

The first of these portages is that path of which I have already spoken several times (and which I never tire of letting my imagination travel again), the one over which Nicolet must have passed from the Fox

[1] A. B. Hulbert, "Historic Highways of America," 7 : 49.

River into the Wisconsin River, if he got so far on his way to Muscovy—the path to which Father Dablon said the way was as through a paradise, but was as hard as the way to heaven[1]—the path which the coureurs de bois Radisson and Groseilliers doubtless followed; the path which La Salle may have found in those two years of mysterious absence in the valley; the path Marquette and Joliet and hundreds after them certainly took on their way from Montreal to the Mississippi or from the Mississippi back to Montreal. You would not know this narrow strip—not a mile wide—to be a watershed dividing the continent, the north from the south; you would not know it for the threshold to the Mississippi Valley. The plain which the path crosses seems to the eye as level as a table. Undoubtedly before the tipping of the bed of the lakes the water flowed over this path. Indeed, La Salle in one of his letters refers to the portaging here of canoes past an "oak grove and across a flooded meadow." The tree of which he speaks, with two canoes clumsily drawn upon it by the savages, to mark the beginning of the portage at the Wisconsin, has gone, but a monument of red granite now stands there with the names of Marquette and Joliet upon it. At the other end of the now macadamized "path" there is a little red bridge that leads across the Fox to where a portage fort grew later into an important trading-post; but now there is no trace of those monuments of war and trade. There is a farmhouse on their site whose tenants are in fear only of drought and early frosts.

---

[1] "If the country . . . somewhat resembles an earthly paradise in beauty, the way leading to it may be said to bear some likeness to the one depicted by our Lord as leading to Heaven."—"Jesuit Relations" (Thwaites), 55 : 191.

A canal crosses this little isthmus and once it inter-
locked the east and west, the arctic plains with the
subtropic cane fields; but it has given over its work
to the railroads, having served, however, I have no
doubt, to water the roots of the beautiful town that
bears the generic name of all those places where
burdens were borne between waters. "Wauona," the
Indians called it, more euphoniously, but with the
same significance as "Portage"—in the State that has
taken the name of the river that carried the burdens
on to the Mississippi—Wisconsin. This town has
lately crept modestly into our western literature as
"Friendship Village."[1]   Except that it has a more
comely setting than most towns of the plains—even of
those northern plains with their restful undulations—
and has a brighter, cleaner aspect—since a light-
colored brick is used instead of the red so much in
favor where wood is forbidden by the fire laws—it
is a typical western town—the next size larger than
"Aramoni"; and so I must stop here for a moment
where Marquette, son of Rose de la Salle of Rheims,
and Joliet, the wagon maker of Quebec, came up out
of the twisting little stream that is still one of the
fountains of the Atlantic.

For none the less is this village, standing beside
this fountain (again more euphoniously called the Kaka-
ling or Kaukauna), itself touching the Atlantic shores
and even mingling with currents that reach the European coasts.   There was born in this village the historian[2] who has written so well of the rise of that
western country that he has been called to the pro-

---

[1] Zona Gale, "Friendship Village."   Macmillan, New York, 1908.
[2] Frederick Jackson Turner.

fessorship of American history at Harvard University, a literal son of the portage, who has rediscovered the west to the world.   And recently all the valley, and other valleys, too, have been reading the stories of this place of portage (called, as I have said, "Friendship Village"), written by a young woman whose windows look out from her home upon the Wisconsin River not many paces from Marquette's place of embarkation—a true daughter of the portage.

The French, who have given the new continent this portage path out of Europe into the very heart of America, should read with some gratification of the more intimate life that dwells there back of and in the midst of the bustling, tireless, noisy industry of the valley.

"The long Caledonian hills" [the same which La Salle describes], "the four rhythmic spans of the bridge" [a bridge of iron, not of vines and flowers such as Châteaubriand describes], "the nearer river, the island where the first birds build—these teach our windows the quiet and the opportunity of the home town, its kindly brooding companionship, its doors to an efficiency as intimate as that of fairy fingers."[1]   And this is but one of thousands of "home towns" in that great basin, towns with Daphne streets and Queen Anne houses, and gloomy court-houses and austere churches and miniature libraries, towns that taper off into suburban shanties, towns that have in these new bottles, of varied and pretentious shapes, the best wine of that western world.

The author of "Friendship Village" has vision of the more beautiful towns into which these towns will

[1] "Friendship Village," p. vii, author's note.

some day grow, as yours have grown more beautiful
with age. "All the way," she writes, seeing the sunset from that same river of the portage as Marquette
saw it, "I had been watching against the gold the
jogging homeward of empty carts. . . . Such a procession I want to see painted upon a sovereign sky. I
want to have painted a giant carpenter of the village
as I once saw him, his great bare arms upholding a
huge white pillar, while blue figures hung above and set
the acanthus capital. . . . Some day we shall see these
things in their own surprising values and fresco our
village libraries with them."[1] That appreciation and
expression of the beautiful is something that the French
explorers in that other world—the valley reached of
the pioneers of the seeing eyes and the understanding
hearts—have carried and will continue to carry over
those same portages, to give that virile life of the
west some of those higher satisfactions of which this
daughter of the portage is the prophetess.

Another portage path of importance is that which
Marquette may also have trodden, or may even have
been carried over by his faithful attendants, Pierre
Porteret and Jacques, on his death journey from the
land of the Illinois to the mission of Michilimackinac,
which he did not reach alive—a journey, the latter
part of which was like that of King Arthur borne in a
barge by his faithful knight, Sir Bedivere, to his last
resting-place, the Vale of Avalon. This portage, varying in length with the season from three to five miles,
was the St. Joseph-Kankakee Portage. La Salle,
Tonty, and Hennepin passed over it in 1679 on a less
spiritual errand to the same land whose inhabitants

[1] Zona Gale, "Friendship Village Love Stories," p. 47.

Marquette had tried to instruct in the mystery of the faith. And it was well worn by adventurous and pious feet in the century that followed.

What traffic in temporal and spiritual things was here carried over, is intimated by relics of that century found in the fields not far away, where for many years a French mission house stood with enough of a military garrison to invite for it the name "Fort St. Joseph." In the room of the Northern Indiana Historical Society at this portage there are to be seen some of these relics, sifted from the dirt and sand: crucifixes, knives, awls, beads—which I am told are clearly the loot of ancient Roman cities, traded to the Indians for hides—iron rings, nails, and hinges—these with flint arrow-heads and axes, relics of the first munitions of the stone and iron ages out on the edges of civilization.

This portage path between the rivers is now obliterated by railroads, paved streets, furrows, graves, factories, and dwellings; but down by the St. Joseph River there stands a withered cedar, perhaps several hundred years old, which bears scars that are believed to be the blaze marks of the broad-bladed axes of the French explorers—made to indicate the place where the portage out of the river began, the place which La Salle missed when lost in the forest but afterward found, where Father Gabriel made several crosses, as Hennepin records, on the trees—perhaps these very marks—and where La Salle left letters for the guidance over the prairie of those "who were to come in the vessel"—thinking of the captain of the *Griffin* who was ordered to follow him to the Illinois on his return.

It is only a little more than a league from this landing at the bend of the river (which has given the name "South Bend" to the town) across the "large prairie" to the wet meadows in whose ooze the tortuous Kankakee River became navigable, in La Salle's day, a hundred paces from its source, and increased so rapidly in volume that, as he says in a letter, "in a short time it becomes as broad and deep as the Marne"—the Marne which he knew in his boyhood and for which any but his iron heart must have longed.

Charlevoix walked across those unchanged fields of St. Joseph a half century (1674–1720) after La Salle, and Parkman made the same journey nearly a century after Charlevoix, finding there what he called "a dirty little town." To-day a clean, industrious, eager city of over fifty-three thousand, with a world horizon, as well as a provincial pride, throws its shadow in the early morning across the path. Through its outskirts I tried years ago to trace this portage path and there with my companion (who was always the "Tonty" of my voyages on those western streams), put my boat in the river and paddled and poled the seventy-five miles down the St. Joseph River to the lake, where, as I wanted to believe, Marquette had made his last journey. Hearing, some time after, of the blaze marks on the cedar-tree, I went again to the portage, and from this old red cedar-tree again traced the probable course of the French to the fields of corn, or maize, yellow in the autumn sun that hid the fountains of the Kankakee. This time, having but little leisure, I rode in an automobile from one end to the other through and along the path, looking occasionally toward the sky for air-ships that were due to alight there on their way from Chicago to New York.

In La Salle's packs, carried over that portage, were blacksmith's tools—forge, bellows, anvil, iron for nails —and carpenter's and joiner's tools. One might easily believe that they were left there—such have been the products of that portage strip, two or three miles wide.

First, there has grown there the largest wagon factory in the world. The path of the pack and the burden has here produced as its peculiar contribution to civilization that which is to carry burdens, instead of the backs of men, the world round.

Second, here stands the world's largest plough factory—a place from which ploughs are sent to every arable valley that civilization has conquered and made to feel its hunger.

Third, here spreading its acres, or arpents, of buildings across the high ground between the two rivers, is the largest factory in the world for the making of certain parts of the sewing-machine; in every community of any size in the world it has an agency.

And here, last of all, besides more than a hundred minor industries, is what is, to my great surprise, said to be the largest toy factory in the world.

The gift of wagons for the bearing and easing of men's burdens; the gift of the steel plough that has lifted man from the primitive subsistence of the hoe; the gift of the shuttle which has released woman from the tyranny of the needle; the gift of toys to the children of all races; has not this portage prairie, this meadow of St. Joseph, had some element mixed with its loam and clay from the spirit of those Gallic precursors of American energy, something that has given this industry a wider venture, if not peculiar expression? At any rate, its gifts to its time have

been far beyond common, of the tangible at least; and
as to the intangible, the day that I last spent on this
portage an art league was being formed to foster an
interest in art and bring the best examples available
to what were, but a little time ago, dreary meadows
half covered with snow and strewn with skulls and
bones of the buffalo. The most modern schools are
being developed and maintained by the public, and
the University of Notre Dame and the College of St.
Mary look across the river to this portage field and
city.

One might have passed this portage so difficult to
discern, as La Salle did, and yet have found another
way to the lower Mississippi, with a short portage
from this same stream to the Wabash River. A still
shorter way than any of these, and doubtless known to
La Salle from his first years of wanderings in the
eastern end of the Mississippi Valley, led from the west
end of Lake Erie up the Maumee and then by portage
to the Wabash and the Ohio. This was the path that
Céloron followed homeward on his memorable plate-
planting journey. But the portage was so long that he
burned his shattered canoes near the source of the
Miami and was furnished with boats at the French
fort near the headwaters of the Maumee. The hostility of the Iroquois, as we have seen, made perilous
to the French in the earlier days this path, so important among Indian highways as often to be called the
"Indian Appian Way."

Excepting the portage paths farther up the valley,
notably that of St. Esprit, and important chiefly as
fur-trading paths, there remains but one other historic
portage path across the ridge of stone and swamp and

prairie from which are pendent, on the one side, all the silver streams of the Mississippi Valley and, on the other side, all the Great Lakes and all the rivers that flow into them.

This remaining path is the tenuous trail through the fields of wild onions that led from the river or creek called Chicago (the Garlic River—Rivière de l'Ail) into a stream that still bears a French name but of a pronunciation which a Parisian would not accept—the Des Plaines. This path, too, traversed a marsh and flat prairie so level that in freshet the water ran both ways and was once in the bed of a river that ran from the lake to the gulf. But it has been hallowed beyond all others of these trails, for it was beside this portage that Marquette suffered through a winter, detained there by a serious sickness when on his way to minister to the Illinois Indians a hundred miles below. His hut was the first European habitation upon its site—the site of the future city of Chicago.

In a book-shop not a league from where that hut stood I found a volume valued at its weight in gold[1] giving the account of the journey in which Marquette had passed up this portage on the way to Green Bay after the discovery of the upper Mississippi with Joliet. It tells in its closing paragraphs of the rich prairies just beyond this portage, but it recites with greater satisfaction the baptizing of a dying child brought to the side of his canoe as he was setting out for the mission house. "Had all this voyage," he said, "caused but the salvation of a single soul I should

---

[1] Thevenot, "Recueil de Voyages," with 2 folding maps and 14 plates, complete. Crown 8vo, white pigskin. Paris 1682. Contains Marquette's and Joliet's Discoveries in North America, etc. For an account of the various editions, see "Jesuit Relations," 59 : 294-9.

deem all my fatigue well repaid, and this I have reason
to think. For, when I was returning, I passed by the
Indians of Peoria, where I was three days announcing
the faith, in all their cabins, after which, as we were
embarking, they brought me on the water's edge a
dying child which I baptized a little before it expired,
by an admirable providence, for the salvation of an
innocent soul."[1]

That was in 1673. It was more than a year before
he again entered the Chicago River, wishing to keep
his promise to minister to the Illinois savages and
eager "to do and suffer everything for so glorious an
undertaking." In the "Jesuit Relations"[2] the story
of those winter days at the Chicago portage has been
kept for all time. All through January his illness
obliged him to stay in the portage cabin, but early in
February he "commenced Novena (Neufuaine) with a
mass, at which Pierre and Jacques [his companions],
who do everything they can to relieve me, received com-
munion—to ask God to restore my health." His ail-
ment left him, but weakness and the cold and the ice
in the rivers kept him still at the portage until April.
On the eve of his leaving for the Illinois the journal
ends with this thoughtful word of the French: "If
the French procure robes in this country, they do not
disrobe the savages, so great are the hardships that
must be endured to obtain them."[3]

In the dusk of an autumn day I went out to find
the place where the Novena had worked the miracle
of his healing. As I have already intimated, few of all

[1] Shea, "Discovery and Exploration of the Mississippi Valley," 2d
ed., p. 55.
[2] 59: 165-183.   [3] "Jesuit Relations" (Thwaites), 59 : 183.

the hundreds of thousands there in that great city
have had any consciousness of the background of
French heroism and suffering and prevision in front
of which they were passing daily, but I found that the
policemen and the watchmen on the railroad near the
river knew at least of the great black cross which
stands by that drab and sluggish water, placed there
in memory of Marquette and Joliet. The bit of high
ground where the hut stood is now surrounded by great
looming sheds and factories, which were entirely tenantless when I found my way through a long unlighted
and unpaved street in the direction of the river. The
cross stood, in a little patch of white, black as the
father's cowl, against the night with its crescent moon.
I could not make out the inscription on the river side
of the monument and, seeing a signal-lantern tied to a
scow moored to the bank near by, I untied it and by
its light was able to read the tribute of the city to the
memory of the priest and the explorer "who first of
known white men had passed that way," having travelled, as it recites, "two thousand five hundred miles
in canoes in one hundred and twenty days." The
bronze plate bears a special tribute to the foresight
of Joliet, but it commemorates first of all the dwelling
of the frail body and valorous soul of Father Marquette,
the first European within the bounds of the city of
Chicago. I wish there might be written on Mississippi maps, in that space that is shown between the
Chicago and the Des Plaines, or the "Divine River,"
as it was sometimes called, the words: "Portage St.
Jacques." That were a fitter canonization than to
put his name among the names of cities, steamboats
on the lake, or tobaccos, as is our custom in America.

The crescent moon dropped behind the shadows that now line the portage "like a sombre forest," but it is only a few steps through the darkness back into the light and noise of the city of more than two million people.

Out of the black loam of this dark portage path fringed by marshes, in the field of wild onions, the newest of the world's great cities has sprung and spread with a promise that exceeds any other on the face of the planet, though within the life of men still living it was but a stretch of lake shore, a marshy plain with a path from its miniature river or creek toward the crescent moon.

A metropolis was doubtless predestined on or near the very site of Chicago by natural conditions and the peopling of the lands to the northwest; but Louis Joliet was its first prophet. The inscription on the tablet at the foot of the black cross recites that in crossing this site Joliet recommended it for its natural advantages and as a place of first settlement. And he first suggested the lakes-to-the-gulf waterway—a prospect of which La Salle speaks with disfavor but which over two hundred years later was in some measure realized.

The "Jesuit Relation" of August 1, 1674, reporting the conversation of Joliet, who had lost all his precious papers in the Lachine Rapids, makes this interesting prophecy:[1] "It would only be necessary to make a canal by cutting through half a league of prairie, to pass from the foot of the Lake of the Illinois [Michigan] to the River St. Louis [Mississippi]. . . . A bark [built on Lake Erie] would easily sail

[1] Thwaite's edition, 58 : 105.

to the Gulf of Mexico." The monument to him stands by the canal that has been cut through not merely a league but many leagues (thirty-eight miles) and lets the waters of Michigan flow southward to the Illinois.

Of this site Joliet is quoted as saying, "The place at which we entered the lake is a harbor, very convenient for receiving vessels and sheltering them from the wind;"[1] and of the prairies back of the harbor: "At first when we were told of these treeless lands I imagined that it was a country ravaged by fire, where the soil was so poor that it could produce nothing. But we certainly observed the contrary, and no better soil can be found, either for corn, for vines, or for any fruit whatever. . . . A settler would not there spend ten years in cutting down and burning the trees; on the very day of his arrival he could put his plough into the ground, and if he had no oxen from France, he could use those of this country, or even the animals possessed by the western savages, on which they ride, as we do on horses. After sowing grain of all kinds, he might devote himself especially to planting the vine, and grafting fruit-trees, to dressing ox-hides, wherewith to make shoes; and with the wool of these oxen he could make cloth, much finer than most of that which we bring from France. Thus he could easily find in the country his food and clothing, and nothing would be wanting except salt; but, as he could make provision for it, it would not be difficult to remedy that inconvenience."[2] If Marquette was the first martyr of the Illinois, Joliet was the first prophet of that great city of the Illinois.

[1] "Jesuit Relations" (Thwaites), 58 : 107.
[2] "Jesuit Relations" (Thwaites), 58 : 107-9.

What he could not foresee was that Lake Michigan would make the Chicago of to-day not so much by giving it a waterway to the markets of the east and Europe as by standing as an obstacle in the way of a straight path to the sea from the northwest fields and so compelling those fertile lands to send all their riches around the southern end of Lake Michigan. He overestimated the economic importance, to be sure, of the buffalo. But if domesticated cattle be substituted for the wild species, he again showed remarkable prevision of the future of a city which has enjoyed a world fame by reason of its cattle-market— its stock-yards.[1]

Chicago is a city without a past, save for that glow of adventure which is almost as hazy as the myths or legends that lie back of Europe. It is just eighty-one years since it came into existence as a town,[2] and but twenty-eight voters voted for the first board of trustees of the town; its population was variously estimated at from above two hundred to three hundred and fifty. As a city, it is seventy-seven years old,[3] beginning its legal life as such with fewer than five thousand people. It was of its first mayor, William B. Ogden— though some years later than his administration—that Guizot, looking upon the portrait of his benevolent face, said: "That is the representative American, who is the benefactor of his country, especially the mighty West; he built Chicago." But the Chicago which he administered was but a small town in size. Its officials from treasurer to scavenger were appointed by the

---

[1] Of the importance of the lakes-to-the-gulf waterway we have already spoken.

[2] August 12, 1833.   [3] Chartered March 4, 1837.

common council and obliged to serve or pay certain fines. Every male resident over twenty-one was obliged to work three days each year on the streets and alleys or pay one dollar for each day. Fire wardens had no compensation except release from jury or military service. There was at first meagre school provision,[1] no public sanitary provision, no considerable public service of any sort. It was a neighborly but unsocialized place, where the individual had little restraint save of his own limitations and his personal love of his neighbors. What social functions the city performed were self-protective and not self-improving in motive. For example, fire might not be carried in the street except in a fire-proof vessel.[2] The aboriginal frog croaked on the very site of the place where grand opera is now sung.

The city's development was largely left to the haphazard, unrestrained, but whole-souled, big-hearted, self-confident individualism, such as has been potent in Pittsburgh. The restrictions were mainly those of the prohibitory Mosaic commandments. And so this city, increasing its population by a half-million in each of the last three decades, has come to stand next to Paris in population and first of all great American cities in the constructive activity of its civic consciousness and urban imagination. The city is still smoke-enwrapped (when the wind does not blow from the lake); its streets run out into prairie dust and mud;

---

[1] The money derived from the sale of school lands in 1833 was distributed among the existing private schools which thus became free common schools. Less than $40,000 was received for lands now worth much more than $100,000,000.

[2] S. E. Sparling, "Municipal History and Present Organization of the City of Chicago," University of Wisconsin Bulletin, No. 23, 1898.

its harbor, of which Joliet spoke in praise, merits
rather the disparagement of La Salle; there are offend-
ing smells and sights everywhere. But in the midst
of it all and over it all is moving now, as a healing
efficacy in troubled waters, a spirit of democratic
aspiration. What Louis XIV or Napoleon I or Napoleon III, king and emperors, planned and did, compelling the co-operation of a people in making the
city of Paris more beautiful, more habitable, that a
people of millions out upon the prairies of Illinois are
beginning to do out of their own desire and common
treasury.

It is of interest that the sovereign of France who
gave her empire of those great stretches of plain, gave
to Paris "those vast reaches of avenue and boulevard
which to-day are the crowning features of the most
beautiful of cities." But it must quicken France's interest further to know that this first systematic planning for a city, as an organic whole, by Louis XIV and
Colbert, Le Notre and Blondel is now being followed
out on that plain by a self-governing people, who have
been making cities for barely half a century, to bring
order and form and beauty, and better condition of
living out of that grimy collection of homes and
shops and beginnings of civic enterprise and great
private philanthropies. A great deal has been already
accomplished, such as the widening of the leading
avenue, the addition of acres upon acres to the park
space on the lake shore, the establishment of an efficient
small park system; but it is only the beginning of a
scheme that thinks of Chicago as a city that will some
day hold ten millions of people. The prophecy of one
statistician (now of New York) predicts for Chicago a

population of thirteen million two hundred and fifty thousand souls in 1952;[1] and the great railroad builder, James J. Hill, has estimated that "when the Pacific coast shall have a population of twenty millions, Chicago will be the largest city in the world."

The specific plans for its improvement have been developed by a small body of public-spirited citizens, but they are simply that great urban democracy thinking and speaking, trying to express itself. It has developed with less interference or compulsion on the part of the State than any other great city of America, and now it is moving voluntarily to the noblest as well as the most practical of improvements.

Under like leading it built the "White City," the ephemeral city of the World's Fair, in the celebration of the four-hundredth anniversary of the discovery of America, and that splendid achievement of the black, unkempt city back of it gave first hint, in the co-operation that made this possible, of what a community could do and at the same time gathered to it the teaching of the older cities of the earth from their long striving for the city beautiful.

The city provides its own water-supply, it lights its streets, it has recently acquired control of its street-car lines, and every passenger is notified as a shareholder that 55 per cent of the profits comes into the city treasury. And now under this inspiration and yet of its own will it has begun a transformation of itself into the likeness of what it dreamed in those evanescent buildings and courts and columns and statues and frescoes out by the opalescent waters of

[1] Bion J. Arnold, "Report of the Engineering and Operating Features of the Chicago Transportation Problem," pp. 95, 96.

its sea. It saw the reflection of that "White City" in the lake and then the image of its own workaday face—and it has not forgotten what manner of city it was.

Remember again that what is and what is promised have come in a lifetime. Walking in the streets of that city early one morning a few years ago, as the trains were emptying the throngs who sleep outside along the lake and out on the prairie, into the canyons made by its tall buildings, I found myself immediately behind a robust old man, a civil engineer, who was born before Chicago had a hundred inhabitants. He was much older than the city whose buildings now reach out miles from the lake (one of its streets thirty-two miles long) and thirty and forty stories into the air. One hundred years ago it was the French wilderness untouched. Eighty years ago most of its citizens bore French names. The portage path has literally yielded a harvest of streets.

Chicago, the city of the French portage, Chicago, which despite all that casual visitors see and say of it, was, I contend, best defined by Harriet Martineau as a "great, embryo poet," moody, wild, but bringing about results, exulting that he—for he is a masculine poet—has caught the true spirit of things of the past and has had sight of the depths of futurity. But it is only now that the brooding poet is coming to express himself in verses that are recognized for their beauty.

Chicago, the field of the wild onions, threaded by La Rivière de l'Ail, the place of the shambles, the capital of the golden calf. That is her fame.

Only recently I read in a book which I found in Paris, written by an English traveller, that Chicago stands apart from all other cities in that "her people are really on earth to make money"; that, magnificent as she is in many ways, chiefly in distances, she is "too busy money-making to attend to civic improvements" or to have a "keen affection for worthier things."

I have gone a hundred times in and out of that dirty, unkempt city, swept only by the winds, one would think, and I know its worst, its physical, moral, political worst. But if the people there have worshipped the golden calf in their wilderness, they have now drunk of the dust of their first image, and I should be disposed to say that nowhere among American cities is there a keener affection for worthier things showing itself.

Again I shall have to admit that this "affection" is not the spontaneous expression of the entire democratic community. As in Pittsburgh, a comparatively few men have voluntarily, and at their own expense, undertaken to study not only the conditions that make for better and cheaper travel, more profitable commercial intercourse and greater productiveness, but for a more wholesome and a higher spiritual existence. And again it is so with the hope that the great self-governing community will out of its desire and treasury bring about these conditions.

These few men and women, possessed both by a love of that still uncouth city and an ideal objectively learned in the days when the "White City" stood between it and the lakes, have already spent a half-million francs in study and in making plans—in addition to all the months and years of volunteer, unpaid service.

The principal items of this great scheme are:

1. The improvement of the lake front.

2. The creation of a system of highways outside the city.

3. The improvement of railway terminals and the development of a complete traction system for both freight and passengers.

4. The acquisition of an outer park system and of parkway circuits.

5. The systematic arrangement of the streets and avenues within the city, in order to facilitate the movement to and from the business districts.

6. The development of centres of intellectual life and of civic administration, so related as to give coherence and unity to the city.

Is there not hope for democracy if in the places of its greatest strain and stress, in the midst of its fiercest passions, there is a deliberate, affectionate, intelligent striving toward cities that have been revealed not in apocalyptic vision but in the long-studied plans of terrestrial architects and engineers and altruistic souls, such as that of Jane Addams, cities that to such amphionic music shall out of the shards of the past build themselves silently, impregnably—if not in a diviner clime, at any rate in a diviner spirit—on shores and slopes and plains of that broad valley of the new democracy, conterminous in its mountain boundaries with New France in America?

A little while ago some workmen who were digging trenches for the foundations of a new factory or warehouse along that portage path thrust their spades into a piece of wood buried sixteen feet below the surface. It was found to be a fragment of a French bateau, lying on one of whose thwarts was a sword—probably of one who had met his death on the edge of the portage—a sword with an inscription showing that it probably belonged to an early French voyageur.

And so again in these relics but newly brought to light I find new words to remind ourselves that the roots of that mighty, virile, healthiest, most aspiring of America's great cities are entwined about the symbols of French adventure and empire in the west— the sword and the boat, and doubtless there was a crucifix not far away.

CHAPTER XIII

FROM LA SALLE TO LINCOLN

I ONCE heard a public lecturer in America telling a New York audience of an experience in the Mississippi Valley, where he asked an audience of children what body of water lay in the middle of the earth—wishing them to name to him, of course, the Mediterranean Ocean—and unexpectedly got the serious answer from a lad of deep conviction but narrow horizon, "the Sangamon River." I told the amused lecturer, who had never heard of this river, at any rate as locally pronounced, that the lad spoke more truly than the lecturer knew. For to those of even wider horizons, whose greatest and most beloved hero in history lived and was buried near the banks of the Sangamon, it is the middle water of the earth.

It is but a little river, and it is but one of the rivers of the valley of a hundred thousand streams, truly the Medimarenean Land, since all the oceans are now being gathered about it. The Sangamon flows into the Illinois, the Illinois into the Mississippi, and the Mississippi is now to flow into all the seas, even as the life of Lincoln is to flow into all history.

How little competent I am to speak dispassionately of this great incarnation of the spirit of those western waters the distorted geography of the untravelled lad whom the alien lecturer found on the prairies will suggest, for the river of the home and the fame of Lincoln empties into the river of my birth.

It was along this latter river—the Illinois—as we
know, that La Salle and his men, in midwinter of 1682,
dragged on the ice their canoes, baggage, and disabled
companions from the Chicago River, all the way to the
site of Fort Crèvecœur, where they found open water,
and thence in their canoes made their way past the
mouth of the Sangamon (which first appears on the
maps of the new world in 1683, just after La Salle's
journey, as the River Emicouen) and on into the Mississippi. We recall their "adventurous progress" and
the unveiling to their eyes more and more of the vast
new world, where the warm and drowsy air and hazy
sunlight succeeded the frosty breath of the north. We
see them floating down the winding water path. We
see the red children of the sun—the Indian sun-worshippers—clothed in white cloaks, receiving the white
heralds of Europe; we hear the weather-beaten voyageurs chant on the shores of the gulf solemn, exulting
songs learned in church and cloister of France; we
hear the faint voice of their leader crying his claim to
all the great valley from the mouth of the river to its
source beyond the country of the Nadouesioux—the
voice not of a human throat alone but of a vision in
the wilderness. We discern after long years the
sounds of its realization. We see the iridescence of the
John Law bubble shining over the turbid waters of
that river for a moment. We see the raising and lower-
ing of flags of various colors. We hear Napoleon's representative saying: "May the inhabitants of this valley
and a Frenchman never meet upon any spot of the
globe without feeling brothers!"   We see the general
who is later to embody the west's crude democratic
ideals, Andrew Jackson, victorious in the last struggle

of independence from Europe. We see the red worshippers of the sun in their white cloaks crossing the
river, vanishing toward its setting; and we see the
black shadows of men, the negro slaves, creeping out
of Africa after the white heralds of Europe in America.
Seeing and hearing all this, we have seen and heard
the intimations of the glory of France in the new
world, the birth of a world-power, the United States,
the infancy of a new democracy, the disappearance of
the aboriginal Indian, the menace of the black shadow
that had made a nation half slave and half free, and
the prophecy of the triumphant coming of the new-age
producers and poets, the men of the Land of the Western
Waters.

It is out of this light and shade gathered by the
Father of Waters—the Mississippi—along its banks,
that there comes silently one day in 1831, the lank,
bony, awkward figure of Abraham Lincoln, then a
young man of twenty-two, guiding a flatboat laden
with prairie products down this same tortuous waterway, from the Sangamon to the sea. He was six feet
four inches tall, homely, sad-faced, handy, and as
little promising outwardly as any other pilot or boatman of those days. It is still remembered in prairie
legends, however, that at the beginning of the voyage,
his boat being stuck midway across a dam, he had in-
geniously managed to release it and save all from
shipwreck. It seems now an incident fraught with
prophecy. And it is said that many years later he
made designs of a contrivance that would lift flatboats
over shoals and even let them navigate on ice—an
intimation of the resourcefulness of men left to fight
alone with the forces of nature.

He was not a "Yankee," as one writing me in Paris characterized the men of that valley. This awkward landsman on water was born in a cabin in the Kentucky wilderness, a house replaced by one of unhewn timber, without door or floor or window, probably not better than the meanest of the gypsy houses just outside the fortifications of Paris. He accompanied his restless, migratory father from one squatter home to another until he settled in Illinois, where the timberland and prairie meet, near the Sangamon, and there built another cabin, made rails to fence ten acres of land—which gave him the sobriquet the "rail-splitter"—"broke" the ground, and raised a crop of corn on it the first year. You may remember that Joliet made report of such a possibility there.

Lincoln's origin you will recognize as typical of that frontier, except that the character which asserted itself in the son, if there is transmission of acquired character, seems to have come from the mother and the nurturing of his stepmother rather than from the shiftless, paternal pioneer who gave the wilderness environment and soil to the nurturing of this stock and was as little paternalistic as the government. Perhaps this ne'er-do-well father is to be classed as one of those rough coureurs de bois who, in his ambassadorship from his ancestors to their frontier posterity, forgot the conventions and manners of the ancestral life in the temptations of the open country to a man without a slave. When he started down the Ohio into Indiana with his family, his carpenter's tools, his household goods, and a considerable quantity of whiskey, he was going to treat, not as the coureurs de bois, with the Indians, the savage men of the forests;

he was going to treat with the savage forces of nature themselves. And one must, as I have said of Nicolet and Perrot and Du Lhut, judge charitably these men who made the reconciliations of the edges of things. They made the paths to western cities; he, to a western character; that only need be remembered.

Certain trees depend for the spread of their kind on seeds equipped with spiral wings that when they fall they may reach the ground outside the shadow of the parent tree and so have a chance to grow into wide-spreading trees. Thomas Lincoln, the father of Abraham, was as the spirals that carried the precious seed where it could have free air and an unshadowed soil to grow in.

And there the tuition of the experiences that made all men kin and so made a natural democracy possible began. He had little teaching of the formal sort. Six months or a year in a log schoolhouse probably measured its duration. He had the sterner discipline of the fields, the waters, and the trees, for their very temptations became disciplines to those who resisted, as his father did not. He learned his parables of the fields and of the natural instincts of his neighbors. He knew both physical and human nature about him, and this he illustrated, expressed, in such manner as to make him a faithful and favorite exponent of its coarseness, its kindliness, its gallantry, its sympathies, and its heroisms.

These neighborly fellowships, not affected but genuine, equipped him not only with a vital and never-failing sense of brotherhood but with a faith in those whom he called the "plain people," the common man. His creed was, if not innate, innurtured. That fellow-

ship and that faith were at the bottom of his democracy
—not merely patient love of his neighbors but faith
in their ultimate judgments—democracy that made him
a nationalist and a world humanist.

But in the making of Lincoln there were more than
the usual disciplines. He had also the tuition of the
"solemn solitude," as Bancroft says. He sought the
fellowships of the past—of that "invisible multitude
of the spirits of yesterday." He read every book that
he could get within fifty miles, it is said. But what is
more certain is that he read thoroughly and "inwardly
digested" a few books. He knew the Bible, Shakespeare, and Burns, Æsop's "Fables," Bunyan's "Pilgrim's Progress," and "Robinson Crusoe." He read a
history of the United States and a life of Washington,
and he learned by heart the statutes of the State of Indiana. Moreover, he studied without guidance algebra
and geometry. It is said that later in life, when his
political career was beginning, he continued his studies
even more seriously and attempted to master a foreign
language.

So he had companionship of the patriarchs and
prophets and poets of Israel. And it was the experience of many another prairie boy that he knew intimately these Asiatic heroes of history before he consciously heard of modern or contemporary heroes. I
knew of Joshua before I was aware of Napoleon, and I
remember carving upon a primitive arch of triumph—
which was only the stoop at the roadside, but the most,
conspicuous public place accessible to my knife—the
name of one of the cities taken in the conquest of
Canaan, an instinct of hero-worship—so splendidly illustrated in French art and monuments.

Lincoln the youth had not only those ancient companionships but the intimate counsel of the greatest of teachers of democracy. He knew, too, the homely wisdom of Greece as well as he knew the treasured sayings of his own people handed on from generation to generation. He was as familiar with the larger-horizoned gossip and philosophies of Shakespeare's plays as with those which gathered around the post-office of Clary's Grove, where later this youth as postmaster carried the letters in his hat and read the newspapers before they were delivered. He loved Burns for his philosophy that "a man's a man for a' that." So with these and others he found his high fellowships, even while he "swapped" stories (enriched of his reading) with his neighbors at the store or his fellow lawyers at the primitive taverns.

But there were less personal associations. He made the fundamental laws of a wilderness State an acquisition of his instincts. There is preserved in a law library in New York the much-worn copy of the statutes of Indiana enacted in the first years of the existence of that State. It is stated that he learned these statutes by copying extracts from them—and from the Declaration of Independence, the Constitution of the United States, and the Ordinance of the Northwest, included in the same volume—on a shingle when paper was scarce, using ink made of the juice of brier-root and a pen made from the quill of a turkey-buzzard, and shaving the shingle clean for another extract when one was learned, till his primitive palimpsest was worn out. But whatever the medium of their transmigration from matter to mind, they became the law of his democracy, sacred as if they had been brought

to him on tables of stone by a prophet with shining
face.   It was in that school, I believe, that he learned
his nationalism, his devotion to the Constitution—to
which in maturer years he gave this famed expression: "I would save the Union, I would save it in the
shortest way under the Constitution. . . .   My par-
amount object in this struggle is to save the Union.
If I could save the Union without freeing any slave I
would do it; and if I could save it by freeing all the
slaves, I would do it; and if I could save it by freeing
some and leaving others alone, I would also do that.
What I do about slavery and the colored race, I do
because I believe it helps to save the Union, and what
I forbear, I forbear because I do not believe it would
help to save the Union."[1]
     And when he had freed the negro by a proclamation
that violated the letter of the Constitution, it was
still that boy of the woods speaking in the man—the
boy who had learned his lesson beyond all possibility
of forgetting or misunderstanding—"I felt that measures otherwise unconstitutional might become lawful
by becoming indispensable to the preservation of the
Constitution through the preservation of the nation."
     It was from those shingles that he learned, too, the
place of the State in this nationalism.   Its paternalism
has grown tremendously since 1824, when democracy
was a negative, a repressive and not a positive, aggressive political and social spirit, but, as it was, it gave
him the foundation of the political structure within
whose lines he had to build later.
     And with all this was a self-discipline in the two
great knowledges by which men have climbed from

[1] Letter to Horace Greeley, August 22, 1862.

savages to gods—language and mathematics. He was
told one day that there was an English grammar in a
house six miles from his home, and he at once walked
off to borrow it. And he studied geometry and algebra
alone. This may seem to you an inconsequential thing,
but having myself on those same prairies not far away
from the Sangamon acquired my algebra with little
teaching and my solid geometry with only the tuition
of a book and of the sun or a lamp, I am able to appreciate what the hardship of that self-schooling was.
It was more agreeable to watch the clouds while the
horses rested at the end of the furrow, to address, as
did Burns, lines to a field-mouse, or to listen to the song
of the meadow-lark, than to learn the habits of the three
dimensions then known, of points in motion, of lines
in intersection, of surfaces in revolution, or to represent
the unknown by algebraic instead of poetic symbols.

But his private personal culture, as one[1] has observed,
had no "embarrassing effects," because he shared so
completely and genuinely the amusements and occupations of his neighborhood. No "taint of bookishness"
disturbed the local fellowships which gave him opportunity to express in "familiar and dramatic form" of
story and illustration his more substantial philosophy
and so find for it the perfect speech. His neighbors
called him by homely, affectionate names, thinking he
was entirely one of them—a little more clever, a little
less ambitious in the usual channels of business and
enterprise. He had no "moral strenuousness of the
reformer" and no "exclusiveness" of learning. He
"accepted the fabric of traditional American political

[1] Herbert Croly, Lincoln as more than an American in his "Promise of
American Life," pp. 89–99.

thought." He seemed "but the average product," and yet, as this same writer has said, "at bottom Abraham Lincoln differed as essentially from the ordinary western American of the middle period as St. Francis of Assisi differed from the ordinary Benedictine monk of the thirteenth century."[1] He was not, like Jackson, simply a large, forceful version of the plain American trans-Alleghany citizen; he made no clamorous, boastful show of strength, powerful as he was physically and intellectually. He shared genuinely, with no consciousness of his own distinction, the "good-fellowship of his neighbors, their strength of will, their excellent faith, and above all their innocence." But he made himself, by discipline of his own, "intellectually candid, concentrated, and disinterested and morally humane, magnanimous and humble." This is not the picture of a conventional, generic democrat; and this is not, we are assured by the earlier writers, the picture of the westerner of that period. Indeed, Mr. Croly insists that while these Lincolnian qualities are precisely the qualities which Americans, in order to become better democrats, should add to their strength, homogeneity, and innocence, they are just the qualities (high intelligence, humanity, magnanimity, and humility) which Americans are "prevented by their individualistic practice and tradition from attaining or properly valuing." "Their deepest convictions," he contends, "make the average unintelligent man the representative democrat, and the aggressive, successful individual the admired national type." To them Lincoln is simply "a man of the people" and an example of strong will.

[1] Croly, "Promise of American Life," p. 90.

But the man who said this did not know that land of Lincoln—which was the valley of La Salle, and even before that the valley of the tribe of men—for I believe its inhabitants knew that he was the embodiment of what they coveted for themselves; that he was not their ordinary average but their best selves.

Their individualism has been, I must say again, under practical compulsions and has had fruits that deceive the eye. It is so insistent upon national productivity, but none the less is it joined to a high idealism that worships just the qualities that were so miraculously united in Abraham Lincoln. To be sure, some remember for their own excuse his coarse stories; some recall for their own justification his acceptance of the political standards that he found; but the great body of the people keep him in reverence and affection as the incarnation of patience, honesty, fairness, magnanimity, humility; not for his strength of will primarily, but for his strength of charity and honesty, and in so doing they reveal the ideal that is in and under their own individual struggle.

Montalembert said that "a social constitution which produced a Lincoln and others like him is a good tree whose sure fruit leaves nothing to envy in the product of any monarchy or aristocracy." Lincoln was not, we want to believe, a freak, a sport of nature, but the "sure fruit" that should not only leave nothing to envy in others, but leave nothing to question in the soundness of a democracy that gives evidence of its spirit in remembering Abraham Lincoln more tenderly, more affectionately, more reverentially than any one else in its history. It is less to his praise but more accurate, I think, that, as his biographer put it: "His day and generation uttered itself through him." He expressed their ugliest forms and their most beautiful developments.

None the less is it remarkable that not only should the virility and nobility of the frontier have been exhibited in him, but that the consummate skill and character known to the world's centres of culture should have had, in his speech and intellectual attitude and grasp, a new example.

When he wrote his letter in acceptance of the nomination to the presidency, he showed it to the superintendent of public instruction in Illinois, whom he called "Mr. Schoolmaster" (and who was years after my own beloved schoolmaster) saying: "I am not very strong on grammar and I wish you would see if it is all right." The schoolmaster had only to repair what we call a "split infinitive." But the great utterances of his life had no tuition or revision of schoolmasters. They were his own in conception and expression. He sent his Cooper Union speech in advance to several for advice, and they, I am told, changed not a word.

Of his debates with Douglas (1858), his speech in Cooper Union, New York, 1860, his oration at the dedication of the Soldiers' Cemetery at Gettysburg, and of his second inaugural address, it has been said that no one of them has been surpassed in its separate field. Goldwin Smith said of the Gettysburg speech: "Saving one very flat expression, the address has no superior in literature."[1] These appraisements I would hesitate to repeat in France, where all letters come finally to be adjudged, if I did not know that this last

[1] Goldwin Smith, "Early Years of A. Lincoln." In R. D. Sheppard, "Abraham Lincoln," p. 132.

document (the Gettysburg speech), at least, had been admitted to the seat of the immortal classics. It is said to have been written on scraps of paper, as the great care-worn man rode in the car from Washington to Gettysburg, and I have been told by one who was present at the ceremonies that the quiet had hardly come over the vast audience, stirred by the eloquence of Edward Everett's oration which had lasted two hours, before this briefest and noblest of American orations, spoken in a high and unmusical voice by the great lank figure, consulting his manuscript, was over. It is heard now in the memory of millions of school-children from the Atlantic to the Pacific:

"Fourscore and seven years ago our fathers brought forth on this continent a new nation, conceived in liberty and dedicated to the proposition that all men are created equal.

"Now we are engaged in a great civil war, testing whether that nation or any nation so conceived and so dedicated, can long endure. We are met on a great battle-field of that war. We have come to dedicate a portion of that field as a final resting-place for those who here gave their lives that that nation might live. It is altogether fitting and proper that we should do this.

"But in a larger sense, we cannot dedicate—we cannot consecrate—we cannot hallow—this ground. The brave men, living and dead, who struggled here have consecrated it far beyond our poor power to add or detract. The world will little note nor long remember what we say here, but it can never forget what they did here. It is for us, the living, rather, to be dedicated here to the unfinished work, which they who fought

here have thus far so nobly advanced.   It is rather for
us to be here dedicated to the great task remaining
before us—that from these honored dead we take increased devotion to that cause for which they gave the
last full measure of devotion; that we here highly
resolve that these dead shall not have died in vain;
that this nation, under God, shall have a new birth of
freedom; and that government of the people, by the
people, for the people, shall not perish from the earth."

Bronze tablets bearing this oration for their inscription have been put on the walls of schoolhouses
and public buildings all the way across the continent—
plates in renewal of possession, that are another fruitage of the valley where the French planted their plates
of possession and repossession a century before.

But I would also have read—especially in France,
where letters are still being written that have the
quality of literature—a letter of this frontiersman.   The
professor of history in the College of the City of New
York, showing me his museum, would have me read
again this letter in the hand of Abraham Lincoln; and
I would have those beyond America, as well as in that
valley, hear what a man of the western waters could
write before the coming of the typewriter:

"DEAR MADAM: I have been shown in the files of
the War Department a statement of the Adjutant-
General of Massachusetts that you are the mother of
five sons who have died gloriously on the field of
battle.   I feel how weak and fruitless must be any
words of mine which should attempt to beguile you
from the grief of a loss so overwhelming.   But I cannot refrain from tendering to you the consolation that

may be found in the thanks of the Republic they died to save. I pray that our heavenly Father may assuage the anguish of your bereavement and leave you only the cherished memory of the loved and lost and the solemn pride that must be yours to have laid so costly a sacrifice upon the altar of freedom.

"Yours very sincerely and respectfully,

"ABRAHAM LINCOLN." [1]

These two examples illustrate not only the form of his speech and writing, but the sympathy and the temper of the soul of the man. They need only the supplement of a comment on the strength of his thought in expression. It is said of his Cooper Union speech (his first speech before a large eastern urban audience, I think): "From the first line to the last, from his premises to his conclusion, he travels with a swift, unerring directness which no logician ever excelled, an argument complete and full, without the affectation of learning. . . . A single, easy, simple sentence . . . contains a chapter of history that, in some instances, has taken days of labor to verify and which must have cost the author months of investigation to acquire. . . . Commencing with this address as a political pamphlet, the reader will leave it as an historical work, brief, complete, profound, truthful—which will survive the time and occasion that called it forth and be esteemed hereafter, no less for its intrinsic worth than its unpretending modesty." [2]

---

[1] "Lincoln, Complete Works" (Nicolay and Hay edition), 2 : 600. To Mrs. Bixby, Boston, Mass., November 1, 1864.

[2] Pamphlet edition with notes and prefaces by C. C. Nott and Cephas Brainerd, September, 1860. Quoted in Nicolay and Hay, "Abraham Lincoln," 2 : 225.

His first wide fame grew from a speech which he delivered on October 16, 1854, in Peoria, the city that had grown on the Illinois River by the side of La Salle's Fort Crèvecœur. "When the white man governs himself," he said there, "that is self-government; but when the white man governs himself and also governs another man, that is more than self-government—that is despotism."[1] Two years later he made near there an address so irresistible in its eloquence that the reporters forgot why they were there and failed to take notes. So there are but fragments preserved of what is known as "the lost speech."

The minor anecdotes of his life that are treasured and the stories which he is said to have told would fill a volume—perhaps volumes. They all tell of a genius who through adversity became resourceful, who through the neighborly exchanges of a village learned a sympathy as wide as humanity, and who with an infinite patience and kindliness and good sense dealt with a divided people.

The world outside the valley at first thought him a buffoon because it heard only the echo of the hoarse laughter after his stories. They found when he spoke in Cooper Union that he had a mind that would have sat unembarrassed and luminous in the company of the men of the age of Pericles. But he had a sense of humor that, had he been there, would have saved Socrates from the hyssop. Mr. Bryce says, that all the world knows the Americans to be a humorous people.[2] "They are," he has said, "as conspicuously the purveyors of humor to the nineteenth century as

---

[1] "Lincoln, Complete Works," ed. by Nicolay and Hay, 2 : 227.
[2] Bryce, "American Commonwealth," 2 : 286.

the French were the purveyors of wit to the eighteenth.
. . . [This sense] is diffused among the whole people;
it colors their ordinary life and gives to their talk that
distinctively new flavor which a European palate en-
joys." And he adds: "Much of President Lincoln's
popularity, and much also of the gift he showed for
restoring confidence to the North at the darkest moments of the war, was due to the humorous way he
used to turn things, conveying the impression of not
being himself uneasy, even when he was most so."
Yet it was no mask, it was instinctive.

On one of those days when the anxiety was keenest
and the sky darkest a delegation of prohibitionists
came to him and insisted that the reason the north
did not win was because the soldiers drank so much
whiskey and thus brought the curse of the Lord down
upon them. There was, we are told, a mischievous
twinkle in his eye when he replied that he considered
it very unfair on the part of the Lord, because the
southerners drank a good deal worse whiskey and more
of it than the soldiers of the north.

Most of these stories and parables had a flavor of
the west and of the fields where they were collected in
the days when, as a lawyer, he followed the court from
one town to another, and spent the nights in talk around
the tavern stove.

When asked one day how he disposed of a caller
who had come to him in a towering rage, he told of the
farmer in Illinois who announced one Sunday to his
neighbors that he had gotten rid of a great log in the
middle of his field. They were anxious to know how,
since it was too big to haul out, too knotty to split,
too wet and soggy to burn. And the farmer announced:

"I ploughed around it." "And so," he said, "I got rid of General ———. I ploughed around him, but it took me three hours to do it."

This, then, was the lank boatman who came down the river (that was once the River Colbert) and who, seeing the horrors of the slave markets in New Orleans, went back to the Sangamon with a memory of them that was a "continual torment," as he said, and with a vow to hit that institution hard if ever he had a chance. It was this boatman who was twenty years later to have, of all men, the chance.

One cannot tell here, even in outline, the story of that irrepressible conflict in which this western plough-man and lawyer became commander-in-chief of an army of a million men and carried on a war involving the expenditure of three billion dollars. One need not tell it. It need only to be recalled that it was this man of the western waters who first saw clearly, or first made it clearly seen, that the nation could not endure permanently half slave and half free. "I do not expect the Union to be dissolved," he said, "but I do expect it will cease to be divided. It will become all one thing or the other." And it was he who more than any one single force brought the fulfilment of his prophecy—of a nation reunited and all free.

He hated slavery. "If slavery is not wrong," he said, "nothing is wrong." But he wanted to get rid of it without injustice to those to whom it was an in-herited, if cherished, institution. If he saw a venomous snake in the road he would take the nearest stick and kill it, but if he found it in bed with his children, "I might hurt the children," he said, "more than the snake and it might bite them." He was as tender and considerate of the south as ever he was of an erring neighbor in Illinois, where it is remembered that he carried home with his giant strength one whom his comrades would have left to freeze, and nursed him through the night. So he sat almost sleepless, sadhearted, through the four dark years, but resolute, cheering his own heart and those about him with a broad humor that came as "Æsop's Fables" out of the fields and their elemental wisdoms.

One summer's day, when ploughing in the fields of that land of Lincoln, I heard a sound of buzzing in the air and, looking up, I saw a faint cloud against the clear sky. I recognized it as a swarm of bees making their way from a hive, they knew not where, and with an instinct born of the plains at once I began to follow them and to throw up clods of earth to stop their flight, bringing them down finally on the edge of the field upon a branch of a tree, where they were at evening gathered into a new hive and persuaded back to profitable industry instead of wasting their substance in the forest. So this great ploughman used the clods of earth, the things at his hand, illustrations from the fields, to bring the thoughts of his countrymen down to contentful co-operation again.

"You may," said Alcibiades, speaking of Socrates, "imagine Brasidas and others to have been like Achilles, or you may imagine Nestor and Antenor to have been like Pericles; and the same may be said of other famous men. But of this strange being you will never be able to find any likeness, however remote, either among men that now are or who ever have been —other than . . . Silenus and the Satyrs, and they represent in a figure not only himself but his words.

For his words are like the images of Silenus which open.
They are ridiculous when you first hear them. . . .
His talk is of pack-beasts and smiths and cobblers and
curriers. . . . But he who opens the bust and sees
what is within will find they are the only words which
have a meaning in them and also the most divine,
abounding in fair images of virtue, and of the widest
comprehension, or rather extending to the whole duty
of a good and honorable man."[1]

The twenty-three centuries since Socrates do not
furnish me with a fitter characterization of Lincoln.
His image was as homely as that of Silenus was bestial.
His talk was of ploughs and boats, polecats and
whiskey. But those who opened this homely image
found in him a likeness as of no other man, and in his
words a meaning that was of widest and most ennobling
comprehension. And, as Crito said for all ages, after
the sun that was on the hilltops when Socrates took the
poison had set and darkness had come: "Of all the men
of his time, he was the wisest and justest and best."
So has the poet of that western democracy given to
all time this phrase, sung in the evening of the day of
Lincoln's martyrdom, at the time when the lilac bloomed
and the great star early dropped in the western sky
and the thrush sang solitary: "The sweetest, wisest
soul of all my days and lands."[2]

We ask ourselves if he was the gift of democracy.
And we find ourselves answering: his peculiar excel-
lence could have come of no other order of society. We
ask ourselves anxiously if democracy has the unerring
instinct to find such men to embody its wishes, or did

---

[1] Plato, "Symposium," Jowett's trans., I : 592.
[2] Walt Whitman, "When Lilacs Last."

it take him only for a talented rail-splitter—an average man? But we have no certain answer to this
anxious questioning. What gives most hope in new
confusions and problems, unknown to his day, however,
is that the more clearly his disinterestedness and for-
bearance and magnanimity and humility are revealed,
the wider and deeper is the feeling of admiration and
love for his character, which perhaps assures us, after
all, better than anything else, of the soundness and
nobility of the ideals of democracy.

They carried this man at death over into the valley
of his birth, into the land of the men of the western
waters that was Nouvelle France, and there buried
him among his neighbors, of whom he learned his
spirit of democracy, in the midst of scenes where he
had mastered its language, in the very ground that
had taught him his parables, by the side of the stream
that gave him sight of his supreme mission. It is the
greatest visible monument to his achievement that the
"Father of Waters . . . goes unvexed to the sea"[1]
through one country instead of the territory of two or
more nations and that the slavery he witnessed is no
more. But it is a greater monument to him, as it is
a nobler monument to those who have erected it in
their own hearts, that he is revered the length of the
course of the river first traced by La Salle, and through
all the reach of the rivers of his claim from its source,
even as far as its mouth at the limitless sea.

[1] Letter to John C. Conkling, August 25, 1863.

CHAPTER XIV

THE VALLEY OF THE NEW DEMOCRACY

FRANCE evoked from the unknown the valley that may, in more than one sense, be called the heart of America. Her coureurs de bois opened its paths made by the buffalo and the red men to the shod feet of Europe. Her explorers planted the watershed with slender, silent portage traces that have multiplied into thousands of noisy streets and tied indissolubly the lakes of the north to the rivers of the south from which they were long ago severed by nature. Her one white sail above Niagara marked the way of a mighty commerce. Her soldiers sowed the molten seeds of tumultuous cities on the sites of their forts, and her priests and friars consecrated with their faith and prayers forest trail, portage·path, ship's sail, and leaden plate.

But that is not all—a valley of new cities like the old, of new paths for greater commerce, of more altars to the same God! The chief significance and import of the addition of this valley to the maps of the world, all indeed that makes it significant, is that here was given (though not of deliberate intent) a rich, wide, untouched field, distant, accessible only to the hardiest, without a shadowing tradition or a restraining fence, in which men of all races were to make attempt to live together under rules of their own devising and enforcing. And as here the government of the people by the people was to have even more literal interpretation than in that Atlantic strip which had traditions of property suffrage and church privilege and class distinctions, I have called it the "Valley of the New Democracy."

When the French explorers entered it, it was a valley of aboriginal, anarchic individualism, with little movable spots of barbaric communistic timocracy, as Plato would doubtless have classified those migratory, predatory kingdoms of the hundreds of red kings, contemporary with King Donnacona, whom Cartier found on the St. Lawrence—communities governed by the warlike, restless spirit.

The French communities that grew in the midst of those naked timocrats, whose savagery they soothed by beads and crucifixes and weapons, were the plantings of absolutism paternalistic to the last degree. One cannot easily imagine a socialism that would go further in its prescriptions than did this affectionate, capricious, generous, if unwise, as it now seems, government of a village along the St. Lawrence or the Mississippi, from a palace by the Seine where a hard-working monarch issued edicts "in the fulness of our power and of our certain knowledge."

The ordinances preserved in the colonial records furnish abundant proof of that parental concern and restraint. They relate to the regulation of inns and markets, poaching, preservation of game, sale of brandy, rent of pews, stray hogs, mad dogs, matrimonial quarrels, fast driving, wards and guardians, weights and measures, nuisances, observance of Sunday, preservation of timber, and many other matters.

Parkman cites these interesting ordinances, which illustrate to what absurd lengths this jealous, paternalistic care extended:

"Chimney-sweeping having been neglected at Quebec, the intendant commands all householders promptly to do their duty in this respect, and at the same time fixes the pay of the sweep at six sous a chimney. Another order forbids quarrelling in church. Another assigns pews in due order of precedence."[1]

One intendant issued a "mandate to the effect that, whereas the people of Montreal raise too many horses, which prevents them from raising cattle and sheep, 'being therein ignorant of their true interest, . . . now, therefore, we command that each inhabitant of the côtes of this government shall hereafter own no more than two horses or mares and one foal—the same to take effect after the sowing season of the ensuing year (1710), giving them time to rid themselves of their horses in excess of said number, after which they will be required to kill any of such excess that may remain in their possession."[2]

And, apropos of the trend toward cities, there is the ordinance of Bigot, issued with a view, we are told, of "promoting agriculture and protecting the morals of farmers" by saving them from the temptations of the cities: "We prohibit and forbid you to remove to this town (Quebec) under any pretext whatever, without our permission in writing, on pain of being expelled and sent back to your farms, your furniture and goods confiscated, and a fine of fifty livres laid on you for the benefit of the hospitals."[3]   There is even a royal edict

---

[1] Parkman, "Old Regime in Canada," p. 341.
[2] Parkman, "Old Regime in Canada," p. 341.
[3] Parkman, "Old Regime in Canada," p. 342.

designed to prevent the undue subdivision of farms which "forbade the country people, except such as were authorized to live in villages, to build a house or barn on any piece of land less than one and a half arpents wide and thirty arpents long."[1]

And this word should be added in intimation of the generosity of the paternalism:

"One of the faults of his [Louis XIV's] rule is the excess of his benevolence, for not only did he give money to support parish priests, build churches, and aid the seminary, the Ursulines, the missions, and the hospitals, but he established a fund destined, among other objects, to relieve indigent persons, subsidized nearly every branch of trade and industry, and in other instances did for the colonists what they would far better have learned to do for themselves."[2]

Like Æneas, therefore, these filial emigrants, seeking new homes, not only carried their *lares et penates* in their arms but bore upon their shoulders their father Anchises.

Succeeding savage individualism, this benevolent despotism gave the valley into the keeping of an individualism even purer and less restrained than that which it succeeded, for the sparse pioneer transmontane settlements were practically governed at first by only the consciences or whims of the inhabitants, instructed of parental commandments learned the other side of the mountains, and by their love of forest and of their prairie neighbors.

And when formal government came—a pure democracy, social and political—it came of individual in-

---

[1] Parkman, "Old Regime in Canada," p. 342.
[2] Parkman, "Old Regime in Canada," p. 347.

terest and neighborly love and of no abstract philosophical theory or of protest against oligarchy; it came
from the application, voluntary for the most part, of
"older institutions and ideas to the transforming influence of land," free land; and such has been the
result, says Professor Turner,[1] that fundamentally
"American democracy is the outcome of the American
people in dealing with the West," that is, the people
of this valley of the French pioneers.

The democratical man, as Socrates is made to define
him in Plato's "Republic," was one in whom the
licentious and extravagant desires have expelled the
moderate appetites and love of decorum, which he
inherited from his oligarchical father. "Such a man,"
he adds, "lives a life of enjoyment from day to day,
guided by no regulating principle, but turning from
one pleasure to another, just as fancy takes him. All
pleasures are in his eyes equally good and equally
deserving of cultivation. In short, his motto is 'Liberty
and Equality.'"

But the early "democratical man" of that valley,
even if he came remotely from such oligarchical sires
as Socrates gives immediately to all democratical men,
reached his motto of "Liberty and Equality" through
no such sensual definition of life.

It is true that many of those first settlers migrated
from places where the opportunities seemed restricted
or conventions irksome or privileges unequal, but it
was no "licentious or extravagant desire" or flitting
from pleasure to pleasure that filled that valley with

[1] See his "Significance of the Frontier in American History," in "Fifth
Yearbook of the National Herbart Society, 1899," also his "Significance
of the Mississippi Valley in American History," in "Mississippi Valley
Historical Association Proceedings, 1909-10."

sober, pale-faced, lean-featured men and tired, gentle
women who enjoyed the "liberty" not of a choice of
pleasurable indulgences but of interminable struggles,
the "equality" of being each on the same social, economic, and political footing as his neighbor. The
sequent democracy was derived of neighborliness and
good fellowship, the "natural issue of their interests,
their occupations, and their manner of life," and was
not constructed of any theory of an ideal state. Nor
were they frightened by the arguments of Socrates,
who found in the "extravagant love of liberty" the
preface to tyranny. And they would not have been
frightened even if they had been familiar with his
doctrine of democracy. They little dreamed that they
were exemplifying the doctrines of a French philosopher or refuting those of a Greek thinker.

Those primitive democratic and individualistic conditions had not yet been seriously changed when, in
that bit of the valley which lies in the dim background
of my own memory, there had developed a form of government more stern and uncaressing. But there was
not a pauper in all the township for its stigmatizing
care. There was not an orphan who did not have a
home; there was not a person in prison; there was only
one insane person, so far as the public knew, and she
was cared for in her own home. The National Government was represented by the postmaster miles away;
the State government by the tax assessor, a neighbor
who came only once a year, if he came at all, to inquire
about one's earthly belongings, which could not then
be concealed in any way; and the local government
by the school-teacher, who was usually a man incapaci-
tated for able-bodied labor or an unmarried woman.

The citizens made and mended the public roads, looked after the sick in a neighborly way, bought their children's schoolbooks, and buried their own dead. I can remember distinctly wondering what a "poor officer" was, for there were no poor in that society where none was rich.

It was a community of high social consistency, promoted not by a conscious, disinterested devotion to the common welfare but by the common, eagerly interested pursuit of the same individual welfares, where there was room enough for all.

It is well contended in a recent and most profound discussion of this subject by Professor Turner (of whom I spoke as born on a portage) that this homogeneity of feeling was the most promising and valuable characteristic of that American democracy.[1]

And it was, indeed, prolific of mighty consequences:

First of all, it made it possible for the United States to accept Napoleon's proffer of Louisiana.

Second, it compelled the War of 1812 and so confirmed to the United States the fruits of the purchase, demonstrating at the same time that the "abiding-place" of the national spirit was in the west.

And, third, that spirit of nationalism took into its hands the reins of action in the time when nationality was in peril. Before the end of the Civil War the west was represented in the National Government by the President, the Vice-President, the Chief Justice, the Speaker of the House, the Secretary of the Treasury, the Postmaster-General, the Attorney-General, the General of the Army, and the Admiral of the Navy. And it furnished, as Turner adds in summary, the

[1] See his "Significance of the Mississippi Valley in American History."

"national hero, the flower of frontier training and ideals."

While the mere fact of office-holding does not indicate the place or source of power, it is noteworthy that the Presidents since the war—to the election of Wilson—Grant, Hayes, Garfield, McKinley, Harrison, and Taft all came from this valley. Cleveland went over the edge of it, when a young man, to Buffalo and left it only to become governor and President; Arthur, who succeeded to the presidency through the death of President Garfield, and President Roosevelt, who also came first to the presidency through the death of a President and was afterward elected, were both residents of New York, though the latter had a ranch in the far west and seems rather to belong to that region than the place of his birth. Thus of the elected Presidents there was not one who had not a middle-western origin, experience, or association. The Chief Justices since the war have been without exception western men, and so with few exceptions have been the Speakers of the House. And practically all these Presidents, Chief Justices, Speakers, were pioneers or sons of pioneers in that "Valley of the New Democracy" or, at any rate, were nurtured of its natural fellowships, its one-man-as-good-as-another institutions, and its unhampered ambitions.

It is not mere geographical and numerical majorities that are connoted. It is the dominancy of the social, democratic, national spirit of the valley—the supremacy of the average, the useful man, his power and self-sufficiency when standing squarely, firmly upon the earth. It was the secret of the great wrestler Antæus, the son of Terra, that he could not be thrown even by

Hercules so long as his feet touched the earth. How intimately filial to the earth and neighborly the middle-west pioneers were has been suggested. And it was the secret of their success that they stood, every man in his own field, on his own feet, and wrestled with his own arms in primitive strength and virtue and self-reliant ingenuity.

Democracy did not theorize much, and when it did it stumbled. If it had indulged freely in the abstractions of its practices, it would doubtless have suffered the fate of Antæus, who was finally strangled in mid-air by a giant who came over the mountains.

As it was, this valley civilization apotheosized the average man. Mr. Herbert Croly, in his "Promise of American Life," makes this picture of him: "In that country [the very valley of which I am writing] it was sheer waste to spend much energy upon tasks which demanded skill, prolonged experience, high technical standards, or exclusive devotion. The cheaply and easily made instrument was the efficient instrument, because it was adapted to a year or two of use, and then for supersession by a better instrument; and for the service of such tools one man was as likely to be good as another. No special equipment was required. The farmer was required to be all kinds of a rough mechanic. The business man was merchant, manufacturer, and storekeeper. Almost everybody was something of a politician. The number of parts which a man of energy played in his time was astonishingly large. Andrew Jackson was successively a lawyer, judge, planter, merchant, general, politician, and statesman; and he played most of these parts with conspicuous success. In such a society a man who per-

sisted in one job and who applied the most rigorous
and exacting standards to his work was out of place
and was really inefficient. His finished product did
not serve its temporary purpose much better than did
the current careless and hasty product, and his higher
standards and peculiar ways constituted an implied
criticism upon the easy methods of his neighbors.
He interfered with the rough good-fellowship which
naturally arises among a group of men who submit
good-naturedly and uncritically to current standards."[1]

Is this what democracy, undefiled of aristocratic conditions and traditions, has produced? it will be asked.
Has pure individualism in a virgin field wrought of its
opportunity only this mediocre, all-round, good-natured,
profane, rough, energetic, ingenious efficiency? Is this
colorless, insipid "social consistency" the best wine
that the valley can offer of its early vintages?

I know those frontier Antæi, who, with their feet on
the prairie ground, faced every emergency with a
piece of fence wire. They differed from their European
brothers in being more resourceful, more energetic, and
more hopeful. If it be true that "out of a million well-
established Americans taken indiscriminately from all
occupations and conditions," when compared to a
corresponding assortment of Europeans, "a larger proportion of the former will be leading alert, active, and
useful lives," though they may not be wiser or better
men; that there will be a "smaller amount of social
wreckage" and a "larger amount of wholesome and
profitable achievement," it may be safely said that, if
the middle-west frontier Americans had been under
consideration, the proportion of alert achievement

[1] Herbert Croly, "Promise of American Life," pp. 63, 64.

would have been higher and the social wreckage smaller —partly because of the encouragement of the economic opportunity, and partly because of the encouragement of a casteless society.

I cannot lead away from those familiar days without speaking of other companionships which that valley furnished beyond those intimated—companionships which did not interfere with the rough frontier fellow-ships that made democracy possible. For it was in these same fields that Horace literally sat by the plough and sang of farm and city. It was there that Livy told his old-world stories by lamplight or at the noon-hour. It was there that Pythagoras explained his ancient theorem.

I cannot insist that these companionships and intimacies were typical, but they were sufficiently numerous to disturb any generalizations as to the sacrifices which that democracy demanded for the sake of "social conditions" and economic regularity.

The advancing frontier soon spent itself in the arid desert. The pioneer came to ride in an automobile. The people began to jostle one another in following their common aspirations, where once there was freedom for the energy, even the unscrupulous energy, of all. Time accentuated differences till those who started together were millions of dollars apart. Failures had no kinder fields for new trials. Democracy had now to govern not a puritanical, industrious, sparsely settled Arcady but communities of conflicting dynamic successes, static envies, and complaining despairs.

It met the new emergencies at first, one by one, with no other programme than the most necessary restraints, encouragement of tariffs for the dynamic, improved transportation for the static, and charity for the despairful; but all with an optimism born of a belief in destined success.

To this has succeeded gradually a more or less clearly defined policy of constructive individualism, under an increasingly democratic and less representative control. The paternal absolutism of Louis XIV has evolved into the paternal individualism of a people who are constantly struggling in imperfect speech to make their will understood and by imperfect machinery to get it done—and, as I believe, with increasingly disinterested purpose. It is, however, I emphasize, the paternalism of a highly individualized society.

I described in an earlier chapter a frontier community in that valley. See what has come in its stead, in the city into which it has grown. The child coming from the unknown, trailing clouds of glory, creeps into the community as a vital statistic and becomes of immediate concern. From obliging the nurse to take certain precautions at its birth, the State follows the newcomer through life, sees that he is vaccinated, removes his tonsils and adenoids, furnishes him with glasses if he has bad vision, compels him to school, prepares him not only for citizenship but for a trade or profession, prevents the adulteration of his food, inspects his milk, filters his water, stands by grocer and butcher and weighs his bread and meat for him, cleans the street for him, stations a policeman at his door, transports his letters of business or affection, furnishes him with seeds, gives augur of the weather, wind, and temperature, cares for him if he is helpless, feeds him if he is starving, shelters him if he is homeless, nurses him in sickness, says a word over him if he dies friendless, buries him in its potter's field, and closes his account as a vital statistic in the mortality column.

And there are many agencies of restraint or anxious care that stand in a remoter circle, ready to come in when emergencies require. I have before me a report of legislation in the States alone (that is, exclusive of national and municipal legislation) for two years. I note here a few characteristic and illustrative measures out of the thousands that have been adopted. They relate to the following subjects:

Health of women and children at work; employer's liability; care of epileptics, idiots, and insane; regulation of dentistry and chiropody; control of crickets, grasshoppers, and rodents; exclusion of the boll-weevil; the introduction of parasites; the quenching of fires; the burning of débris in gardens; the destruction of predatory fish; the prohibition of automatic guns for hunting game; against hazing in schools; instruction as to tuberculosis and its prevention; the demonstration of the best methods of producing plants, cut flowers, and vegetables under glass; the establishment of trade-schools; the practice of embalming.

I introduce this brief but suggestive list as intimating how far a democratic people have gone in doing for themselves what Louis XIV at Versailles in the "fulness of power" and out of "certain knowledge" did for the trustful habitants of Montreal, who were "ignorant of their true interest."

And, of course, with that increased paternalism has come of necessity an army of public servants—governors and policemen, street cleaners and judges, teachers and factory inspectors, till, as I have estimated, in some communities one adult in every thirty is a paid servant of the public.

Such paternalism is not peculiar to that valley. I remember, years ago, when I was following the legislation of an eastern State, that a bill was introduced fixing the depth of a strawberry box, and another obliging the vender of huckleberries to put on the boxes a label in letters of certain height indicating that they were picked in a certain way. And this paternalism is even more marked in the old-age pension provision in England, where the "mother of parliaments," as one has expressed it, has been put on the level of the newest western State in its parental solicitude.

But nowhere else than in this valley, doubtless, is that paternalism so thoroughly informed of the individualistic spirit. Chesterton said of democracy that it "is not founded on pity for the common man. . . . It does not champion man because man is miserable, but because man is so sublime." It "does not object so much to the ordinary man being a slave as to his not being a king." Indeed, democracy is ever dreaming of "a nation of kings."[1] And that characteristic is truer of the democracy that came stark out of the forests and out of the furrows than of the democracy which sprang from protest against and fear of single kings.

The constitution east of the mountains was made in fear of a system which permitted an immediate and complete expression of the will of the people. The movement in American democracy which is most conspicuous is the effort to get that will accurately and immediately expressed—that is, a movement toward what might be called more democracy—toward

[1] G. K. Chesterton, "Heretics," p. 268.

a direct control of "politics" by the people—and that movement has had its rise and strength in the Mississippi Valley and beyond.

But who are the people who are to control? Only those who are living and of electoral age and other qualification? I recall again Bismarck's definition: "They are the invisible multitude of spirits—the nation of yesterday and to-morrow." And that invisible multitude of yesterday and to-morrow, whose mouths are stopped with dust or who have not yet found human embodiment, must find voice in the multitude of to-day —the multitude that inherits the yesterdays and has in it the only promise of to-morrow.

There may be some question there as to its being always the voice of God, but no one thinks of any other (except to add to it that of the woman). The "certain knowledge" and the "fulness of power" of Louis XIV have become the endowments of the average man— and the average man is one-half or two-thirds of all the voting men of the community or nation, plus one. But that average man, forgetful of the multitude of yesterday and ungrateful, has none the less wrought into his very fibre and spirit the uncompromising individualism, the unconventional neighborliness, and the frontier fellowships of yesterday. It is of that that he is consciously or unconsciously instructed at every turn. And he is now beginning to think more and more of the invisible multitude, the nation of to-morrow.

It is deplored that the so-called individuality developed in that valley is "simply an unusual amount of individual energy, successfully spent in popular and remunerative occupations," that there is "not the remotest conception of the individuality which may reside in the gallant and exclusive devotion to some disinterested and perhaps unpopular moral, intellectual, or technical purpose," as has such illustrious exhibition in France, for example. This is, we are told, one of the sacrifices to social consistency which menaces the fulness and intensity of American national life. And the most serious problem is to make a nation of independent kings who shall not exercise their independencies "perversely or irresponsibly."

Men have been always prone to make vocational pursuits the basis of social classification. In the Scripture record of man he had not been seven generations in the first inhabited valley of earth before his descendants were divided into cattlemen, musicians, and mechanics. For the record runs that Lamech had three sons, Jabal, Jubal, and Tubal—Jabal who became the father of those who live in tents and have cattle, Jubal the father of those that handle the harp and the organ, and Tubal the father of those who work in brass and iron. And we do not have to turn many pages to discover the social distinctions that grew out of the vocational. The first question of that western valley is, "Who is he?" and the answer is one which will tell you his occupation. No one who has not an occupation of some regularity and recognized practical usefulness is, as Mr. Croly intimates, likely to have much recognition.

On the other hand, within the limits of approved occupations, there is, except in great centres, no marked social stratification based on vocation, as in old-world life and that of the new world more intimately touched by the old. The man is recognized for his worth.

In the midst of that valley is a college town,[1] planted
by a company of migrants from an older State seventy-five years ago who bought a township of land,
founded a college,[2] and built their homes about on
the wild prairie. It has now twenty thousand inhabitants and is an important railroad as well as educational centre. It was nearly fifty years old when I
entered it as a student. That I studied Greek did not
keep me from knowing well a carpenter; that in spare
hours I learned a manual trade and put into type my
translation of "Prometheus Bound" did not bar me
from the homes of the richest or the most cultured.
Once, when a student, because of some little victory, I
was received by the mayor and a committee of citizens,
but the men at the engines in the shops and on the
engines in the yards blew their whistles. When I went
back to that college as its president it was not remembered against me that I had sawed wood or driven
a plough. I knew all the conductors and most of the
engineers on the railroads. I knew every merchant
and nearly every mechanic, as well as every lawyer,
judge, and doctor. Men had, to be sure, their pref-
erential associations, but these were personal and
not determined of vocation or class. A recent mayor
of this city of two colleges was a cigar maker and, I
was assured by a professor of theology in a local
university, the best mayor it has had in years, and
he died driving a smallpox patient to a pest-house. I
received when in Paris, by the same mail as I recall,
a resolution of felicitation from a Protestant body of
which I was a member in that town, and a letter
of like felicitation from the Catholic parish priest of

[1] Galesburg, Ill. [2] Knox College.

that same city. I do not know how better to illustrate, to those who are working at the problem of democracy in other valleys, how democracy has wrought for itself in that valley of neighborliness and resourcefulness and plenty, in the wake of the monarchical, paternalistic affection of France.

CHAPTER XV

WASHINGTON: THE UNION OF THE EASTERN AND THE WESTERN WATERS

WE have followed the French explorers and priests as pioneers through the valleys of the St. Lawrence, the Great Lakes, and the Mississippi to the gulf and the Rocky Mountains. But there remains one further conquest, a conquest of their adventurous imaginations only, for none of their adventurous or pious feet ever travelled over the valley lying south of the St. Lawrence watershed and east of the Alleghanies, though they were probably the first of white men to see those peaks rising in the north of what is now New England, known as the White Mountains.

Standing on the summit of one of the White Mountains a few summers ago, I was shown a dim little indentation of the sky at the northwest which I was told was Mont Real. And since seeing that I have imagined Jacques Cartier in 1535 looking off to the southeast, when his disappointed vision of the west had tired his eyes, and catching first sight of these dim indentations of his sky, the White Mountains, which the colonists from England did not see until a century later and then only from their ocean side.

But whether the master pilot from the white-bastioned St. Malo saw them or not, we have record that

Champlain in his exploration of the Atlantic coast did discern their peaks upon his horizon; and so we may think of the French as the discoverers not merely of the northern and western valleys, of the Adirondacks, in whose shadows Champlain and Brûlé and Father Jogues fought with the Iroquois and suffered torture, and of the snow-capped Rockies at whose feet Chevalier de la Vérendrye was obliged to turn back, but also of the tops of the white hills near the Atlantic coast, which I have often seen lighted at sunrise while the lower slopes and valleys were in darkness or shadow— hills touched by the French, as by that rising sun, only at their tops and by the trails of their eyes.

For the moment those mountains stand upon the horizon as the symbol of the only part of North America east of the Rockies which the French pioneers did not possess before others by the trails of their feet or the paths of their boats. Verrazano of Dieppe had sailed along the Atlantic shore front, but so, perhaps, had Cabot. Ribaut had been "put to the knife" in Florida, but it was the knife of a Spaniard whose compatriots had been there before Ribaut. Étienne Brûlé had wandered all the way from Canada into Pennsylvania along the sources and upper waters of the Atlantic streams, but the colonists of other nations were sitting huddled at the mouths of the streams. And Father Jogues had endured the torturing portage from the shores of Lake George to the Mohawk, but the Dutch were by that time there to succor him from the Iroquois. Only with their eyes had the French beheld first of Europe the America of the eastern waters, whose inhabitants, when they came to put on uniform and fight for its independence, called themselves

"Continentals," as if their little hem of the garment were the continent.

One wonders—if to little purpose—what would have been the consequence if De Monts, whom Champlain accompanied to America in 1604, had planted his little colony at some place farther south in his continental grant made by Henry IV, stretching, as it did, all the way from what is now Philadelphia to the St. Lawrence —if, for example, he had anchored off the Island of Manhattan, as well he might have done, five years before Hudson came up the harbor in the *Half Moon*, had settled there instead of on the sterile island of Ste. Croix in the Bay of Fundy, where, amid the "sand, the sedge, and the matted whortleberry bushes," the commissioners to fix the boundaries between the United States and Canada discovered in 1793—nearly two centuries later—the foundations of the "Habitation de l'isle Ste. Croix" that the French had built in the gloom of the cedars. Or if, when the scurvy-stricken colony left that barren site, they had followed Champlain to the mouth of the Charles, la rivière du Guast —the site of Cambridge or Boston—or even to the Bay St. Louis—which is remembered in Champlain's journal as the place where the friendly Indians showed him their fish-hooks made of barbed bone lashed to wood, but which has become better known as Plymouth Bay where the Pilgrims landed fifteen years later—there instead of Port Royal, where even Lescarbot's "Ordre de Bon-Temps" could not overcome the evil reports in France concerning a "churlish wilderness"! Or if Champlain, instead of seeking later the Rock of Quebec—whose rugged charms he could not forget even in the presence of the site of

Boston or in the streets of Paris—had laid the foundations of his faith and his courage on the Susquehanna, for example! In any one of these contingencies there might have been a more prosperous Acadia. New England might conceivably have become Nouvelle France, and New York City might be bearing to-day the name of a seventeenth-century French prince.

An idle conjecture, but it does, I think, help us to appreciate the happy destiny (or by whatever name the sequence of events may be called) not that kept France out of that narrow Atlantic-coast strip but that put her in a position to become the power that should in a very true sense force the jealous, many-minded colonies of that strip into a union, make possible the erection of that feeble union into a nascent nation, give it, though under certain compulsion, territory to become a world-power, and finally furnish it, if grudgingly, with a great western, overmountain domain in which to develop a democratic and a nationalistic spirit strong enough to hold a continent-wide people in one republic. These services, intended and unintended, negative and positive, grudging and voluntary, performed, however, all in unsurpassed sacrifice and valiance not only of the explorers and priests but of the exiled soldiers, intimate how, out of all the misery of finding the northern water gate and keeping it and following the northern waterway and fortifying it, came the harvests—even if France did not gather them into her own granaries—of those who "sow by all waters."

We might not have had some of the institutions we do have if Champlain or Poutrincourt had anticipated the English Pilgrims at Plymouth, but we might still be a colony or a cluster of republics, even with all that we have got by way of those and other English migrants, except for these hardy men who kept battling with the ice and snow and water and famine at the north.

But what I wish to emphasize here—and I am much indebted to the young western historian Mr. Hulbert, for this view—is that France, struggling to keep the empire of her adventure and faith in the northern and western valleys of America, gave to the world George Washington. She made him, all unconsciously to be sure, first in war. She saved him, consciously, from the fate of an unsuccessful rebel. And she made it possible for him to be first in peace. These are all defensible theses, however much or little credit France may deserve in her purposes toward him.

Up in those same White Mountains there rises one that bears his name, taller than the rest. It stands in a presidential range that has no rivalling peak. A singular felicity in the naming of the neighboring mountains has given the name Lafayette to the most picturesque of all. There are well-known and much-travelled trails to the austere peak of Mount Washington. There is even a railroad now. Doubtless no mountain in America is known in its contour to more people, though there are many of loftier height and of more inviting slopes.

So the outlines of the life of Washington are known more widely than those of any other American. The trails to the height of his achievement and genius have doubtless been learned in the histories of France. And asking my readers to travel over one of those well-worn trails again, I can offer no better reason than that I may on the way call attention to objects and outlooks that should be of special interest to the eyes of a company of men and women whose geographical or racial ancestors gave us him in giving us the west.

Washington was born a British colonist. His great-grandfather settled in Virginia at about the time that La Salle was making his way up the St. Lawrence to the seigniory of St. Sulpice above the Lachine Rapids. His father, grandfather, and great-grandfather were frontiersmen, farmers, or planters. He had himself the discipline of the plantation, but he learned surveying and had also the sterner experiences of its frontier practice. Then came his appointment at nineteen as an adjutant-general of colonial militia in Virginia and with that office the still sterner disciplines beyond the frontier, where France was tutor, without which tuition he would doubtless have become and remained a successful colonial Virginia planter and general of militia.

I have estimated that all the young men in America of approximately Washington's age at that time could probably have been gathered into the Roman colosseum back of the Pantheon; at any rate, into an American university stadium. They could have been reached by the voice of one man. (Which will intimate how small America was—one-fourth the size of Paris when he was born, one-half the size of Paris when he became a major of militia.)

They were practically all country-born. There were, indeed, no great cities in which to be born. New York was little more than a town with only eight or nine thousand inhabitants; and Boston, the largest city at that time, had but thirteen thousand in the year 1732.

They were men, as Kipling says of the colonials in the Boer War, who could "shoot and ride." And Washington was a strong athletic youth of fiery passions, which, given free rein, would have made him a successful Indian chief. (Indeed, the Indians admired him and called him Ha-no-da-ga-ne-ars—"the destroyer of cities"—and at last admitted him, as a supreme tribute, to their Indian paradise, the only white man found worthy of such canonization.) But, rugged, country-born men though they were, it was in no such neighborly democracy as Lincoln knew that they were bred. Washington had his slaves, his coat of arms, and the occupations and leisures and pleasures, so far as the frontier would permit, of an English gentleman. And it is no such slouchy, shabbily dressed figure as Lincoln's that Washington presents. I saw a few years ago a letter in Washington's own hand, in which he gave directions to the tailor as to the number of buttons that his coat should have, the shape of its lapel, and the fit of its collar. He was most insistent upon the conventions, though if such an assembly had been held, as I have suggested, of the young men from the eastern waters, there would have been no such uniformity of costume as now makes an audience of men in America, or in Europe, so monotonously black and white.

These young men did not dress alike; they did not spell alike. Washington's letters show that he did not even spell consistently with himself. And that first man of the eastern waters to follow the French in establishing a settlement on the western waters, Daniel Boone, left this memorial of his orthography on a tree in Kentucky: "C-I-L-L-E-D A B-A-R."

They did not dress alike, they did not spell alike, they did not think alike. It was a great, and it must have seemed a hopeless, motley of men who were all unconsciously to lay the foundations of a new national structure.

They were all of immigrant ancestors, and most of them of most recent immigrant ancestry, or of foreign birth. Though much more homogeneous in their lineage than the present immigration, they had not the unifying agencies that now keep Maine and Florida within a few minutes of each other by telephone or a few hours by rail.

But there were in all, immigrants and sons of immigrants, hardly more in number than now enter that same land as aliens in one or two years. I spoke a few years ago at a dinner of the descendants of the *Mayflower* and was told that they numbered in all the country, as I recall, about three thousand—three thousand descendants in three hundred years of a hundred colonists, half of whom perished in the first winter; which leads one to wonder what the land of the *Mayflower* and the nation of George Washington will be in three hundred years, when the descendants of each shipload of immigrants of to-day will have increased in like ratio. From a single steerage passenger cargo, of the *Lusitania* or *Mauretania*, let us say, we shall have twenty, thirty, or forty thousand Lusitanians or Mauretanians as descendants; and from a single year's immigration thirty millions. The descendants of the colonial ships will be lost in this mighty new progeny of the ships of Europe and will numerically be as negligible as the North American Indian is in our census to-day.

But to come back to Washington: the appointment
of the stripling as adjutant-general with rank of major
was two years after the humpbacked Governor Galissonnière had sent Céloron down the Ohio on that
historic voyage of plate-planting, the news of which
had finally reached the ears of the governor of Virginia, who with many planters of Virginia (Washington's family included) had a prospective interest in
lands along that same river.   Then came the word
through Indian and trader (the only long-distance
telephones of that time) that forts were beginning to
grow where the plates had been planted.

It was then that the young farmer, surveyor, soldier,
just come of age, was chosen to carry a message to
the commander of the nearest French fort in the
valley—Fort Le Bœuf, which I have already described
—about fifteen miles from Lake Erie on the slight elevation from which the waters begin to flow toward the
Mississippi.   The commander was Legardeur de St.
Pierre, a one-eyed veteran of wars, but recently come
from an expedition out across the valley toward the
Rockies.

Parkman has made this picture of the momentous
meeting of France and America in the western wilderness, which in its peopling has kept only a single tree
of those forests, a tree pointed out to me as the Washington tree, though it, too, may have come with the
migrants:

"The surrounding forests had dropped their leaves,
and in gray and patient desolation bided the coming
winter.   Chill rains drizzled over the gloomy 'clearing,'
and drenched the palisades and log-built barracks, raw
from the axe.   Buried in the wilderness, the military

exiles [Legardeur and his garrison] resigned themselves
as they might to months of monotonous solitude;
when, just after sunset on the eleventh of December, a
tall youth [and he was only an inch shorter than Lincoln, six feet three inches] came out of the forest on
horseback, attended by a companion much older and
rougher than himself, and followed by several Indians
and four or five white men with packhorses. Officers
from the fort went out to meet the strangers; and,
wading through mud and sodden snow, they entered
at the gate. On the next day the young leader of the
party, with the help of an interpreter, for he spoke
no French [a deficiency which he laments with greatest regret later in life], had an interview with the
commandant and gave him a letter from Governor
Dinwiddie. St. Pierre and the officer next in rank,
who knew a little English, took it to another room
to study it at their ease; and in it, all unconsciously,
they read a name destined to stand one of the noblest
in the annals of mankind, for it introduced Major
George Washington, Adjutant-General of the Virginia
Militia."[1]

At the end of three days the young British colonial
officer of militia started on his perilous journey homeward, having been most hospitably entertained by the
one-eyed veteran, bearing on his person a letter which
St. Pierre and his officer had been the three days in
preparing. The brave, courteous, soldierly lines of the
frontier deserve to be heard to-day both in France and
America:

"I am here by Virtue of the Orders of my General;
and I entreat you, Sir, not to doubt, one Moment, but

[1] Parkman, "Montcalm and Wolfe," 1 : 136–7.

that I am determined to conform myself to them with all the Exactness and Resolution which can be expected from the best Officer. . . . I don't know that in the Progress of this Campaign [of repossession] anything passed which can be reputed an Act of Hostility or is contrary to the Treaties which subsist between the two Crowns. . . . Had you been pleased, Sir, to have descended to particularize the Facts which occasioned your Complaints I should have had the Honor of answering you in the fullest, and, I am persuaded, most satisfactory Manner."

In the spring the two hundred canoes which Washington saw moored by the Rivière aux Bœufs carried the builders of Fort Duquesne and a garrison for it down La Belle Rivière, and a little later is heard the volley of the Virginia backwoodsmen up on the Laurel ridges a little way back from Duquesne, the volley which began the strife that armed the civilized world —the backwoodsmen commanded by the Virginia youth, George Washington.

It is in that lonely ravine up among the ridges which I have described in an earlier chapter that the union of the eastern and western waters began. And there should be a monument beside Jumonville's to keep succeeding generations mindful of the mighty consequence of what happened then.

This fray of the mountains was one of the most portentous of events in American history. It was not only the grappling of two European peoples and two systems of government out upon the edges of the civilized world—the stone-age men assisting on both sides—a fray in which Legardeur de St. Pierre, Coulon de Jumonville, and de Villiers, his avenging brother, were France, and Washington was England. It was the beginning of the making of a new nation, of which that tall youth, who found the whizzing of bullets a "charming sound," was to be the very corner-stone.

He was here having his first tuition of war. De Villiers let him march back from Fort Necessity unharmed, when he might, perhaps, have ended the career of this young major in the great meadows where they fought "through the gray veil of mists and rain." Washington was taught by France, in these years of border warfare—for he went four times over the mountains—he was spared by France in the end to help take from France the title of the west, or so it seemed when, in 1763, the war which his command had begun was ended in the surrender of that vast domain to England. But we know now that the struggle had other issue.

The steep path of the years when the colonies were taught their first lessons of federation by their common fear of the French and their allies, led by the tall young man who emerged from the woods back of Fort Le Bœuf and later assisted by the moral and pecuniary sympathy of France, by the presence of her ships along their menaced coasts, by the counsels of her admirals and generals, and by the marching and fighting of her soldiers side by side with theirs, you know. It is a path so marked by memorials as to need no spoken word. Only one vista in this trail of gloom with overhanging clouded sky need detain us a moment. It lets us see Benjamin Franklin rejoicing in Paris after the news of the surrender of Burgoyne at Saratoga in 1777. We see Beaumarchais rushing away from Franklin's lodgings in Passy to spread the good news, and in such mad haste that he upset his carriage and dislocated his arm. And when we next look out from the path we see the British soldiers passing in surrender between two lines drawn up at Yorktown, the American soldiers on one side with Washington at their head, and on the other the French soldiers under Count Rochambeau.

Washington and Legardeur de St. Pierre at Fort Le Bœuf, Washington and Rochambeau at Yorktown! You have been told again and again that except for the France of Rochambeau the War of Independence would probably have failed and that the colonies would have remained English colonies. But let us remember that except for the France of Legardeur de St. Pierre there would probably not have been, as Parkman says, a "revolution"; and by the France of Legardeur I mean the spirit of France that had illustration in his lonely, exiled watching of the regions won by her pioneers.

The French man-of-war *Triumph* brought to Philadelphia in May of 1783 the treaty of Paris. In the December following General Washington said farewell to his officers and returned to Mount Vernon, his estate on the Potomac. There he was busied through the next few months in putting his private affairs in order, in superintending the reparation of his plantation, and in receiving those who came to him for counsel or to express their gratitude. It was as a level bit of the mountain trail from which the traveller catches glimpses of a peaceful valley. And that is all that the traveller usually sees.

But there is a farther view. From that level path

one can see over the Alleghanies the great valley so familiar to our eyes from other points of view, stretching toward the Mississippi.

In the autumn of 1784 (eight months after his farewell to the army) Washington leaves his home, as it appears, to visit some lands which he had acquired as one result of his earlier and martial trips out beyond the Laurel Hills. He had title to forty thousand acres beyond the mountains. He had even purchased the site of this first battle in the meadows, where he had built Fort Necessity and where he was himself captured by the French, but from which he was permitted to go back over the mountains with his flags flying and his drums beating. A "charming field of encounter" he called the place in his youthful exuberance before the battle in 1753. "Much Hay may be cut here When the ground is laid down in Grass; and the upland, East of the Meadow is good for grain," he wrote in his unsentimental diary, September 12, 1784. For over the mountains he went again on what was thought but a trip of personal business. But on the third day of the journey, September 3d, he writes, incidentally, as explaining his desire to talk with certain men: "one object of my journey being to obtain information of the nearest and best communication between the Eastern and Western Waters." And as he advances this becomes the possessing object.

Here are a few extracts from that diary still preserved in his own hand which give the intimation of a prescience that should in itself hold for him a grateful place in the memory of the west and of a concern about little things that should bring him a bit nearer to our human selves:

September 6. "Remained at Bath all day and was showed the Model of a Boat constructed by the ingenious Mr. (James) Rumsey for ascending rapid currents by mechanism. . . . Having hired three Pack horses to give my own greater relief. . . ."

September 11. "This is a pretty considerable water and, as it is said to have no fall in it, may, I conceive, be improved into a valuable navigation. . . ."

September 12. "Crossing the Mountains, I found tedious and fatieguing [*sic*]. . . . In passing over the Mountains I met numbers of Persons and Pack horses . . . from most of whom I made enquiries of the nature of the Country. . . ."

September 13. "I visited my Mill" [a mill which he had had built before the Revolution]. . . .

September 15. "This being the day appointed for the Sale of my moiety of the Co-partnership Stock many People were gathered (more out of curiosity I believe than from other motives). My Mill I could obtain no bid for. . . ."

September 19. "Being Sunday, and the People living on my Land, apparently very religious" [these were Scotch-Irish who had squatted on a rich piece of land patented by Washington], "it was thought best to postpone going among them till to-morrow. . . ."

September 20. "I told them I had no inclination to sell; however, after hearing a good deal of their hardships, their Religious principles (which had brought them together as a society of Ceceders [*sic*]) and unwillingness to seperate [*sic*] or remove; I told them I would make them a last offer. . . ."

September 22. "Note—In my equipage Trunk and the Canteens—were Madeira and Port Wine—Cherry bounce—Oyl, Mustard—Vinegar—and Spices of all sorts—Tea, and Sugar in the Camp Kettles (a whole loaf of white sugar broke up about 7 lbs. weight). . . . My fishing lines are in the Canteens. . . ."

September 23. "An Apology made to me from the Court of Fayette (thro' Mr. Smith) for not addressing me."

The Cheat at the Mouth is about 125 y^{ds} wide—the Monongahela near d^{ble} that—the colour of the two Waters is very differ^t, that of Cheat is dark (occasioned as is conjectured by the Laurel, among which it rises, and through which it runs) the other is clear, & there appears a repugnancy in both to mix, as there is a plain line of division betw^n the two for some distance below the fork; which holds, I am told near a Mile.— the Cheat keeps to the right shore as it descends, & the other the left.

September 25. "At the crossing of this Creek McCulloch's path, which owes its origen [*sic*] to Buffaloes. . . . At the entrance of the above glades I lodged this night, with no other shelter or cover than my cloak & was unlucky enough to have a heavy shower of Rain."

September 26. "We had an uncomfortable travel to one Charles Friends, about 10 miles; where we could get nothing for our horses, and only boiled Corn for ourselves."

October 1. "I had a good deal of conversation with this Gentleman on the Waters, and trade of the Western Country."

October 4. "I breakfasted by Candlelight, and Mounted my horse soon after daybreak. I arrived at Colchester, 30 Miles, to Dinner; and reached home before Sun down."[1]

[1] A. B. Hulbert, "Washington and the West," pp. 32-85.

In this revelation of Washington out of the laconic misspelled entries of his diary we have not only a most human portrait but an intimation of his practical far-seeing statesmanship. He looms even a larger figure as he rides through the fog of the Youghiogheny, for there he appears as the prophet of the eastern and western waters. In his vision the New France and the New England are to be indissolubly bound into a New America. He had written Chevalier de Chastellux from Princeton, October 12, 1783, after a return from the Mohawk Valley, that he could not but be struck by the immense extent and importance "of the vast inland navigation of these United States," that should bring that great western valley into communication with the east, and that he would not rest contented until he had explored that western country and traversed those lines which have given bounds to a new empire. And as he comes back over the Alleghanies from this journey of six hundred and eighty miles on the same horses he writes: "No well-informed mind need be told how necessary it is to apply the cement of interest to bind all parts together by one indissoluble band." And the indissoluble band is the smooth road and the navigable stream or canal.[1]

England and France had both restrained western migration, and the young provincial republic was doubtless of no mind to encourage it, so far as it then knew its mind. But Washington had a larger, wiser view than any other except Franklin, and even Franklin was not ardent for the canals. Washington was thinking, some will say, of the trade that would come over those paths; and so he was, but it was not primarily for his own advantage, not for the trade's sake, but

[1] A. B. Hulbert, "Washington and the West," p. 100.

for the sake of the weak little confederation of States for which he had ventured all he was and had.

He was (as my old professor of history in Johns Hopkins was the first to point out[1]) the first to suggest the parcelling of the western country into "free, convenient, and independent governments," and here he appears the first not to speculate about but to seek out by fording streams and climbing mountains a practical way to a "more perfect union," and not merely for those jealous States lying along the Atlantic and within reach of its commerce, but for all the territory and people of their new heritage.

And singularly enough this very journey led not only to the establishment of those paths between the east and west, the national road, the canals reaching toward the sources of the rivers, and ultimately the trans-Alleghany railroad, but to the making of that unmatched document, the Constitution of the United States. And in this wise:

Washington called the attention of Virginia and Maryland to the importance of opening a communication between the Potomac and James and the western waters. He writes to Lafayette of being at the meeting of the Maryland Assembly in that interest.[2] These two States appointed commissioners to confer concerning this and other matters. Their recommendations resulted in the calling of a more widely representative convention, and this in turn in the convening of a body to revise the entire federal system.

---

[1] Herbert B. Adams, "Washington's Interests in Western Lands," in *Johns Hopkins University Studies*. Third series, No. 1, 1885.

[2] John Pickell, "New Chapter in the Early Life of Washington in Connection with the Narrative History of the Potomac Company, 1856," pp. 133-4.

So this peaceful journey of the warrior over the mountains to the great meadows and down into the tangled ravines of West Virginia became not only the prophecy of the indissoluble bond between the east and west; it became the first step in that movement which led the original States themselves into that more perfect union.

The sequence, which did not occur to me until I read recently the diary of that trans-Alleghany journey, gives Washington a new, if a homelier, majesty.

Napoleon the Great has spoken his praise of Washington as a general. Many of our own historians agree that it is very doubtful if without Washington the struggle for independence would have succeeded. Other men were important. He was indispensable. This intimates the occasion we have for gratitude that the commander of the French let him march out of Fort Necessity in 1754.

The world has for a century been repeating the eulogies that have outlived the invective of his day— and that are only now becoming humanized by the new school of historians who will not sacrifice facts to glowing periods. Washington is now more of a human being and less of a god than the Washington whom Lincoln found in Weems's "Life."

Yet with all the humanizing is he the austere, rugged, inaccessible mountain, its fiery passions hidden, its head above the forests. And so will he stand in history the justest of men, a man of highest purity of purpose and of greatest practical wisdom; but, if as a mountain, then as one that hides somewhere in its slopes such a path as we have learned to know in our journeys over this course, a portage path between two great valleys which its summit has blessed, for he was as a portage path between the eastern and western waters, between the institutions of New England and the fleur-de-lis fields of Nouvelle France.

I have visited the unmarked field where Fort Le Bœuf once stood, by French Creek, the field where "the most momentous and far-reaching question ever brought to issue on this [American] continent"[1] was put by the stripling Washington to the veteran Legardeur de St. Pierre.

I have, in my worship of the great general, followed through the rain and sleet of a winter's night and in the mud of a country road his famous march from the crossing of the Delaware to Trenton, made in that December night of 1776 when the struggle seemed most hopeless.

And I have been in the place in which—as to at least one historian—he seems to me the most of a man and the most of a prophet, even the most of a god, out in the glades and passes, the rains and fogs, of the Alleghanies, fording the streams and following the paths of buffalo and deer in an attempt to find a way between the east and west.

[1] Parkman, "Montcalm and Wolfe," 1 : 4.

CHAPTER XVI

THE PRODUCERS

ON the wonderful background which the passing
life of that valley has filled with dim epic figures that are now but the incarnations of European longings, as rich in color as that which lies more
consciously back of Greece and Rome or in the fields
of Gaul (the splendors of the court of Versailles shining
through the sombre forests and into the huts of the
simple habitants)—on this I have depicted the rather
shadowy suggestions of a matter-of-fact, drab democracy which is usually made to obscure all that
background with its smoke. But if I have made your
eyes see what I have tried to show, the colors and figures
of the background still show themselves.

I have now to put against that wonderful background, dim as it is, the new habitants. I suggested
earlier the emergence of their gaunt figures from the
forests and the processional of their ships of the prairies
through the tall grass that seemed as the sea itself.

I had in my thought to speak of these new inhabitants as workers, but that word has in it too much of
the suggestion of endless, hopeless, playless labor. Yet
they are workers all—or nearly all. There are some
tramps, vagrants, idlers, to be sure, the spray of that
restless sea. But when a man of great wealth wishes
to give up systematic work he generally goes out of the

valley or begins a migratory life, as do the wild birds of the valley.

But these busy, ever-working people of the valley are better characterized by other names, and they may be divided into three overlapping classes:

I. The precursors, those that run before, the explorers, the discoverers, the inventors, the prophets.

II. The producers, those, literally, who lead forth: the dukes, marshals, generals of democracy, bringers forth of things from the ground, the waters, by brain and muscle; and the transporters of the things brought forth to the places of need.

III. The poets, that is, in the old pristine Greek sense, the makers, the creators, in the generic sense, and not merely in the specific sense of makers of verses.

If you object to my terminology as exalting too much the common man, as putting sacred things to profane use, as demeaning prophecy and nobility and poesy, I shall answer that it is because of the narrowing definitions of convention that only the makers of verses, and not all of those, are poets, that only men of certain birth or ancestry or favor are dukes, and that prophets have entirely disappeared. And I bring to my support the more liberal lexicography of science, whose spectroscopy now admits the humblest elements into the society of the stars; whose microscopy, as Maeterlinck has helped us to become aware, has permitted the flowers to share the aspirations of animal intelligence; whose chemistry has gathered the elements into a social democracy in which no permanent aristocracy seems now to be possible, except that of service to man; whose physics has divided the atom and yet exalted it to a place which would lead Lucretius, were he writing now, to include it in Natura Deorum instead of Natura Rerum.

The son of Sirach, in his Book of Wisdom, has described the man who did the work of the world in ancient times; for "how shall he become wise," begins this essay, "that holdeth the plough, that glorieth in the shaft of the goad, that driveth oxen, and is occupied in their labors, and whose discourse is of the stock of bulls? He will set his heart upon turning his furrows, his wakefulness is to give his heifers their fodder. So is every artificer and work-master that passeth his time by night as by day, they that cut gravings of signets; and his diligence is to make great variety; he will set his heart to preserve likeness in his portraiture, and will be wakeful to finish his work. So is the smith, sitting by the anvil, and considering the unwrought iron; the vapor of the fire will waste his flesh, and in the heat of the furnace will he wrestle with his work; the noise of the hammer will be ever in his ears, and his eyes are upon the pattern of the vessel; he will set his heart upon perfecting his works, and he will be wakeful to adorn them perfectly. So is the potter sitting at his work, and turning the wheel about with his feet, who is always anxiously set at his work, and all his handiwork is by number; he will fashion the clay with his arm, and will bend its strength in front of his feet; he will apply his heart to finish the glazing, and he will be wakeful to make clean the furnace. All these put their trust in their hands; and each becometh wise in his own work. Without these shall not a city be inhabited, and men shall not sojourn or walk up or down therein. They shall not be sought for in the council of the people, and in the assembly they shall not mount on high; they shall not sit on the seat of the judge, and they shall not understand the covenant of judgment; neither shall they declare instruction and judgment, and where parables are they shall not be found. But they will maintain the fabric of the world; and in the handiwork of their craft is their prayer."

The wisdom of the scribe, however, he said, "cometh by opportunity of leisure." That wisdom the west, as I have already intimated, has not yet learned. Such a scene as I witnessed a little time ago in the amphitheatre of the Sorbonne, a scene typical of what occurs many times a day there, is not yet to be seen in the valley. I saw that hall filled in the early afternoon with an audience markedly masculine, listening to a lecture on early Greek life, interspersed with readings from the Homeric epics. I cannot visualize, much as I could wish to, a like scene in the Mississippi Valley, except in the atmosphere of a woman's club, or at an assembly on the shore of the lake Chautauqua, which I have described in the narrative of the "sowing of the leaden plates," where men and women are for a little time shut away from their normal occupations in a fenced or walled town; or in a university where attendance upon the lecture is required for a degree. I cannot visualize it even with such a charming and amphionic lecturer as the great scholar who gave the lecture on Greece[1] to which I have referred.

It is that want, in the valley, of appreciation of the value of leisure and of its wisdoms, it is that worship of what the son of Sirach called the "wisdom of business," or busyness, it is that disposition not to listen

[1] Dean Croiset.

to the voices of the invisible multitude of spirits of the past (who after all help to constitute a nation no less than the multitude of spirits of the present, and of the future), it is that inability to credit disinterested, materially unproductive, purposes and pursuits, and fit them into the philosophy of a perfectibility based on material prosperity—it is all of these that intimate the shortcomings of that life of the Valley of Hurry.

I saw another great and, as it seemed, non-university audience in the same amphitheatre in Paris listening just after midday to a lecture on Montesquieu, and I had not sufficient imagination to picture such an audience as near the Stock Exchange of Chicago as the Sorbonne is to the Bourse—in that western city where men take hardly time at that hour of day to eat, much less to philosophize. They will not pause to hear Montesquieu remind them that "democracy is virtue" or to hear Homer speak of virtue as the ancients conceived it.

But, on the other hand, and there is another side, they will give up private business, eating, and all to stop a patent dishonesty, to improve the mail service, to discuss the smoke nuisance that happens to be choking their throats, or get rid of the beggar at the door, or to go to a ball game.

They do not there in any great number appreciate the wonderful, indefatigable, disinterested efforts of scholars, artists, poets, in the narrower sense—the wisdoms of seeming idleness or leisure. On the other hand, I am sure that the poetry and prophecy of those who (again in the language of the son of Sirach) are "building the fabric of the world" are not appreciated either in Paris or Chicago, partly because of convention and inadequate representation in the old world, and because of the smoke and noise and the thought of the "unwrought iron" in the new world.

Of the geographical precursors of that valley I have spoken. But there are others who have enlarged the boundaries and increased the size of acres discovered by the first precursors. Let me without fatiguing statistics give intimation of what I mean in one or two illustrations of the successors of the coureurs de bois, the runners before, the later prophets of the valley.

Out of a trough up in the Alleghany Mountains— one of those troughs occupied by the sinewy Scotch-Irish pioneers who first, after the French, as you will recall, crept down into the great valley—there journeyed one day, a century after Céloron, a young man on horseback. He rode as many miles as La Salle went on foot in that memorable heart-breaking journey from Fort Crèvecœur to Fort Frontenac. He rode through the territory which La Salle had so appealingly described to Louis XIV, now yellow with ripe wheat. Men and women, children and grandmothers, were toiling day and night with scythes and sickles to harvest it by hand, but could not gather it all, and tons were left to rot under the "hoofs of cattle."[1]

This precursor came with a sword, beaten not into a ploughshare but into a something quite as indispen-

---

[1] "He saw hogs and cattle turned into fields of ripe wheat, for lack of laborers to gather it in. The fertile soil had given Illinois five million bushels of wheat, and it was too much. It was more than the sickle and the scythe could cut. Men toiled and sweltered to save the yellow affluence from destruction. They worked by day and by night; and their wives and children worked. But the tragic aspect of the grain crop is this—it must be gathered quickly or it breaks down and decays. It will not wait. The harvest season lasts from four to ten days only. And whoever cannot snatch his grain from the field during this short period must lose it."— H. N. Casson, "Cyrus Hall McCormick," pp. 65, 66.

sable, a sickle—a vibrating sickle driven by horses, that
would in a day do the work of a dozen, twenty, thirty,
forty men, women, children, and grandmothers. In
his eastern home he had, like La Salle, suffered from
creditors, from jeering neighbors who thought him
visionary, if not crazed, and from fearful laborers who
broke his machines; but there in that golden western
valley he found sympathy, and, on the Chicago portage, a site for the making of his sickles, fitted into
machines called harvesters—there where the French
precursor's boat and sword were found not long ago.
Seventeen years later, on his imperial farm, Napoleon
III (whose royal ancestors had given the very site for
the factory) fastened the cross of the Legion of Honor
upon the breast of this prophet.

There were others who went with him or followed
him into that richer valley, adding the self-rake to the
sickle, then putting a platform on the harvester so
that the men who bound the sheaves had no longer
to walk and bend over the grain on the ground, as they
had done since before the days of Ruth and Naomi,
then devising an iron arm to take the place of one of
flesh, and finally putting a piece of twine in the hand
of that iron arm and making it do the work of the
binder. I cannot help wondering what Tonty of the
iron hand would have said could he have seen that
half-human machine cutting the wheat, and with its
iron hand tying it in bundles, there in the fields of
Aramoni, just back of the Rock St. Louis.

But I do not need to idealize or emphasize to men of
France the service of this particular precursor, who was
for years considering the unwrought iron, making experiment after experiment before he came down into

that golden valley, literally to multiply its acres a hundredfold; for the French Academy of Science declared that he had "done more for the cause of agriculture than any other living man," and a late President of the French Republic is quoted as saying that without this harvester "France would starve." The King of Spain, the Emperor of Germany, the Czar of Russia, the Sultan of Turkey, and the Shah of Persia have added their tributes to those of the President of the French Republic, and all the nations of the earth are literally bringing their glory and their honor into that city of the portage strip, which, in a sense, has leading across and out of it paths to all the other golden valleys of the earth, for we are told that the sickles are reaping the fields of "Argentina in January, Upper Egypt in February, East India in March, Mexico in April, China in May, Spain in June, Iowa in July, Canada in August, Sweden in September, Norway in October, South Africa in November, and Burma in December."

When in France, walking one afternoon from Orange to Avignon, the first object I saw as I entered that charming city of the palace of the Pope was a sign advertising the McCormick harvester.

I do not mean to intimate that all the sickles, that is, harvesters, are made on that portage strip, for if all the factories and coal lands (twenty thousand acres) and timber lands (one hundred thousand acres) and ore lands (with their forty million tons of ore) and railway tracks that unite to make these harvesters were brought together around that portage strip there would be no place for the city itself; but through one building on that strip the myriad paths do run, connecting all the tillable, grain-growing valleys of this planet; and yet a recent, most observing English critic, Mr. Wells, saw as he left that city only a "great industrial desolation" netted by railroads. He smelled an unwholesome reek from the stock-yards, and saw a bituminous reek that outdoes London, with vast chimneys right and left, "huge blackened grain-elevators, flame-crowned furnaces, and gauntly ugly and filthy factory buildings, monstrous mounds of refuse, desolate, empty lots, littered with rusty cans, old iron, and indescribable rubbish. Interspersed with these are groups of dirty, disreputable, insanitary-looking wooden houses."[1] Nothing but these in a place whose very smoke was a sign of what had made it possible for the nations of the earth even to subsist at all in any such numbers, or if at all, on anything better than black bread.

And, after all, this precursor, this runner before, was but one of hundreds of later Champlains, Nicolets, and La Salles, in the wake of whose visions came the producers, those who led forth the corn and wheat from the furrows, the trees from the forests, the coal from the ground, the iron from the hills, the steel from the retorts, the fire from the wells, the water from the mountains, electricity from the clouds and the cataract —dukes, field-marshals, generals, demigods whom no myth has enhaloed or poetry immortalized.

Prometheus, bringing fire to mortals, did in a more primitive way what they have done who have led forth the oil of the rocks (petroleum) to light the lamps of the earth. Orpheus, who sang so entrancingly that mortals forgot their punishments and followed him, and Amphion, who drew the stones into their places

[1] H. G. Wells, "Future in America," p. 59.

in the walls by his music, performed no more of a miracle than a lad who tips a Bessemer converter. Hercules is remembered as a hero of the garden of the Hesperides for all time, whereas he probably but imported oranges from Spain to the eastern Mediterranean, and is hardly to be mentioned by the side of such a Mississippi Valley transporter and importer as Mr. Hill.

But let us follow more particularly the producers of the fields, whom we call the farmers there, the men whom the son of Sirach had in mind when he said in the ancient days: "How shall he become wise that holdeth the plough, that glorieth in the shaft of the goad, . . . and whose discourse is of the stock of bulls?" It was a farmer's son who invented the harvester, and four-fifths of the men (whom the writer, to whom I am indebted for many of these facts about the farmer, calls "harvester kings")—along with the plough kings and wagon kings of whom democracy has been dreaming—were farmers' sons. The plough, the self-binder, the thresher were all invented on the farm.

The son of Sirach said: "They shall not be sought for in the council of the people, and in the assembly they shall not mount on high"; but fourteen of the first twenty-six Presidents were farmers' sons, and that statistic gives but merest suggestion of the farmer's part in all the councils of the people.

Here are a few significant, graphic facts which would furnish interesting material for a new edition of Virgil's "Georgics" and "Bucolics" or lead Horace to revise his verses on rural life.

There are practically five times as many farmers (under the early man-power definition of the farmer) as the census shows, for the farmer now works with the old-time power of five men.

Six per cent of the human race (and the larger part of that six per cent is in the Mississippi Valley) produces one-fifth of the wheat of the world, two-thirds of the cotton, and three fourths of the corn (and this takes no account of its reapers and mowers that gather the crops in other valleys).

It would cost three hundred million dollars more to harvest the world's wheat by hand, if it were possible, than it costs now by the aid of the harvester and reaper.[1]

Some years ago in a trial made in Germany in the presence of the Emperor and his ministers, it was shown that a Mississippi Valley harvester driven by one man could do more in one day than forty Polish women with old-fashioned sickles.[2]

The precursor of the harvester saw grandmothers and mothers in the fields working day and night to cut and gather the harvest, but he could not now (except among the new immigrant farmers) see that spectacle. I cannot recall that, until I met that old-world population coming over the mountains as I made my first journey east out of that valley, over twenty years ago, I ever saw a woman at work in the fields.

The gallantry of that primitive pioneer life kept her in the cabin, which was the castle, and, while her labor was doubtless not less than her husband's, it had the sanctity of its seclusion and its maternal ministries to life. In the new industrialism that has invited the daughters of the Polish women harvesters into the

[1] H. N. Casson, "Romance of the Reaper," p. 178.
[2] H. N. Casson, "Romance of the Reaper," pp. 134, 135.

factories yonder there is this constant and increasing concern which is insisting upon a living wage, wholesome sanitary environment, and on shorter hours of labor for women and children—this purpose that will ultimately bring skies and sunsets without exposure or back-breaking labor.

On my way to a provincial university in the north of France not long ago, I saw a peasant mother standing in the misty morning at the mouth of a small thresher, feeding into it the sheaves handed her by her husband, the horse in a treadmill furnishing the power. When I passed in the misty morning of the next day she was still feeding the yellow sheaves into the thresher; and I thought how much better that was than the flail.

On a farm in the northwest, a hundred miles square, as long ago as 1893, three hundred self-binders were reaping the wheat at the cost of less than a cent a bushel—with practically no human labor beyond driving,[1] and there are seven thousand harvesting machines made each week[2] by the one great harvester company alone.

The time needed to handle an acre of wheat has been reduced by the use of machinery from sixty-one hours to three; of an acre of hay from twenty-one to four; of oats from sixty-six to seven; of potatoes from one hundred and nine to thirty-eight—which is significant in its promise of the wisdoms of leisure.[3]

But machinery has also increased the size of the farm. In France and Germany, I am told, the average farm is but five acres in size, and in England nine;

[1] H. N. Casson, "Romance of the Reaper," p. 178.
[2] H. N. Casson, "Cyrus Hall McCormick," p. 196.
[3] H. N. Casson, "Romance of the Reaper," p. 179.

while in the United States it is one hundred and thirty-eight acres, and in the States west of the Mississippi two hundred and eleven acres.

And the product? One harvest, in the picturesque words of Mr. Casson, would buy Belgium, two would buy Italy, three would buy Austria-Hungary, and five, at a spot-cash price, would take Russia from the Czar. Seven bushels of wheat for every man, woman, and child of the ninety or more millions in America and a thousand million dollars' worth of food to other nations! That is the sum of the product—of what has been led forth in a single year.

But the leader forth, the producer, the man who set his heart upon "turning his furrows," whose "wakefulness was to give heifers their fodder," he has himself risen. He has, as I said of the farmers of Aramoni (the sons of the first settlers who are still turning up occasionally a flint arrow-head in the fields)—he has his daily paper, his daily mail, his telephone. He "pays his taxes with a week's earning " He ploughs, plants, sows, cultivates, reaps by machinery. The poet Gray could find only with difficulty in that valley a footsore ploughman homeward wending his weary way, and Millet would in vain look for a sower, a man with a hoe, a woman reaper with a sickle, a man with a scythe or cradle. The new-world peasant is not only maintaining more than his per-capita share of the "fabric of the world" but he is taking his place in the councils of men.

What is most promising now is that these followers of the old pioneers of France in that valley are beginning to add to their acres new dominions, discovered by the new pioneers of France, such as the chemists

Lavoisier and Berthelot, forerunners of the modern schools of agricultural chemistry and physical chemistry. One hundred years after La Salle completed the waterway journey to the gulf through that valley, Lavoisier made a discovery of the composition of water itself that has been of immense benefit, I am told, to the farmer of that valley and of other valleys. And then came Berthelot with his teaching of how to put together again, to synthetize, what man has wastefully dissipated. France's men of the lens and the retort have become precursors where France's men of the boat and the sword went first, and have opened paths to even richer fields than those in which the harvesters have reaped.

There are as many agricultural colleges in the United States as there are States; there are at least fifty agricultural experiment stations, and there is ever new provision for scientific agricultural research.

Here is a partial catalogue of the enactments and appropriations of the legislature in the valley States for two years only:

LAWS AND APPROPRIATIONS SHOWING WORK DONE IN AGRICULTURAL EXPERIMENT AND EXTENSION WORK BY CERTAIN OF THE STATES, 1911–14.

ALABAMA

1912.—$27,000, experiments with fertilizers, combating boll-weevil, plant breeding, horticultural investigations, agricultural extension, etc.

1913.—Same as for 1912.

COLORADO

1911–12.—$5,500, experiments with potatoes.
5,000, experiments with alfalfa, grain, etc.
3,500, dry farming.

1913.—$47,500, experimental work in dry farming, dairying, etc.

1913–14.—County commissioners, on petition of one hundred taxpayers, to appoint county agriculturist; salary paid by county and expenses by county, State, and United States.

ILLINOIS

1913.—Authorized counties to appropriate $5,000 annually for soil and crop improvement.
See "American Year Book, 1913," p. 466.

IOWA

1913.—$500, cross-breeding of fruits and edible nuts. Authorizing establishment of county corporations for improvement of agriculture.

40,000, experiment station.

10,000, veterinary investigation.

17,000, experimental farm.

40,000, agricultural extension.
See "American Year Book, 1913," p. 465.

KANSAS

1913–14.—$55,000, experiment station.

15,000, production and dissemination of improved seeds.

102,500, for six branch stations, two of which are new.

125,000, pumping-plants at experiment station.

LOUISIANA

1912.—Police juries of several parishes authorized to appropriate not to exceed $1,000 annually in aid of farmers' co-operative demonstration work; also to acquire and establish experimental farms.

MICHIGAN

1912.—Authorizing and regulating county agricultural departments for advice and assistance to farmers.

MINNESOTA

1913.—$60,000, maintenance of county agricultural agents; counties each to pay $1,000.

MISSOURI

1913–14.—$25,000, county farm advisers.
    20,000, soil experiments.
    30,000, agricultural investigations.
    5,000, promotion of corn growing.
    12,000, soil survey.
    50,000, hog-cholera serum work.
    2,500, orchard demonstration.
    10,000, agricultural laboratories.
    12,000, animal husbandry.
    5,000, dairying.

MONTANA

1912.—$20,000, demonstration of dry-land farming.
1913.—County commissioners may, upon vote of 51 per cent
    of electors, appropriate $100 per month for
    agricultural instructor, remainder of salary to
    be paid by State and United States.

NEBRASKA

1911–12.—$100,000, establishment of school of agriculture.
    3,000, agricultural botanical work.
1913–14.— $3,000, agricultural botanical work. County to
        employ farm demonstrator on petition
        of 10 per cent of farm-land owners.
    1,250 (maximum), annually to each accred-
        ited high school teaching agriculture,
        manual training, and home economics.
    85,000, for fireproof building for agronomy,
        horticulture, botany, and entomol-
        ogy.

OHIO

1913.—$229,200, aggregate of station appropriation.

OKLAHOMA

1913.—Counties authorized to appropriate $500 annually
    for farmers' demonstration work.
    See "American Year Book, 1913," pp. 465–6.

TEXAS

1911.—Authorizing county commissioners' courts to estab-
        lish experimental farms.
1913.—Railroads may own and operate experimental farms.

WISCONSIN

1913.—Beginning January 1, 1914, $10,000, county agricul-
        tural representatives, agricultural develop-
        ment, etc.

WYOMING

1912.—$4,000, agriculture and soil-culture experiments.
1913.—$4,000, experiments along lines of agriculture and soil
        culture.
        5,000, purchase and maintenance of experimental
        farm.
1914–15.—$5,000, dry-farm experiments.
        See "American Year Book, 1913," p. 466.

And nearly every State availed itself by specific act
of certain appropriations under a federal grant. In
addition to all this, appropriations are generally made
for the holding of farmers' institutes at which instruction is given by experts and farmers exchange experiences.

The agricultural colleges have a total of over one
hundred thousand graduates, men and women, and it is
they, and those who follow in increasing numbers, who
are to cultivate the valley of Lavoisier and Berthelot
even as the pioneers and producers of the past have
cultivated for the world the valley of Marquette and
La Salle.

It is not all as bright and promising as this rather
generalized picture may seem to indicate. There are
still isolations, there are bad crops in unfavorable
places and untoward seasons. There are human fail-

ures. It is an intimation of the darker side that President Roosevelt appointed a commission[1] a few years ago to see what could be done for the ignorances, the lonesomenesses, the monotonies of country life in America, and to prevent the migration to cities, even as Louis XIV. But all that I have described is there —aggressively, blusteringly, optimistically there—and is going most confidently on. It is for the most part a temperate life. All through that valley there has swept a movement, moral, economic, or both, which has closed saloons and prevented the sale of intoxicating drink of any sort in States or communities all the way from the lakes to the gulf.

But, singularly enough, there is promise of a new age of alcohol, I am told. Farmers can distil a variety of alcohol from potatoes at a cost of ten cents a gallon and use it in gasolene engines most profitably, which leads one who has written most informingly and hopefully of the American farmer to foreshadow the day when the farmer "will grow his own power and know how to harness for his own use the omnipotence of the soil" and get its fruits most beneficially distributed.

That there is a strong utilitarian spirit possessing all the valley I do not deny. But I often wonder whether we are not conventionally astigmatic to much of the beauty and moral value of such utilitarian life and its disciplines. There is intimation of this in a recent statement of a western economist to the effect that there was as great cultural value in developing the lines of a perfect milk cow as in studying a Venus de Milo, and in growing a perfect ear of corn as in rep-

[1] Commission on Country Life.

resenting it by means of color or expressing the rhythm of its growth in metered words. But, I believe that there is as much beauty and poetry there as among the isles of Greece, if only it were interpreted by the disinterested spirit and skill of the artist, the scholar, and the poet.

If we turn for a moment to the precursors who have led the way to the valley that lies beneath, the valley of the strata of coal and iron, with its subterranean streams of precious metal, its currents of gold and silver, and its lakes of oil and gas, and from these precursors to the producers and transporters who have led these elements forth to the uses of man, we shall find a like story—another chapter of democracy's dreaming of kings.

The same author whom I have quoted liberally above has written what he calls "The Romance of Steel" in that valley. It begins with an Englishman of French ancestry, Bessemer, and one Kelly, an Irish-American, born on the old Fort Duquesne point. They had discovered and developed, each without the knowledge of the other, the pneumatic process of treating iron—that is, of refining it with air and making steel. Bessemer's name became associated with the process. But the industry has made Kelly's birthplace, the site of the old French fort, its capital (with another of those poetic fitnesses that multiply as we put the present against the past).

France not only gave to Pittsburgh her site but the crucibles in which her fortunes lay. Bessemer was the son of a French artist living in London in poverty. Young Bessemer had invented many devices, when Napoleon III, one day in a conversation, complained to him that the metal used in making cannon was of poor quality and expensive. He began experiments in London at the Emperor's suggestion and later sent the Emperor a toy cannon of his own making. It was in this experimenting, as I infer, that the idea struck him of making malleable iron by introducing air into the fluid metal. But his first experiments were not particularly encouraging, and when he read a paper on the process of manufacturing steel without fuel before the British Association for the Advancement of Science, it is said that every British steelmaker roared with laughter at the "crazy Frenchman" and that it was voted not to mention his silly paper in the minutes of the association.[1]

To-day, on the same authority, "there are more than a hundred Bessemer converters in the United States," and they "breathe iron into steel at the rate of eighteen billion pounds a year"—"two and a quarter millions of pounds every hour of the day and night."

With their companion open-hearth converters and

[1] "On the 13th of August, 1856, the author had the honor of reading a paper before the mechanical section of the British Association at Cheltenham. This paper, entitled 'The Manufacture of Malleable Iron and Steel without Fuel,' was the first account that appeared shadowing forth the important manufacture now generally known as the Bessemer process.

"It was only through the earnest solicitation of Mr. George Rennie, the then president of the mechanical section of this association, that the invention was, at that early stage of its development, thus prominently brought forward; and when the author reflects on the amount of labor and expenditure of time and money that were found to be still necessary before any commercial results from the working of the process were obtained, he has no doubt whatever but that, if the paper at Cheltenham had not then been read, the important system of manufacture to which it gave rise would to this hour have been wholly unknown."

Henry Bessemer, "On the Manufacture of Cast Steel: Its Progress and Employment as a Substitute for Wrought Iron." British Association for the Advancement of Science, Report, 1865. Mechanical Science Section, pp. 165–6.

attendant furnaces and mills, they not only hold the site of the old fort but make a circle of glowing fortresses around the valley—in Buffalo, in Birmingham, Alabama, and in the "red crags" of the Rockies at Pueblo, beneath Pike's Peak. And within ten years a whole new city,[1] not far from Chicago, on Lake Michigan, has been made to order. A river was turned from its course, a town was moved, and an entirely new city was constructed with homes for nearly twenty thousand workmen near a square mile of furnaces and mills.

The attention of the world has been centred upon the millionaires whom this mighty trade has made. The very book which I have quoted so literally carries as its luring subtitle, "The Story of a Thousand Millionaires." "A huge, exclusive preoccupation with dollar-getting," says H. G. Wells. But an occupation that finds the red earth and the white earth, carries it hundreds of miles to where the coal is stored or the gas is ready to be lighted, assembles the labor from Europe, and converts that red earth, with almost human possibilities, into rails and locomotives (that have together made a republic such as the United States possible), into forty-story buildings and watch-springs, into bridges and mariners' needles, into battle-ships and lancets, into almost every conceivable instrument of human use, can hardly be rightfully called a preoccupation with dollar-getting, though it has brought the perplexing problem that has so much disturbed the hopes of democracy, dreaming of such masterful children, producers, and poets, yet dreading the very inequalities that their energies create.

[1] Gary, Indiana.

There comes constantly the question as to how all this initiative which has been so titanic is to be reconciled with the general good—a world-wide and insistent problem, which will be more serious there when the neighborliness is not so intimate. But the new neighborly element will be found, we must believe, as an element has been found for the strengthening of steel.

I was told by a chemist, when visiting the mills in Pittsburgh, that every steelmaker knows that a little titanium mixed with the molten iron after its boiling in air multiplies its tensile strength immeasurably, though no one knows just why it is so. Perhaps, in the plans for the new cities of Pittsburgh and Chicago, we have sign of the social titanium that will increase the tensile strength of democracy in the places where the stress and strain are greatest.

But my concern just now is that the reader shall see how the valley first explored by the French has given and is giving bread to the world, and has postponed the dread augury of the Malthusian doctrine; how the larger valley of the explorers of the lens and crucible, Lavoisier and Berthelot, is opening into infinite distances; and how the under valley, when breathed upon by the air, has given its wealth to the over valley —and through this all to realize that France's geographical descendants are out of those three valleys evoking, making, a new world.

For they are a people of makers—of new-age poets, not mere workers glorying in the shafts of their goads, wakeful to adorn their work and keep clean the furnace, and making their "craft their prayer" (an impossibility in these days of the high division of labor) but rough, noisy, grimy, braggart creators, caring not for the straightness of the furrow unless it produces more, the beauty of the goad unless it promotes speed, the cleanliness of the furnace unless it increases the output, or the craft itself; but only of the product, the thing led forth, and its value to the world. If so much is said of the dollar, it is because the dollar is the kilo-watt, the measure of the product. And while we have not yet found the ideal way of distributing what has been led forth, do not let that fact obscure the world service of these new-world Prometheans, who have carried the fire to a mortal use which even the gods of Greece could not have imagined and have turned the air itself into fuel to feed it.

A young man, born son of a stone-mason in that valley, who has been successively a student, clerk, lawyer, solicitor-general of a great railroad, its presi-dent, and later the head of an industry that is carrying electricity over the world, said to me not long ago that he was building a trolley-line in Rome. It seemed a profanation. But if the titular function of the official who holds the highest spiritual office there was once the care of bridges (Pontifex Maximus), will the higher utilization of those bridges not be some day made as poetic, as spiritual, as high a function of state and society?

I see that son of the stone-mason, with blanched face and set jaw, facing and quelling a body of strikers threatening to tear up the tracks along the Chicago River, as brave as Horatius at the bridge across the Tiber. There is a vivid picture of democracy's great-est problem in that valley. Then I see him flinging almost in a day a new bridge across the Tiber. There is a companion picture, a gleam of democracy's poesy.

One writing of the habitants of one of those smoky valley cities said: "They are not below poetry but above it." Rather are they making it—rough, virile, formless, rhymeless. It reminds me of some of Walt Whitman's verses that at first seem but catalogues of homely objects on his horizon but that by and by are singing, in some rough rhythm, a song that stirs one's blood.

Oil of rocks, led from cisterns in the valley, that Bonnecamp found so dark and gloomy on the Céloron journey, to the lamp of the academician and the peasant; wheat from millions of age-long fallow acres to keep the world from fear of hunger; flour from the grinding of the mills of the saint to whom La Salle prayed; wagons, sewing-machines, ploughs, harvesters from the places of the portages; bridges, steel rails, cars, ready-made structures of twenty stories from the places of the forts; unheard-of fruits from the trees of the new garden of the Hesperides (under the magic of such as Burbank); flowers from wildernesses! Would Whitman were come back to put all together into a song of the valley that should acquaint our ears with that rugged music—that rugged music wakened by the plash of the paddle and the swirl of the water in the wake of the Frenchman's canoe! As he is not, I can only wish that you who have read these chapters may have intimation of it, as not long ago in New York, standing before a rough, unsightly, entirely isolate frame in a university corridor—where there were heard normally only the noises of closing doors and shuffling feet—I put a receiver to my ears and heard, in the midst of these nearer, every-day noises, some distant cello whose vibrations were but waiting in the air to be heard. Some said there was but the slamming of doors, but I had evidence of my own ears that the music was there. I have not imagined this song of the valley, nor have I improvised it. Its vibrations which I myself feel are but transmitted as best an imperfect, detached frame in the midst of other sounds and interests can.

CHAPTER XVII

THE THOUGHT OF TO-MORROW

THE clearing in the forest for the log schoolhouse
where Lincoln got his only formal schooling il-
lustrates the beginning of the field of public
provision for culture, a territory then made up in that
valley largely of the white acres set apart from the domain of Louis XIV for the maintenance of public
schools. I can tell you out of my own experience how
meagre that provision was. Out on the open prairie
a frame building—the successor of the log cabin—was
built. I think the ground on which it stood had never
been ploughed. I remember hearing, as if yesterday,
a farmer's boy reciting in it one day what we thought
a piece of lasting eloquence: "Not many generations
ago where you now sit encircled by all the embellishments of life, the wild fox dug his hole unscared and the
Indian hunter pursued the panting deer; here lived and
learned another race of beings"—little realizing that,
except in the encircling embellishments, we were sitting on such a site, and that we were the "new race of
beings" and much nearer to the stone-age man than
were they who built the ancient wall just back of the
Pantheon in Paris.

The thought of the nation for to-morrow was tangibly represented only by that hut twenty feet square,
with its few nourishing acres, most primitively furnished, a teacher of no training in the art of teaching,

a few tons of coal in a shed, a box of crayons, and perhaps a map. The master made his own fires and
swept unaided, or with the aid of his pupils, the floor.
When, years later, in a larger building on the same
site I came to be master of the same school, and
gathered for work at night the farmers' sons who could
not leave the fields by day, except in winter, I even
paid the expense of the light. Now, if not on that
site, certainly on thousands of others, in schools springing from such beginnings, the community provides not
only chalk and electric light, but pencils, paper, books,
lenses, compasses, lathes, libraries, gymnastic ap-
paratus, pianos, and even food, if not free, at any rate
at cost, in addition to trained teachers, trained in public
normal schools, and janitors, and automatic ventila-
tors to insure pure air, and thermostats to preserve an
even temperature. The public has become father,
mother, physician, and guild master as well as teacher
of the new generation.

The public has even become the nurse, for in most
of the large cities the kindergarten has become transformed into a public institution which takes the child
from the home, sometimes almost from the cradle,
but more often from the street, at the age of four,
five, or six years, and keeps it until it is ready for the
tuitions of the elementary grades. In St. Louis, just
across and up the river from Fort Chartres, where the
initial municipal experiment was made, there are now
more than two hundred and eighty-three such schools.

It has, moreover, gone beyond these serious maternal
employments. The strenuous civilization of the west
has insisted that every man shall work. But now
that it has succeeded in this, it is not only beginning

to insist that he shall not work too much—the maximum hours of labor in many employments being fixed by law—but he is being taught how to play wisely. One of the most stirring books that I have read recently, "The Spirit of Play and the City Streets," is an appeal written by Miss Addams, of Chicago, whose noble work has been for years among the people who live close by Marquette's portage hut—an appeal for the recognition of the play instincts and their conversion into a greater permanent human happiness. There are statistics which intimate that the per-hour efficiency of men in some parts of America, whose number of hours of labor has been lessened, has also been diminished—diminished because of their imprudent use of their leisure, of their play time. So the thought of social experts is turning to teaching children to play wisely, they whose ancestors were compelled to leave off playing.

I speak of this here to intimate how far in its thought of the man of the future, the nation of to-morrow, that valley has travelled—first of all in its elementary training, and within much less than a half century, from chalk to grand pianos, and from inexpensive tuitions in reading, writing, and arithmetic to the dearer tuitions in singing, basket-weaving, cooking, sewing, carpentering, drawing, and the trained teaching of the old elementary subjects, with the addition of history, algebra, physiology, Latin, and modern languages.

When the State of Iowa was admitted into the Union, in 1846, there were 100 log schoolhouses in use, valued each at $125. The latest statistics I have at hand show that in 1912 the average value of the 13,870 school properties in the State was $2,170, that the average expenditure for each pupil was $28.86, and for each inhabitant $6.58, and that of the 507,109 pupils enrolled in the State only six per cent were in private schools—the average for the States of the west varying from less than one per cent to sixteen per cent.

The elementary school followed the frontier at even pace. It was usually the first public building of every community, large or small. That everybody saw it for what it was, I cannot maintain; but that it was the symbol of the nation of to-morrow, borne daily before the people of the present is certain. The westerners carried rails in the Lincoln campaign, in their pride of his humble birth and vocation; they carried miniature log cabins in another campaign in exaltation of another frontier hero. They pictured ploughs and axes on the shields of their commonwealths. But if one were to seek a symbol for the democracy of that valley, one could find none more appropriate than the image of a frontier schoolhouse. It is the most poetical thing of all that western landscape, when it is seen for what it is, though it is not always architecturally imposing. A signal-box, says an English essayist, such as one sees along the railroads, is only called a signal-box, but it is the house of life and death, a place "where men in an agony of vigilance light blood-red and sea-green fires to keep other men from death." A post-box is only called a post-box; it is a sanctuary of human words, a place to which "friends and lovers commit their messages, conscious that when they have done so they are sacred, and not to be touched not only by others but even by themselves."[1] And so a school-

[1] G. K. Chesterton, on Mr. Rudyard Kipling, in his "Heretics," p. 41.

house is only called a schoolhouse, but it is a place where the invisible spirits of the past meet in the present the nascent spirits of the future—the meeting-house of the nation of yesterday and to-morrow.   And I would show that image of the schoolhouse upon a field of white, as suggesting those white acres conse-crated of the domain of Louis XIV to the children of the west.

Some years ago, when walking across the island of Porto Rico in the West Indies, just after its occupation and annexation by the United States, I met in the in-terior mountains one morning a man carrying upon his shoulders a basket filled with flowers, as it seemed to me at a distance.   As he approached, however, I saw that he was bearing the dead body of his child, with flowers about it, to burial in consecrated ground miles away.   The first task of the new government there, as in the western States, was to make fields con-secrated for the living child, to set apart sites for schoolhouses—the place for the common school.

That the common school has not in itself brought millennial conditions to the valley we are aware, even as universal man suffrage has not brought the full fruits of democracy.   French philosophers and American pa-triots alike have expected too much perhaps of an im-perfect human nature.   But they have made their high demand of the only institution that can give in full measure what is sought in a democracy.

First, it teaches the child the way and the means by which the race has come out of barbarism and some-thing of the rigor of the disciplines by which civilization has been learned.

Second, it gives this teaching to the whole nation

of to-morrow. There are over ten million children in the public schools of that valley alone in America, and, as I stated above, less than eight per cent in the private schools; in the State of Indiana, where Lincoln had his slight schooling, less than three per cent are in private schools—that is, practically the entire people of the coming generation will have had some tuition of the common school, some equality of fitting.

Third, as is to be inferred from the second fact, children of rich and poor, of banker and mechanic, doctor and tradesman, come together, and in a perfectly natural companionship, though in the great cities, where there is less homogeneity, this mingling is somewhat disturbed by social stratification and the great masses of immigrants.

So is the motto of the French Republic written the length and breadth of that valley, though it may never actually be seen upon a lintel or door-post: the "liberty" of access to the knowledges which are to assist in making men as free as they can be; an elevating "equality" such as a State can give to men of unequal endowments, capacities, and ambitions; and a "fraternity" which is unconscious of else than real differences.

I gave intimation in an earlier chapter of the cosmopolitan quality of the human material gathered into those houses of prophecy. There is separation of Caucasian from African in the south, and there is more or less unwilling association of Caucasian and Oriental in places of the far west on the Pacific slope, but except for these and for individual instances where, for example, the social extremes are brought together, these minglings are but microcosms of the State itself.

The schools are not in that valley, in any sense, places provided by wealth for poverty, by one class for another —charity schools; they are the natural meeting-houses of democracy, with as little atmosphere of pauper or class schools as the highways, on which even the President must obey the custom which controls the humblest.

And let me say in passing: there is no body of men and women in America more useful to the State, more high-minded, more patriotic, than the army of public school-teachers—our great soldiery of peace.

They are a body six times the size of our standing army—more than a half-million in number (547,289) —recruited from the best stock we have and animated by higher purposes, more unselfish motives than any other half-million public or private vocationalists of America. The total expenditure for the common schools is but four and a half times the appropriation for the standing army, though the number of teachers is six times (which intimates how little we pay our public school-teachers relatively—seventy-eight dollars per month to men, fifty-eight dollars to women teachers). These men and women, who take the place of father, mother, adviser, and nurse in the new industrial and social order—receive about one and a quarter cents a day per inhabitant, man, woman, and child—a little more than two sous per day.

It is this two-sous-per-day army that is our hope of to-morrow. It is primarily upon its efficient valor that the future of democracy depends. For it is they, rather than the parents, especially in the great cities and in communities of large foreign elements, who have its making in their hands. Without them the nation of to-morrow would be defenseless. She would have to increase her standing army of soldiers, and even then, with the multitudes of individual ignorances, malices, selfishnesses growing in her own valleys and being disembarked by millions at her ports, she would be powerless to defend her ideals.

One whom I have already quoted as speaking so disparagingly of Chicago said that the most touching sight he saw in America was the marching of the phalanxes of the nation of to-morrow past one of the generals or colonels of that standing army of teachers. It was not in Chicago, but it might have been. This particular phalanx had not been in America long. They were singing "Sweet Land of Liberty" as they marched, swishing their flags, and then they paused and repeated in broken speech:

"Flag of our great republic, inspirer in battle, guardian of our homes, whose stars and stripes stand for bravery, purity, truth, and union, we salute thee! We, the natives of distant lands who find rest under thy folds, do pledge our hearts, our lives, and our sacred honor to love and protect thee, our country, and the liberty of the American people forever."[1] A little florid, you may say. "But think," said the English visitor, even as he passed out into the filthy street, "think of the promise of it! Think of the flower of belief that may spring from this warm sowing!"

And what gives most promise now is that this tuition has assumed a more positive interest in the nation of to-morrow. The pioneer school was a place of discipline, a place of fraternity, and it had the co-operation of the home discipline and of the discipline of the primitive industrial life in which the boy joined

[1] H. G. Wells, "Future in America," p. 205.

even during his school years.   But that tuition was in a sense as unsocialized as was the democracy of that day.   It was assumed that this meagre training would equip the boy with all the tools of citizenship. . Being able to read, write, and cipher, his own instincts and interests would somehow procure good government and happiness.   Whatever patriotic stimulus his school gave him, as I recall out of my experience, was through a history which engendered a feeling of hostility toward England.   That is being succeeded by a positive programme that thinks very definitely of the boy's fullest development and of his social spiritualization.   The schoolhouse has become, or is in the way of becoming, the civic centre of the nation.

But on top of the eight years' training of the elementary school, which was considered at first the full measure of the obligation of the community, the State in that region came to build additional years of discipline—the high schools, first to equip young men for colleges or universities and then to fit them for the meeting of the more highly complex and specialized problems of life.   These schools multiplied in the upper Mississippi Valley at an extraordinary rate after the elementary schools had prepared the way.   In the northern part of that valley alone sixteen hundred were established between 1860 and 1902.   And there is hardly a community of five thousand inhabitants that has not its fully organized and well-equipped high or secondary school; while even towns of a thousand inhabitants or less have made such provision.

Near the site of the village of the Illinois Indians, the village where Père Marquette went from hut to hut in his ministries just before his death journey;

where La Salle gathered about his rock-built castle his red allies to the number of thousands and attempted to build up what La Barre, in his letter to Louis XIV, characterized as an imaginary kingdom for himself—there is a beautiful river city, bearing the Indian name of "Ottawa," and in the midst of it a large building that was for me the capital of an imaginary kingdom, my one-time world, though it is called a township high school. I speak of it because it is typical of the instruction and influence that have come out of the long past, and that are looking into the long future, in thousands of the towns and cities that have each about them as many aspiring men, women, and youth as La Salle had savage souls about his solitary castle in the wilderness.

These are the new Rocks St. Louis, these the eagles' nests of the new Nouvelle France—I have visited scores of them—at Peoria, that was Fort Crèvecœur; at Joliet, where is now one of the best-equipped schools in the valley; at Marquette, upon Lake Superior; at Chicago, where I spoke one day to four thousand high-school boys and girls, for in most of these schools the boys and girls are taught together. The valley has one of these schools every few miles, where are gathered for the higher, sterner disciplines of democracy those who wish to prepare themselves for its larger service.

Their courses are four years in length, and, though varying widely, have each a core of mathematics, English, foreign languages, and either science or manual training or commerce. In some large cities the schools are differentiated as general, manual training, and commercial.

But the States of that valley have not stopped here. With the encouragement of national grants—again from the great domain of Louis XIV—they have established universities with colleges of liberal arts and sciences, and schools of agriculture, forestry, mining, engineering, pharmacy, veterinary surgery, commerce, law, medicine, and philosophy. There is not a State in all that valley that has not its university in name and in most instances in fact. They admit both men and women and there is no fee, or only a nominal fee, to residents of the State. These are the great strategic centres and strongholds of the new democracy.

A little way back from Cadillac's fort on the Detroit River is one, the oldest, the University of Michigan—founded in 1837—with 5,805 students. A few years ago I addressed there, at commencement, over eight hundred candidates for degrees and diplomas in law, medicine, pharmacy, liberal arts and science.

A little way from the Fox-Wisconsin portage is another, the University of Wisconsin, with 5,970 students. A few years ago I sat in that beautiful seat of learning among men from all parts of the world offering their congratulations at its jubilee. And they sat in silk gowns only less ornate than Nicolet's when he came over the rim of the basin to treat with the Winnebagoes—whom he had supposed to be Chinese mandarins. I heard, too, the graduates receive their degrees on theses ranging from the poetry of a lesser Greek poet to the "pancreas of a cat." I spent a month in its library at a later time and found it superior for my purposes to any other in America.

No higher institution of learning in America is more strongly possessed by the spirit of the ministry of scholarship directly to the people. It needs sorely advice of the arts that centre in Paris, as most of those universities do. It needs advice not of industry but of the indefatigable disinterestedness of the French.

Behind the Falls of St. Anthony in the Mississippi River, first described and named by Father Hennepin, is the University of Minnesota, with 6,642 students. The principal deity of the Sioux was supposed to live under these falls, and Hennepin, the priest of Artois, speaks in his journal of hearing one of the Indians at the portage around the falls, in loud and lamenting voice haranguing the spirit to whom he had just hung a robe of beaver-skin among the branches of a tree. The buildings that are and are planned to be on this site would tell better than a chapter of description what a single State has done and is purposing at this portage of St. Anthony of Padua, where hardly more than a lifetime ago the savage was sacrificing beaver-skins to the god of the Mississippi. There are many great laboratories and academic buildings upon that high shore at present, but a score more are in prospect for this mighty democratic university of letters and science, law and medicine, that will house in other centuries perhaps not merely the appeased spirit of the Mississippi but such learning as is in Paris or was in Padua, whose saint is still remembered by the falls; for the university has the necessary means. When the Église of the Sorbonne, which Richelieu had consecrated, was being built, the French priests out along the shores of Superior were preparing the way for this new-world university. Certain lands in that iron region which they first explored were given by the nation as dowry to the university. These were not

thought to be valuable, as at the time of the grant the
most valuable timber and farming land had been sold.
Fifteen years ago, more or less, a train-load of iron ore
was brought down from that region to Allouez, a town
on the lake named in memory of the priest of St.
Esprit—and now the lands of the university are valued
at from thirty to fifty millions of dollars.[1]

One might follow the River Colbert all the way down
the valley and trace its branches to the mountains on
either side, and find in every State some such fortress:
in Iowa a university with 2,255 students; in Illinois
one with 4,330; and so on to the banks of the river in
Texas where La Salle died—and there learn that the
most extensive of all in its equipment may some day
rise. These, besides the scores of institutions of private
foundation, but compelled to the same public spirit
as the State universities, tell with what thought of
to-morrow the geographical descendants of France are
doing their tasks of to-day, where Allouez and Marquette, Hennepin and Du Lhut, Radisson and Groseilliers, and the Sieur de la Salle wandered and suffered
and died but yesterday.

Their paths have opened and multiplied not only
into streets of cities and highways and railroads but
into curricula of the world's wisdoms, gathered from
Paris and Oxford and Edinburgh and Berlin and
Bologna and Prague and Salamanca, even as their
students are being gathered from all peoples. Perrot
spoke truer than he knew when he said to the savages
of Wisconsin, "I am but the dawn of the day"; and
the Indian chief who first of human beings welcomed
Europeans the other side of the Mississippi River

[1] "Forty Years at the University of Minnesota," p. 243.

spoke in prophecy when he said that the earth had grown more beautiful with their coming.

The common school, the high school, the college and university—the common school compulsory for every child; the high school open to every boy and girl, without regard to race, creed, or riches; the university accessible to every young man and woman who has the ambition, the endurance, to make his way or her way to the frontiers of the spirit and endure their hardships! For I think of these universities as the free lands that were out upon the borders of that valley, except that this frontier of the mind will never, never find its limit. There will always be a frontier beyond, for new settlers, new squatters, of the telescope which makes the universe smaller, of the microscope which enlarges it, of the written word, the spoken word, the unknown quantities, the philosophies of life. Do we not see the illimitable fields opening even beyond the vision of those men of the crucible and retort, who are but leading the new farmers on to visible fields of increasing richness?

Hardly less cosmopolitan are the men of science and letters who are actually in those regions, and only less so those tens of thousands, who, like migrants of the earlier days, are going forward, many to the farthest, lonesomest frontiers of knowledge, but all to something beyond their immediate ancestral lot or field.

I am not thinking of the additions to the world's learning in all this, great as it is but impossible of appraisement. Nor am I thinking chiefly of the industrial and material advantages. I think it was some bacteriological discovery, known as the Babcock test, resulting in a great improvement in the making of

butter, that gave the University of Wisconsin its first
wide sympathetic support. It was the discovery by
a professor in one of the western universities of the
means of inoculating with some fatal disease, and so
exterminating, an insect that destroyed wheat and
oats, which gave that professor a chancellorship, I am
told, and his university more liberal appropriations.
But those achievements and fames, while not to be
belittled, I have no wish to catalogue and recite here.
I am thinking of the social value of this great public
educational system that is thinking constantly of to-
morrow—of the world markets of to-morrow, to some
extent, to which these curricula, as railroads' and ships'
courses, lead; of the world's letters of to-morrow, perhaps; but more specifically and more especially of the
higher happiness of those particular regions and the
success of its democracy. I am thinking of what these
institutions of the people's own devising are doing
toward the making of a homogeneous spirit, in which
individual, disinterested, and varied achievement will
have a liberty to grow—as perhaps in no other soil of
earth.

Democritus said two thousand years and more ago:
"Education and nature are similar. For education
transforms the man, and in transforming him creates
in him a new nature." The State in its three institutions—the common school, the high school, the college
and university—has many in its care and under its
tuitions for fifteen, sixteen, seventeen years, and in
these tuitions has she created in her children a new
nature, whatever their ancestry or place of birth.
Memories of Europe's forges and trees, or fields of
roses and golden mountains, and even of Asia's wil-

dernesses, are in the names of many who enter those doors; the memories of other languages are in the muscles of their tongues or the formation of their organs of speech. Like the ancient Ephraimites at the fords of Jordan, they cannot "frame to pronounce" certain words. And memories of persecution or of vassalage are in the physical and mental attitudes of some. But they are all reborn of a genealogy impersonal but loftier in its gifts than any mere personal heritage—a genealogy which, like that of the children of Deucalion, begins in the earth itself, the free soil.

I have often thought and spoken of how artificial differences disappear when, let us say, Smith (English) and Schmidt (German) and Cohen (Hebrew), Coletti (Italian) and D'Artagnan (French) and McGregor (Scotch) and Olsen (Scandinavian) and McCarthy (Irish) and Winslow (of old America) travel together through the parasangs of the "Anabasis," or together follow Cæsar into Gaul, or together compute a solar parallax, or build an arch, or do any one of a thousand things that have no national boundaries or racial characteristics. This is an extreme but not an unheard-of assembling of elements which the State has the task of assimilating to its own ideals.

I have not spoken, I cannot speak, of methods of that teaching, of its shortcomings, of it crudities in many places, of its general want of appreciation of form and color (of its particular need of France there), of its utilitarian inclinations, and of its eager haste. The essential thing that I have wanted to say is that this valley is not only more democratic socially and politically than any other part of America, unless it be that narrow strip farther west, but is also more consciously and vitally and constantly concerned about the nation of to-morrow.

I spoke of the flaming ingot of steel swinging in the smoky ravine by the site of Fort Duquesne as the symbol of the new human metal that is made of the mingling of men of varied race, tradition, and ideals in the labor of that continent. But above that in a clearer sky shines a more hopeful symbol—the house of the school, the meeting-place of the invisible spirits, the place of prophecy, pictured against a white field.

The historians have traced the origins of these institutions to New England, to England, to Germany, to Greece. It is not remembered that France went first and hallowed the fields. But it is my hope that out in that valley, once a year, school and university may be led to look back to the men who there ventured all for the "greater glory of God" and majesty of France and found a field for the greater freedom and fraternity of mankind.

My own thought goes back to the place by the St. Charles River where Cartier's boat, which he could not take back to St. Malo because so many of his men had died, was left to be buried by the river, the place where Montcalm gathered his shattered army after the defeat on the Plains of Abraham. It was there that a structure once stood, made of planks hewn out of the forest, plastered with mud and thatched with long grass from the meadows. It was the residence of Notre Dame des Anges, the house from which the first martyrs were to go forth toward the west. This was, says Parkman, the cradle of the great mission of New France. And to this my thought goes as the precursor of the university in the Valley of the New Democracy.

CHAPTER XVIII

"THE MEN OF ALWAYS"

IF one travels along the lower St. Lawrence in summer, one sees the narrow strips of the one-time great seigniories, clinging like ribbons of varied colors, green, gold, and brown, to the ancient river, of Cartier and Champlain. There is on each strip, a little way back from the river, a picturesque cottage, usually thatched, not roofed by shingles, with its outbuildings close about, such as Longfellow writes of in Acadia—memories of homes "which the peasants of Normandy built in the reign of the Henries." There is usually on each a section of meadow for the cattle, a section of tilled field for the wheat and corn and vegetables and a section of woodland for the fire-wood —each strip, so divided, being a complete miniature seigniory. Everything is neat. One feels that not a wisp of hay is lost (for it was in haying time that I passed), that every tree is as carefully watched as a child, that whatever is taken from the fields they are not impoverished. The living owners, when they go to their graves, leave their little patches of earth as rich as they found them. There is no hurrying. The habitants go at the pace of their oxen. They are thrifty, apparently contented, conservers of what they have; they spend prudently for to-day; they save for to-morrow—not for the to-morrow of the nation, but for the to-morrow of the family. They are avowedly individualistic, nepotic conservationists and only in effect national.

This is one picture. I put beside it another. Out on the farther edge of the Mississippi Valley one finds the other extreme. Within the past twenty-two years certain tracts of vacant land have been purchased by the government from the Indians (and let me here say that the government has been trying to deal fairly with these people; mistakes have been made, but I should say that the nation had in its recent treatment of them, despite reports I have heard in Paris, pauperized rather than robbed them). These tracts have been opened to settlement—all the rest of the great public domain that was immediately desirable having been occupied, as we have seen. When, in 1889, the first of these tracts, nearly two million acres, was to be opened, twenty thousand people were waiting just outside its borders—some on swift horses, some in wagons or buggies, and some in railroad trains. When the signal was given there was a race across the border and a scramble for farm sites; and on the part of the passengers on the trains, for town lots, when the trains had reached the predetermined sites of cities. At the close of the first day the future capital of what has for many years been a State had a population of several thousand inhabitants living in tents, and within a hundred days a population of fifteen thousand people, mostly men, an electric system in operation, a street-railway under contract, streets, alleys, parks, boulevards, stores, and bridges, four thousand houses under construction, five banks, fifteen hotels, fifty grocery stores, six printing-offices, and three daily papers— about as striking and unpleasant a contrast to that peaceful life on the St. Lawrence as one can well imagine. Practically all of the available land (nearly two million acres) was taken during the course of a few days.

At the later opening of another tract one hundred thousand persons took part in the race for the "last of the people's land." And these scenes but illustrate the rough races to the gold-fields and the iron mountains and the oil-wells, in eagerness to seize whatever earth had to offer and turn it to immediate wealth—rough, restless precursors, producers, poets eager for to-day, yet coming by and by, as we have seen, to be ready to spend for to-morrow, building schools and universities, enlarging the field of public provision and service, and filling the land, once neighborly, individualistic, with institutions of philanthropy.

But the habitant of that farther valley is considerate neither of himself nor of generous nature. He is ready to spend his all, or her all, of to-day for to-day and for to-morrow, and to some extent unselfishly, but not to save it. He lives "angerously" and takes all the risks. His thought of the future is not nepotic or thrifty; it is likely to be altruistic, publicistic. I suppose that the constitution and laws of Oklahoma, whose land was the last to be added to the public domain and its commonwealth among the last to the roll of States, has been more generous-minded toward its children than any other. It set apart not only sections sixteen and thirty-six in every township for the public schools; it reserved two more sections in every township for kindred uses. But in all this, as I pointed out, it is spending for the future, not saving, hoarding.

The nepotic conservationist of the St. Lawrence, fixed in his place, saves because if he leaves but an exhausted field behind him he is robbing his children and grandchildren of their rightful, personal heritage. The "boomer" of Oklahoma exploits and spends lavishly because of a sublime confidence in the illimitability of the resources of nature and in the resourcefulness of the coming generations.

But the natural scientists—the foresters, the physiographers, the geologists—have within a very few years been making themselves heard in warning. They have said that "the mountains of France, of Spain, and China have been denuded of their forests in large measure so that the supply of wood is inadequate to meet the needs of the people,"[1] that "in Spain and Italy, though warm countries, the people suffer more from the cold than in America because of insufficient fuel,"[2] that "one-half of the people of the world go to bed hungry,"[3] or at any rate insufficiently nourished for the next day's work. But few listened to them except in the hills and in the valleys of abandoned farms. France, Italy, Spain, China were remote. The optimism fostered of new teeming acres and newly discovered mines was heedless of the warning. It tore down barns and built bigger, and it gave even more generously to the need of the hour and the day.

But the scientists came even nearer home in their studies and statistics. These are some of the ominous and disturbing facts that are getting to the ears of the people out of their laboratories and experiment stations:

[1] C. R. Van Hise, "Conservation of Natural Resources in the United States," p. 3.
[2] Van Hise, p. 2.   [3] Van Hise, p. 3.

The coal-fields of the United States (which lie almost exclusively in and upon the eastern and western edges of the Mississippi Valley) were, at the rate at which coal was used a few decades ago, practically inexhaustible. But the per-capita consumption has increased from about a ton in 1870 to 5.6 tons in 1907.[1] Up to 1908, 7,240,000,000[2] tons had been mined, but over ten million tons were wasted in the mining of seven billions. You may recall the prophecy which I quoted earlier, that if the mining and wasting go on at the same rate of increase as in the past few decades the supposed illimitable fields will be exhausted in one hundred and fifty years—that is by the year 2050.[3] This is one of the statistics of those watchmen on the walls who, instead of standing in high places with telescopes, sit at microscopes or over tables of figures. That seems a long period of time, one hundred and fifty years, but it was only a little longer ago that a French explorer saw the first signs of coal in that valley along the Illinois, and, as the scientist has intimated, there is no reason why we should not expect a future of thousands of years for the coal that has been thousands or millions of years in the making.

The petroleum and natural-gas fields are also nearly all in that valley or on its edges. (I think it was in the narrow valley of La Belle Rivière, which Père Bonnecamp found so dark on that Céloron expedition, that this oil of the rocks was first found.)[4] If we as-

---

[1] Van Hise, p. 23.   [2] Van Hise, p. 25.   [3] Van Hise, p. 25.
[4] Natural gas and burning springs were early known to the French pioneers and Jesuits who penetrated the Iroquois country, as the following extracts show:
"It was during this interval that, in order to pass away the time, I went

sume that the fields have all been discovered and that
the present rate of exploitation is to continue, the supply of petroleum will be exhausted by 1935 (twenty-
one years), or, if the present production goes on without increase, in ninety years (*i. e.*, eighty-six years),[1]
and that of natural gas in twenty-five years (*i. e.*,
twenty-one years from 1914).[2]

Iron, the metal which the Indians worshipped as
a spirit when they first saw it in the hands of the
French, a substance so precious that their name for
it meant "all kinds of good," has, too, been taken
with feverish haste from its ancient places. Joliet and

with M. de LaSalle, under the escort of two Indians, about four leagues
south of the village where we were staying, to see a very extraordinary
spring. Issuing from a moderately high rock, it forms a small brook.
The water is very clear but has a bad odor, like that of the mineral marshes
of Paris, when the mud on the bottom is stirred with the foot. I applied a
torch and the water immediately took fire and burned like brandy, and was
not extinguished until it rained. This flame is among the Indians a sign of
abundance or sterility according as it exhibits the contrary qualities. There
is no appearance of sulphur, saltpetre or any other combustible material.
The water has not even any taste, and I can neither offer nor imagine any
better explanation, than that it acquires this combustible property by passing over some aluminous land."—Galinee's journal, 1669, in "Marshall
Historical Writings," p. 209.

"... The spring in the direction of Sonnontouan is no less wonderful;
for its water—being of the same nature as the surrounding soil, which has
only to be washed in order to obtain perfectly pure sulphur—ignites when
shaken violently, and yields sulphur when boiled. As one approaches
nearer to the country of the Cats, one finds heavy and thick water, which
ignites like brandy, and boils up in bubbles of flame when fire is applied to
it. It is, moreover, so oily, that all our Savages use it to anoint and grease
their heads and their bodies."—"Jesuit Relations, 1657," 43 : 261.

Pierre Boucher (governor of Three Rivers in 1653–8 and 1662–7) thus
mentions the mineral products of Canada, in his "Histoire véritable et
naturelle de la Nouvelle France" (Paris, 1664), chap. I: "Springs of salt
water have been discovered, from which excellent salt can be obtained; and
there are others, which yield minerals. There is one in the Iroquois Country,
which produces a thick liquid, resembling oil, and which is used in place
of oil for many purposes."—"Jesuit Relations," 8 : 289.

[1] Van Hise, p. 48   [2] Van Hise, p. 56.

Marquette saw deposits of this ore near the mouth of the Ohio in 1673, but it was a century and a half before the harvesting of this crop, down among the rocks for millions of years before, began. And now, if no new fields are found and the increased use goes on at the rate of the last three decades, all the available high-grade ore will have become pig iron and steel billets, bridges, battle-ships, sky-scrapers, and loco-motives, and all kinds of goods, within the next three decades.[1]

The forests of the United States—the forests pri-meval, with the voice of whose murmuring pines and hemlocks Longfellow begins his sad story of the Aca-dians—contained approximately one billion acres,[2] a region not conterminous with, but almost as large as, the Mississippi Valley. Of that great, tempering, be-nign shadow over the continent, tempering its heat, giving shelter from its cold, restraining the waters, there is left about 65 per cent in acreage and not more than one-half the merchantable timber—five hundred million acres gone in a century and a half.[3]

And as to the land itself—the land first symbolized in the tuft of earth that St. Lusson lifted toward the sky that day in 1671 at Sault Ste. Marie, when he took possession of all the land between the seas of the north and west and south—in the first place, the loss each year from erosion is six hundred and ten million cubic yards.[4] This is, of course, inconsiderable in a short period but in a long period of years means a mighty loss of nourishing soil. With this loss is that of nitro-

---

[1] Van Hise, p. 68.   [2] Van Hise, p. 210.   [3] Van Hise, p. 210.
[4] Van Hise, p. 307, quoted from W. J. Spillman, "Report National Con-servation Commission," 3 : 257–262.

gen, potassium, and phosphorus, things of which the
farmer had not even heard the names a few years ago.
The yield of farms in the United States during the
last forty years does not show a decreased average,
but it must be remembered that in this period there
have been brought under cultivation new and virgin
acres, which have in their bountiful yield kept up the
general average.   One authority says that, taking the
country by regions and by districts and considering
what has actually happened, he is led to the conclusion
that the fertility of the soil for 50 per cent of our country has been lessened.[1]

The significance of these facts lies in the desire of
the people to know the truth and seek a remedy.

In a sense the public domain has been exhausted.
The pick of the land has been pre-empted, occupied.
But if it is to grow with all its crops, and to put forth
with all its products such a public spirit as this, France
will have given to America a treasure infinitely more
valuable than the land itself which her explorers gave
to Europe and the world.

The beaver, which the French regarded as the first
opulence of the valley, remains only as a synonym for
industry, one of the States being called the "Beaver
State," perhaps in memory of the beaver days but
now in characterization of the beaverlike activity of
its people.   The hide of the buffalo which La Salle
showed in Paris is now almost as great a curiosity in
the valley as it was in Paris in 1680.   Wild beasts now
slink only in the mountains' margins.   Domestic animals, natives of distant lands, live about the dwellings
of men.

[1] Van Hise, p. 299.

Even the streams of water that bore the French into the valley have dwindled, many of them, or are in despair and tears, between shallows and torrents, longing for the forests, it is said by the scientists—longing for the days of the French, the poet would put it. So are the rivers crying, "In the days of Père Marquette" —the days of the "River of the Immaculate Conception." And so are the prophets of science crying as the prophets of inspiration cried of old: O valley of a hundred thousand streams, O valley of a million centuries of rock and iron and earth, O valley of a century of man! The riches of the gathering of a million years are spent in a day. Baldness has come upon the mountains, as upon Gaza of old. The trees have gone down to the waters. The iron has flowed like blood from the hills. The fire of the ground is being given to the air. The sky is filled with smoke. The soil is being carried into the sea; its precious dust of nitrogen and phosphor blown to the ends of the earth. The fresh lands are no more. There are no mines to be had for the asking. The frontier has become as the centre, the new as the old.

But it is not a hopeless prophecy—an unconstructive, pessimistic, lamentation. The way of reparation is made clear.

If I were to speak only of what has been done under the inspiration of that prophecy, I should have little that is definitely measurable to present, but in making a catalogue of the averting advice of that prophecy, I am giving intimation of what will in all probability be done. For the people of that valley are not wittingly going to give their once fertile lands as stones, even to the sons of others who ask for bread, nor their streams as serpents of pestilence to those who ask for fish.

These are some of the items of their constructive conservation programme:

Coal.—The waste in the mining of coal must be reduced from 50 and 150 per cent of the amount taken out to 25, 15, or 10 per cent by the working of upper beds first, the utilization of slack, etc.[1] The reckless waste of coal in the making of coke can be prevented by the use of the right sort of oven. It is estimated that there would be a saving of $50,000,000 per annum if such a substitution were made.[2] The tremendous loss of the power value,[3] from 20 to 33 per cent, and of illuminating value[4] (99 per cent) in coal because of its imperfect consumption can be greatly reduced by the employment of mechanical stokers and other devices. The use of the gas-engine in the place of the steam-engine,[5] the use of power developed from water, and the diffused carbon dioxide in the air tempering the climate are also intimations of forces that may lengthen the life of the coal, 99 per cent of which still remains in the keeping of the valley. It is not too late.[6]

Petroleum.—Its probable life may be lengthened beyond ninety years by its restriction to lubricating and illuminating uses only and by the prevention of its exportation.[7]

Natural Gas.—Its flame is ephemeral at best, but its light may be kept burning a little longer if the prodigious waste is prevented. During 1907 four hun-

[1] Van Hise, pp. 26, 27.   [2] Van Hise, p. 28.
[3] Van Hise, pp. 29, 30.   [4] Van Hise, p. 32.   [5] Van Hise, p. 31.
[6] See "The Coal Resources of the World," International Geological Congress, 1913.
[7] Van Hise, pp. 50–55.

dred billion feet were consumed and almost as great an amount wasted through uncontrolled wells, leaky pipes, etc.[1]

Iron (*and, in less measure, gold, silver, and other metals*), whose life does not, as coal and oil and gas, perish with the using, but some of whose value is lost in the transformation from one state of use to another, needs only to be more economically mined and used.[2] Non-metallic, inexhaustible materials, as stone, clay, cement, should be employed in their stead when possible.[3] Every scrap of iron should be conserved, cry our constructive prophets, even as the Indians treasured it. We may not need it, but succeeding generations will. It may be recast to their use. We are but its trustees.[4]

Forests.[5]—A reduction of the waste in cutting (this is 25 per cent of the total value of the timber cut); of the waste in milling and manufacture, and in turpentining. This last waste is appalling but preventable in full or large measure. The lessening the demand for lumber by a preservative treatment of all merchantable timber. A utilization of by-products. (Undoubtedly science will be most helpful here.) Precautions against fires and their control. Reforestation. Maintenance of forests on what are called essential areas, such as high altitudes and slopes, as tending to prevent floods and erosion. (France here gives most impressive example in planning to bring under con-

[1] Van Hise, p. 58.   [2] Van Hise, p. 68.

[3] I watched day by day for weeks the erection of a great building in Paris, and I noticed how little iron or steel was used as compared with that in such structures in New York. We shall undoubtedly come to that.

[4] See, "Iron Ore Resources of the World," International Geological Congress, 1910.

[5] Van Hise, pp. 223–262.

trol about three thousand torrential streams in the
Alps, Pyrenees, Ardennes, and Cévennes by means,
partly at least, of afforestation, $14,000,000 out of
$40,000,000 being provided for this purpose.[1] Italy,
because of the greatly increased destruction by the
Po, has begun the reforestation of the Apennines to
the extent of a million acres.) Battle with insect pests
and finally the substitution of other materials for
wood, thus not only saving the trees but diminishing
the losses by fire.

Land.[2]—The control of water to prevent erosion,
deep tillage, and contour ploughing. The restoration
of nitrogen and phosphorus by rotation of crops, phos-
phates, fertilizers, and electricity. The destruction of
noxious insects, mammals, and weeds. The reclamation of wet lands. The introduction of new varieties
of crops.

Water.—A fuller use in the place of other sources
of power that are exhausted in use. It is believed that
of the twenty-six million horse-power now developed
by coal fifteen million could be more economically developed by water, thus saving not only $180,000,000
by the substitution, but 150,000,000 tons of coal for
posterity.[3] The leading of this power through longer
distances, as from Niagara Falls; its impounding for a
more steady supply;[4] the digging of channels of irrigation into arid places;[5] the drainage of wet regions;
the fuller utilization of the carrying power of water to
relieve the costlier use of wheels.[6] Making the escaping, unsatisfying stream of Sisyphus turn the mills of
the gods.

[1] Van Hise, p. 247.   [2] Van Hise, pp. 307–352.
[3] Van Hise, p. 124.   [4] Van Hise, pp. 125–133.
[5] Van Hise, pp. 185–207.   [6] Van Hise, p. 164.

This is, indeed, as the writing of that ancient prophet of Israel who, in his vision of the restoration of his city and his land and the healing of its waters, saw a man with a radiant face, a line of flax in his hand and a measuring reed. And wherever this man of radiant face measured he caused the waters to run in dry places and deep rivers to course where the waters were but ankle-deep; fish to swarm again in the rivers and the seas to be free of pollution; salt to come in the miry places and trees to grow upon the land with un-withering leaves and abundant meat.

So have these modern prophets with optimistic faces written of their vision, only the fulfilment comes not simply of the constructive measuring of statistics. It takes some trees a hundred years to grow; and dams and reservoirs for the deepening of shallow streams are not made over night as once they were by nature, or as they grew in the vision of Ezekiel.

None the less is the prophecy a long way toward fulfilment when the vision is seen. And that it has been seen is intimated by this sentence, too optimistic no doubt, from a book on the subject by one of the major prophets of conservation, recently published in America. "Conservation," he says, "has captured the nation."

It is not the thrifty, nepotic, static conservation of the St. Lawrence habitant, which depends upon the self and family interest of each landholder to keep the fields enriched and to prevent the washing away of the soil. It is a dynamic and paternalistic conserva-tion—a conservation that thinks of great dams for the restraint of waters and reservoirs for their impound-ing to the extent of millions or billions of cubic feet, forestation of great stretches of mountain slope, of restrictions and compulsions of other than personal and family interests—a paternalism that looks beyond the next generation or even two generations and to the feeding of other children than one's own lineal descendants—a paternalism that is not exploiting but fiduciary.

It is interesting to observe again how the beginnings of this conservation have been made in the fields where stood the first hospitals for the sick among the living, the first memorials to the dead, the first schools for the children of to-day that are to be the nation of to-morrow. Here also begin to rise the structures of the thought for the day after to-morrow.

The first notable assembling of men in the interest of conservation, chiefly of men already in public service —the President of the United States, the Vice-President, members of the cabinet, justices of the Supreme Court, members of Congress, the governors of thirty-four States, representatives of the other States, the governors of the Territories, and other public officials, with a number of representatives of societies and a few guests—met in 1908, to discuss questions relative to conservation. Probably not in the history of the nation has there sat in its borders an assembly of men so widely representative. This gathering resulted in the appointment of a National Conservation Commission by the President, but Congress made no appropriation for meeting the expense of its labors; and so private enterprise and providence have undertaken the carrying out of the movement.

A great body of men and women scientists, public-spirited citizens from all parts of the nation, under the presidency of Doctor Charles W. Eliot, former president of Harvard University, began a campaign of education to the end that ultimately and soon—before the riches have gone—this concern for the far future may become fixed in the law and conscious provision of the people.

I spoke in the last chapter of Hennepin's seeing a savage making sacrifice to the spirit of the Mississippi, supposed to live under the Falls of St. Anthony. You will recall the description of the great public university beside it that represents the sacrifice of the democracy of to-day for the nation of to-morrow. Instead of the beaver-skin which the poor Indian hung in the branches of a tree near the falls as his offering, the State has hung its gift of forty million dollars for the highest training of its sons and daughters. But there is still, if possible, a nobler aspiration to put against that primitive background and beside the Indian's beaver-skin, for the gift is as yet little more than an aspiration.

A few miles back from these same falls there was held in 1910 a convention of many thousands from all parts of the Union, the President of the United States and his predecessor among them, assembled under the auspices of the National Conservation Congress to consider, as they avowed, not alone their own affairs, not even the good of their children with theirs, but primarily the welfare of unborn millions as well. It cannot be assumed that all were looking so far ahead, but the declaration of principles which had called this great assemblage had in it this import—something loftier than any declaration of personal rights. It was a declaration of duty—of duty not to the past, not even to the present, but to the long, long distant future.

"Recognizing the natural resources of the country as the prime basis of property and opportunity, we hold the rights of the people in these resources to be natural and inherent and justly inalienable and indefeasible; and we insist that the resources should and shall be developed, used, and conserved in ways consistent with current welfare and with the perpetuity of our people."

When this or a like sentiment is framed out of the consciousness of a free people into a controlling declaration of public policy, we shall have not merely a nobler offering to put beside the beaver-skin and the university, but a document worthy to be put above our Declaration of Independence even, and an interpretation of the words "the people of the United States" in our Constitution that will give them an import beyond the highest conception of its authors.

The movement which embodies this sentiment is as yet chiefly a private effort, as I have said, but its influence is beginning to run through the sentiment of the individualism which has so rapidly exploited the riches of the valley and spent with such generous hand for the immediate future. And the boundaries of public service are already enlarged in making room for the previsions of the "Children of Always," as the mankind now in the thought of conservationists may well be called.

Already millions of acres of coal lands have been withdrawn from private entry, and plans are being made for the leasing of such lands; that is, the people are to keep them for their own.

Like provision has also been made with respect to oil, natural gas, and phosphate fields.

Forest lands to the extent of nearly two hundred million acres have been reserved as a perpetual national domain, and, in addition to this, several States have forest reservations amounting to nearly ten million acres.[1] The volume of forest legislation in the States is unprecedented, providing for forest service, forest study, and the prevention of forest-fires, with a prospect of laws providing for a more rigid public control of private forests.

An increasing public control of waters is another noticeable trend in legislation, and their increased utilization has already been noticed. Joliet's canal has been built. Champlain's is at last completed. A President of the United States has recommended the deepening of La Salle's river. The valley is coming back to the French paths. These and many others are conservation projects only indirectly, but they intimate a thought of the future as do the heavy appropriations for the reclamation of arid and subarid regions, the government having spent seventy million dollars[2] in such undertakings, making "one hand wash the other," as our saying is; that is, making the well-watered regions meet the expense of watering the arid.

And, finally, the States are beginning to take most serious and even radical measures to encourage farmers so to till their fields as to be able to bequeath them unimpoverished to those who come after. I think it not unlikely that eventually the demos, thinking of the future, will be as paternalistic as was Louis XIV, who told the habitant of the St. Lawrence how many horses he should keep.

This review of the resources of the valley of France

---

[1] Van Hise, pp. 216, 217. [2] To June 1, 1912.

in the midst of America, and of the forces that are now assembling to preserve for posterity its vast capital of earth, air, and water, is but an intimation of what might easily be expanded into a volume of itself. Indeed, much of my statistical material I have from a book by Doctor Charles R. Van Hise, president of the University of Wisconsin; but, meagre as this review is, it must give you, as it has given me, a stirring sense of the mighty reach of the paths of those few pioneers of France in those regions where the spirit of conservation is strongest.

While it is true that every human life, as Carlyle has said, stands at the conflux of two eternities—the one behind him, the other before—in a sense have the material preparations, extending during a length of time that to our measurement seems an eternity, converged upon and in those pioneers of Europe in that valley; and from them has diverged a civilization that now begins to look forward in the eyes of her prophets through years that seem as another eternity. Probably, says this eminent scientist of that valley, speaking of the past, "some of the deposits at present being mined are the result of agents . . . a hundred million years ago";[1] and of the future: "We hope for a future . . . not to be reckoned by thousands of years but by tens of thousands or hundreds of thousands or even millions of years. And, therefore, so far as our responsibility is concerned, it is immaterial whether the coal will be exhausted in one hundred and fifty years or fifteen hundred years, or fifteen thousand years. Our responsibility to succeeding generations demands that we reduce its use to our absolute neces-

[1] Van Hise, p. 18.

sities, and therefore prolong its life to the utmost."[1]

Conservation has in such depth of years given a new perspective to the picture we have been painting of the life in that valley. The French were pioneers not merely of an exploiting individualism of a day, or of a hundred or two hundred years, not merely of a democracy thinking of an equality of the men of one generation, but also of the conserving dynamic civilization of hundreds of centuries of a people—to come back again to that best of definitions—who are the invisible multitude of spirits, the nation of yesterday and to-morrow.

The French priest, kneeling over the dying Indian child in the forest hut and stealthily touching its brow with water, had vision of another immortality than that, as we know; the empire which the French explorers and adventurers hoped to build with its capital on the Rock of Quebec, or on the Rock St. Louis of the Illinois, or at the mouth of the Mississippi did not grow in the fashion of their dream, as we of course realize. But we see, on the other hand, what promise of ages has been given to the faith and adventure which found incarnation in a frontier democracy whose energy and spirit made possible the great, lusty republic of to-day, that now begins to talk of a thousand centuries.

Out in that far west, in a recent autumn, the men of the standing army were set to fighting forest-fires. This has seemed to me a happy omen of what the new conservatism of the world may ask of its soldiery— the conserving not of borders but of the resources of human life and of human life itself. And so have I

[1] Van Hise, p. 25.

added another class to the inhabitants of the valley, to the precursors, the producers, the poets, and the teachers of to-morrow—the conservers of the day after to-morrow.

Our great philosopher William James gave expression in one of his last utterances to a hope that every man, rich or poor, may come to serve the State (as now every man in France does his military service) in some direct duty that asks the same obedience, the same sacrifice, the same forgetting of self that is asked of the soldier—that every man by the payment of the blood tax may be able to get and keep the spirit of neighborliness, to know how to sympathize more deeply with his fellow men, and to learn the joy of disinterested doing for the nation.[1]

But in this demand and appeal of the new theory of our common responsibility, of a dynamic conservationism, is the germ of a larger patriotism than any that history has as yet defined—a patriotism that asks the lifetime service of an individualism with an all-time horizon.

[1] "Memories and Studies: The Moral Equivalent of War," pp. 267–296.

CHAPTER XIX

THE HEART OF AMERICA

IN the little town of St. Die in the east of France there was printed in the year 1507 a "Cosmographiæ Introductio"—an introduction to a forthcoming edition of Ptolemy—in which was included an account of the journeys of one Amerigo Vespucci, who is credited with the discovery of a new part of the world—a fourth continent. For this reason, the author recites, "quarta orbis pars, quam quis Americus invenit, Amerigen quasi Americi terram, sivi Americam nuncupare licit." And so the name America (for it was thought proper to give it the feminine form, "cum et Europa et Asia a mulieribus sua sortitæ sint nomina") was probably first pronounced in the mountain-circled town of St. Die, where the scholars of the Vosges, shut away from the sea and its greedy rumors of India, conceived more accurately in their isolation the significance of the western discoveries and made the new-found shores the edge not of Asia but of another continent.

Perhaps this new land should have been given some other name; but that it is futile now to discuss. America it has been these four hundred years and America it is doubtless always to be. And it is particularly gratifying to one who has come to care so much for France to find that the name of his own land—a name most euphonious and delectable to his ears—came of the christening at the font of the River Meurthe, the beautiful French dame of St. Die standing by as godmother, and that that name was first whispered to the world by the trees of the forests of the Vosges, whose wood may even have furnished the blocks to fashion first its letters. So may we go back and write this interesting if not important fact of French pioneering in America.

But let us rehearse to ourselves once more before we separate the epic sequence of adventure and suffering which tells how much more than a name France gave to that continent just rising from the seas when the savants of St. Die touched her face with the baptismal water of their recluse learning.

Again the "boundless vision grows upon us; an untamed continent; vast wastes of forest verdure; mountains silent in primeval sleep; river, lake, and glimmering pool; wilderness oceans mingling with the sky" —the America not of the imaging of the mountain men of St. Die but of the seeing and enduring of the seamen of Dieppe and St. Malo and Rochelle and Rouen.

Again Jacques Cartier stands alone within this "shaggy continent," a thousand miles beyond the banks of the Baccalaos and the Isles of the Demons. Again for a moment Acadia echoes of the Sorbonne and of Arcadian poesy. Again the unblenching "preux chevalier" Champlain stands with his back against the gray cliff of Quebec fighting red and white foe alike, famine and disease, to keep a foothold in the wilderness, with the sublime faith of a crusader and the patient endurance of a Prometheus. Again the zealous but narrow rigor of Richelieu, flowering in his native land in the learning of the Sorbonne and preparing for him in the new world, as Le Jeune wrote, a "dazzling crown in heaven," builds by the St. Charles and the wreckage of Cartier's *Petite Hermine*, the house of Notre Dame des Anges, the "cradle of the great mission of New France." Again the fireflies light the meadow altar of Maisonneuve at Montreal on its birthnight. Again the gray gowns and the black, Le Caron, Brébeuf, Jogues, and Garnier, enter upon their glorious toils, their bare and sandalled feet, accustomed to the smooth walks of the convents of Brouage and Rheims and Paris, begin to climb the rough paths to the west, *ad majorem Dei gloriam.* Again the swift coureurs de bois, half-savage in their ambassadorship of the woods, follow the traces of the most ancient road-makers, the buffalo and deer, and the voyageurs carry their boats across the portage places. Again the *Griffin*—the winged lion of the lakes—flies from Niagara to the island in Green Bay, France's percursor of the million-tonned commerce of the northern seas, but sinks with her cargo of golden fleece in their blue waters. Again Marquette, the son of Laon, beholds with joy unspeakable the mysterious "great water," and yet again, La Salle stands by the lonely sea and cries his proclamation toward the limitless land.

And, seeing and hearing all this again, we have seen a land as large as all Europe emerge from the unknown at the evocation of pioneers of France who stood all or nearly all sooner or later in Paris within three or four kilometres of the very place in which I sit writing these words. Cartier gave to the world the St. Lawrence River as far as the Falls of Lachine; Champlain, his Récollet friars and Jesuit priests and heralds of the woods added the upper lakes; and Marquette, Joliet,

La Salle, Tonty, Hennepin, Radisson, Groseilliers, Iberville, Bienville, Le Sueur, La Harpe, the Vérendrye—father and sons—and scores of other Frenchmen, many of forgotten names, added the valley of the river of a hundred thousand streams, from where at the east the French creek begins, a few miles from Lake Erie, to flow toward the Ohio even to the sources of the Missouri in the snows of the Rockies—"the most magnificent dwelling-place"—again to recall De Tocqueville, "prepared by God for man's abode; the valley destined to give the world a field for a new experiment in democracy and to become the heart of America."

I have not been able to write at any length of that part of all this vast region of France's pioneering and evoking where France is best remembered—remembered in speech that imitates that which is dearest to France's ears; remembered in voices that even in the harsh winds of the north keep something of the mellowness and softness of the south; remembered in the surnames that recall beautiful trees and fields of perfume and hills of vines and things of the sea which surrounded their ancestors; remembered in the appellations of the saints that protect their firesides and their fortunes; remembered in the names that still cling tenaciously to rivers and towns of that land which calls Champlain its father—Canada.

A traveller in the lower St. Lawrence Valley might well think himself east of the Atlantic as he hears the guard on the railway train from Montreal to Quebec call: St. Rochs, Les Éboulements, Portneuf, Pont Rouge, Capucins, Mont Louis, Pointe au Chêne; or hears the speech as he walks at the foot of the gray Rock of Quebec, or even reads the street signs in Montreal. There are memories there on every side, in their very houses and habits—yet memories which I fear are beginning to fade with the allurements of the land of hope to the far west and the northwest of Canada—the "land of hope," the new frontier of America, now of such interest to the people of that other valley, the Mississippi, which was once separated from Canada by no boundaries save watersheds, and these so low that there was reciprocity of their waters.

But even if I could keep you longer I am thinking that I should have asked you to spend it where there are fewer memories than in Canada, in the valley where the old French names, if kept at all, are often obscured in a new orthography or a different pronunciation. Up in the boundary of waters between the two lands there is a lighthouse on an island called "Skilligallee." I was a long time in discovering that this meaningless euphonic name was but the memory of the Isle aux Galets—the island of the pebbles. So have the memories been lost in tongues that could not easily frame to pronounce the words they found when they entered that farther valley where France's pioneering is almost forgotten, but where France should be best remembered.

A catalogue (and this book has been little else) of the reasons for such remembrance has doubtless brought little comfort; indeed, it may have brought some pain, because the recital of the reasons has but emphasized the forgetting and accentuated the loss.

But is France not to find, in a fuller consciousness of what has developed in that valley into which she led Europe, a higher satisfaction than could have come through the formal relationship of mother and colony, or any other that could be reasonably conjectured?

For Turgot's prophecy would have some day been realized, and there would perhaps have been a bitterness where now there is gratitude. I can think of no series of relations that could have been of more profound and momentous import in the history of that continent, or that should give higher satisfaction to France in her thought of America than that which this summation permits us to recall once more.

France not only christened America; she not only stood first far inside that continent at the north and furnished Europe proof of its mighty dimensions; she also gave to this continent, child of her christening, the richest great valley of the world.

This valley she held in the title of her own claim for more than a century from the time that her explorers first looked over its brim, held it by valors and sufferings which would have been gloriously recorded if their issue had been to keep by those waters the tongue in which they could be written and sung.

When France did yield it, because of forces outside the valley, not inside (there was hardly a sound of battle there), she gave it in effect to a new nation. She shared it with the aboriginal American, she gave it to the ultimate American. She got her title from the first Americans who, as Châteaubriand said, called themselves the "Children of Always." She gave it to those who are beginning to think of it as belonging not to them but to the new "Children of Always."

By her very valorous holding she taught the fringe of colonies along the Atlantic the first lessons in union, and she gave them a leader out of the disciplines of her borders, George Washington, whom in the course of time she directly assisted with her sympathy and means to make certain the independence of those same colonies.

He, in turn, in the paths of the Old French War across the Alleghanies, found by a most singular fate not only the indissoluble bond between the eastern and the western waters but in those very paths the practical way to the more "perfect union" of the young nation that was to succeed to this joint heritage of England and of France.

To its estate of hundreds of millions of acres east of the Mississippi Napoleon added a half-billion more out of the one-time domain of Louis XIV and made it possible that the United States should some day develop into a world-power.

The half-valley, enlarged to its mountain bounds through the influence of its free soil on those whose feet touched it as pioneers, nourished a natural democracy founded in the equalities, the freedoms, and the fraternities of the frontier so vital, so powerful that it became the dominant nationalistic force in a continent-wide republic. Aided by the means of communication which a rampant individualism had prepared for it, it held that republic together, expressing itself most conspicuously in the democratic soul of Lincoln—who, following La Salle down the Mississippi, found his high mission to the world—and in the masterful, resourceful generalship of Grant.

The old French forts have grown into new-world cities, the portage paths have been multiplied into streets, the trails of the coureurs de bois have become railroads, and all are the noisy, flaming, smoky places and means of such an industry and exploitation as doubtless are not to be found so extensive and so intensive in any other valley of the earth.

A quantitative analysis has led me to present statistics of its production and manufacture which would seem inexcusably braggart if it were not to remind the French and my own countrymen that it was the geographical descendants of France who, out of the wealth of their heritage of France's bequeathing, untouched from the glaciers and the Indians, were confuting with their wheat the prophecies of Malthus and making the whole world a more comfortable and a somewhat brighter place with their iron, their oil, their reapers, their wagons, and their sewing-machines. It were nothing to be ashamed of unless that were all.

But a careful qualitative analysis discovers in the life of that valley, which has been so widely advertised by its purely quantitative output, a certain idealism that is usually obscured by the smoke of its individualism.

We have seen it in the grimy ravine by old Fort Duquesne, where, like the titanium which, in what way no chemist knows, increases the tensile strength of its steel, this practical idealism gives promise of a democracy that will stand a greater stress and strain.

We have seen it in the plans for the future of the city that has risen from the onion field along the Chicago River, where Marquette's spirit lived in a sick body through a bitter winter.

We have seen it in the setting apart of the white acres in every township for the training of the child of to-morrow, in the higher school that stands in thousands of towns and cities throughout the valley, and in the university supported of every State in that valley, such as that which we saw beside the falls where Hennepin tells of the Indian sacrificing his beaver-skin to the river spirit.

And, finally, we have seen the men of to-day, rising to that highest definition of a people—the invisible multitude of spirits, the nation of yesterday and of to-morrow—forgetting their interests of the moment, listening to the men of the universities speaking out of the past, and planning for the conservation of what they have left to them of the resources of the land for the "interests of mankind"—the true "Children of Always."

This, then, is what France has prepared the way for, in one of the vast regions where she was pioneer in America. Through the venture and the faith of her sons she won the valley with a past of a million of ages; through unrecorded valors she held it as her very own for a century, and, though she lost nominal title to it as a territory, she has a ground-rent interest in it, real title to a share in its human fruitage, which time can neither take away nor cloud but only augment.

The social and industrial life which has developed there by mere coincidence, or of direct cause, is distinctive and peculiar to that part of the United States which has a French background, though it now has made itself felt throughout the nation. And, however little in its feature and language the foreground may seem to take color of it, I shall always believe that the consecration of the rivers and paths, by explorations and ministries that were for the most part as unselfish as France's scholarship is to-day, must in some subtle way have had such a potency as the catalytic sub-

stances which work miracles in matter and yet are beyond the discerning of the scientist.

An English essayist[1] has estimated that we of the
United States are no longer young and finds in the
fact that we have produced great artists the intimations of age. The art of Whistler and the letters of
Henry James are to him the "sweet and startling" but
"unmistakable cry of a dying man." But this essayist
could not have known the men of the valley which is
the heart of the nation as it is the heart of the country, the place of its dominant spirits. That valley, so
rapidly exploited of its resources that it has grown ages
poorer, is yet virile, youthful in its faults and its achievements. It has no "fine futility" as yet, and the cry is
not "sweet" though it may be "startling." It is the
shout of a young god, of a Jason driving the bulls in
the fields of Colchis. The attenuations of distance
may easily deceive one's ears who listens from across
the ocean and the mountains.

I think it was this same essayist who said that to
understand a people one must study them with the
"loyalty of a child" and the patience not of a scientist
but of a poet. I thank him for that, while I excuse his
confounding of sounds that he hears in England from
America, and agree that what we need in that valley
to tell its story, to interpret it, is not a specialist in
statistics nor an annalist, not a critic who looks at the
smoke of the chimneys and visits the slaughter-houses
only, but a poet who will have the patience to consult
both the statistician and the annalist, a patient poet
with the "loyalty of a child" toward his theme.

[1] G. K. Chesterton, "The Fallacy of the Young Nation," in his "Heretics,"
pp. 247-266.

EPILOGUE

FRANCIS PARKMAN

THE HISTORIAN OF FRANCE IN THE NEW WORLD

I MAKE the epilogue of this story my tribute to Francis Parkman, who has in a sense made this all possible for me: first, by reason of the love he gave me long ago for his New France with its primeval forests, its virgin prairies, its glistening rivers, its untamed Indians, its explorers, its gray and black cowls, its coureurs de bois, its stars whose light had never before looked on a white face; and second, by reason of the mass of incident and color which he has supplied for the background of the life I have known in that valley.

On entering a college out in the midst of that region —the middle of the Mississippi Valley—nearly thirty years ago I was assigned, as my first important task in English, the reading and criticism of one of Parkman's books. I think that "The Oregon Trail" was suggested. I read several volumes, however, but found my interest greatest in "The Pioneers of France in the New World" and "The Jesuits in North America." What I wrote I do not now remember (nor do I wish to refresh my memory), but so persistent was the grip of those graphic relations upon my imagination that years later, when leaving the presidency of that same college, I asked to be permitted to take from the library three books (replacing them with fresher copies):

the chapel Bible—from which I had been read to by my president and professors and from which I in turn had read to succeeding students—a copy of Spenser's "Faerie Queene"—which my college's only poet, Eugene Field, had read through—and a volume of Parkman's on the pioneers of France.

So I take the opportunity to pay my tribute to him who long ago put these figures on the frontier of my imagination, and who has prevented my ever speaking in dispassion or without favorable prejudice of them.

When Parkman was leaving America for Paris in 1868, "for medical advice and research," uncertain as to whether he would ever return to take up his unfinished story of the American forest, he left in the hands of a friend a parcel, "not to be opened during his life." It is that parcel, not opened until twenty-five years later—for Parkman lived to return to America and to return again to Paris more than once, and then to go back and finish, after a full half-century of struggle with physical maladies and infirmities, the last book of the plan virtually sketched fifty years before, and with a singular felicity of coincidence named "The Half-Century of Conflict"—it is that parcel which has kept for later generations his remarkable autobiography.

While on his visits in Paris he was known in a wide circle. As he himself said in writing to his sisters, "if able to accept invitations," he "would have had the run of Faubourg St. Germain." I doubt, however, if his personality is remembered by many, much less that strangely tortured life which probably gave little mark of its suffering even to those who knew him best in France.

I therefore recall some of the detail of the years

preceding those days when he appeared in the streets of Paris seeking health, but seeing often Margry, the "intractable yet kindly keeper" of an important department of French archives, who had in his secretive keeping documents most precious to the uses of Parkman.

It is not altogether an agreeable chronicle, this autobiography.[1] It is rather like a "pathological record," and as totally unlike the pages of his books as can be well imagined. But it is an essential document.

The first pages of this biography were withheld by him and so removed from the parcel; the record begins with a general characterization of his childhood. There is no detail. But there are to be found elsewhere the memories of others which tell of his boyish enjoyment of the little wilderness of joyous colors near the school to which he was sent—microcosm of the greater wilderness in which his body and then his imagination were to wander through all his mature days till his death. His own chronicle has forgotten or ignored those elysian days and has not in all its length a joyful note or a bright color.

This is the summary: His childhood was neither healthful nor buoyant. . . . Chemical experiment was his favorite hobby, involving a lonely, confined, unwholesome sort of life, baneful to body and mind. . . . The age of fifteen or sixteen produced a revolution; retorts and crucibles were forever discarded. . . . He became enamoured of the woods, a fancy which soon gained full control over the course of his literary pur-

[1] Printed in "Proceedings Massachusetts Historical Society, 1892-4," series 2, 8 : 349-360.

suits. . . . He resolved to confine his homage to the muse of history. . . . At the age of eighteen (born in 1823) the plan (to whose execution he gave his long life) was, in its most essential features, formed. His idea was clear before him, yet attended with unpleasant doubts as to his ability to realize it to his own satisfaction. . . . The task, as he then reckoned it, would require about twenty years. The time allowed was ample; but here he fell into a fatal error, entering upon this long pilgrimage with all the vehemence of one starting on a mile heat. His reliance, however, was less on books than on such personal experience as should intimately identify him with his theme.

Let me here say that I have found traces of his steps at nearly every site that I have visited. He had been at Fort St. Louis, at the most important portages, and at the places where the French forts once stood. His natural inclinations urged him in the same direction, his thoughts were constantly in the forest, whose features, not unmixed with softer images, possessed his waking and sleeping dreams; he was as fond of hardships as he was vain of enduring them, cherishing a sovereign scorn for every physical weakness or defect. Moreover, deceived by a rapid development of frame and sinews which flattered him with the belief that discipline sufficiently unsparing would harden him into an athlete, he slighted precautions of a more reasonable woodcraft, tired old foresters with long marches, stopped neither for heat nor rain, and slept on the earth without a blanket. . . . He spent his summer vacations in the woods or in Canada, at the same time reading such books as he thought suited to help him toward his object. . . . While in the law school he entered in earnest on two other courses, one of general history, the other of Indian history and ethnology, studying diligently at the same time the models of English style. . . . There developed in him a state of mental tension, habitual for several years, and abundantly mischievous in its effects. With a mind overstrained and a body overtaxed, he was burning his candle at both ends. . . . A highly irritable organism spurred the writer to excess. . . . Labor became a passion, and rest intolerable yet with a keen appetite for social enjoyments. . . . His condition became that of a rider whose horse runs headlong with the bit between his teeth, or of a locomotive, built of indifferent material, under a head of steam too great for its strength, hissing at a score of crevices, yet rushing on with accelerating speed to the inevitable smash. . . . Soon appeared, as a sign of mischief, weakness of sight. Accordingly he went to the Rocky Mountains to rest his failing vision and to get an inside view of Indian life. . . . Reeling in the saddle, he set forth, attended by a Canadian hunter. . . . Joining the Ogallala Indians, he followed their wanderings for several weeks. To have worn the air of an invalid would have been an indiscretion, as he says, since "a horse, a rifle, a pair of pistols, and a red shirt might have offered temptations too strong for aboriginal virtue." So he hunted when he could scarcely sit upright. . . . To the maladies of the prairies other disorders succeeded on his return. . . . Flat stagnation followed, reaching its depth in eighteen months. . . . The desire to return to the prairie was intense, but exposure to the sunlight would have destroyed his sight. . . . When his condition was at its worst, he resolved to attempt the composition of the "History of the Conspiracy of Pontiac," for which he had been collecting material since his days in college. Suffering from extreme weakness of sight, a condition of the brain prohibiting fixed attention, and a nervous derangement, he yet set out upon this labor, using a wooden frame strung with parallel wires to guide his crayon. Books and documents were read to him, but never, without injury, for more than a half-hour at a time, and frequently not at all for days. For the first half-year he averaged six lines of composition a day. And he wrote, I suppose, at least ten hundred thousand lines. His health improving, he dictated, pacing a dark garret. He then entered upon "France in the New World." The difficulties were incalculable. . . . Wholly unable to use his eyes, he had before him the task of tracing out, collecting, indexing, arranging, and digesting a great mass of incongruous material, scattered on both sides of the Atlantic. He was unable to employ trained assistants and had to rely mainly on his own research, though, in some cases, receiving valuable aid of scholars and others. He used to employ as reader of French a public-school girl wholly ignorant of French (who, I suppose, gave English pronunciation to all the words), but with such help and that of members of his own family the work went on. Then came another disaster —an effusion of water on the knee which involved a close confinement for two years; and this in turn resulted in serious nervous disturbance centring in the head. These extreme conditions of disorder continued for many years. . . . His work was wholly interrupted for one year, four years, and numerous short intervals. . . . Later the condition of sight so far improved as to permit reading, not exceeding, on an average, five minutes at one time. By judicious use this modicum of power was extended. By reading for one minute and then resting for an equal time the alternate process could be continued for about half an hour, then, after a sufficient interval, repeated three or four times a day. Working under such conditions he makes this report, 1868, of progress: "Most of the material is collected or within reach; another volume, on the Jesuits of North America, is one-third written; another, on the French explorers of the Great West, is half written; while a third, devoted to the checkered career of Comte de Frontenac, is partially arranged for composition." During this period he had made many journeys in the United States and Canada for material, and had been four times in Europe. . . . He wonders as to the advantage of this tortoise pace, but says in conclusion that, "irksome as may be the requirements of conditions so anomalous, they are far less oppressive than the necessity they involve of being busied with the Past when the Present has claims so urgent, and of holding the pen with the hand that should have grasped the sword" (for he was greatly disappointed that he could not enter the army at the time of the Civil War).

I have made this rather extensive summary of the singular autobiography—and largely in the author's own words—not to prepare your minds for lenient judgments of his work, but to inform them of the tenacious purpose of the man whose infirmities of the knees kept him most of his life from the wild forest trails and streams and compelled him to a wheel-chair in gardens of tame roses; whose weakness of the eyes

408 THE FRENCH IN THE HEART OF AMERICA

allowed him but inadequate vision of the splendor of
the woods and even robbed him of the intimacy of
books; whose malady of mind kept him ever in terror
of devils more fierce than the inhuman tortures of
Jogues and Brébeuf—a tenacious purpose that wrought
its youth-selected, self-appointed work, and so well, so
splendidly, so thoroughly that it needs never to be
done again.

One of his friends, in a memoir of Parkman, recalls
an observation of Sainte-Beuve, in his paper on Taine's
"English Literature," that has found its best illustration in what Parkman accomplished in spite of lame-
ness, blindness, and mental distress: "All things considered, every allowance being made for general or
particular elements and for circumstances, there still
remain place and space enough around men of talent,
wherein they can move and turn themselves with entire freedom. And, moreover, were the circle drawn
round each a very contracted one, every man of talent,
every genius, in so far as he is in some degree a magi-
cian and an enchanter, possesses a secret entirely his
own, whereby to perform prodigies within this circle
and work wonders there."[1]

This autobiography has shown how short was the
radius of the circle. The twelve volumes of his work
attest, under Sainte-Beuve's definition, the degree of
his powers of magic and enchantment. Men of strong
knees, of good eyes, and of brains that do not keep
them from sleep by night or from work by day, have
travelled over this same field, but of most that they
gathered it may be said: "To no such aureate earth
'tis turned as, buried once, men want dug up again."

[1] "Nouveaux Lundis," vol. VIII, English translation in "English Por-
traits," p. 243.

I have sat for days in the Harvard University Library among the books bequeathed to it by Parkman (being the greater part of the library which surrounded him in his work—books of history, of travel, and of biography; books about Indians, flints, and folk-lore; maps and guides—among them several guides to Paris—only twenty-five hundred volumes in all); but they are not the material of his magic. His work was not legerdemain, skilful manipulation, but recreation, and he found the aureate earth in the forests, on the prairies, and in documents contemporary to his theme.

In a cabinet (bearing in its carving suggestions of the fleur-de-lis) in the rooms of the Massachusetts Historical Society, I found some of this precious material, also bequeathed by the historian. Its nature is suggested in the preface to his "Montcalm and Wolfe." "A very large amount," he says, "of unpublished material has been used in its preparation, consisting for the most part of documents copied from the archives and libraries of France and England. The papers copied for the present work ["Montcalm and Wolfe"] in France alone, exceed six thousand folio pages of manuscript, additional and supplementary to the 'Paris Documents' procured for the State of New York. . . . The copies made in England form ten volumes, besides many English documents consulted in the original manuscript. Great numbers of autograph letters, diaries, and other writings of persons engaged in the war have also been examined on this [i. e., American] side of the Atlantic."

But even these were as the dry bones in the valley which Ezekiel saw, till he touched these scattered fragments with his genius.

The process employed by the blind workman is described by Frothingham, one of his friends: "The manuscripts were read over to him, slowly, one by one. First the chief points were considered, then the details of the story were gone over carefully and minutely. As the reading went on, he made notes, first of essential and then of non-essential. After this he welded everything together, made the narrative completely his own, infused into it his own fire, quickened it by his own imagination, and made it as it were a living experience, so that his books read like personal reminiscences."[1]

In a book of Parkman memorabilia of various kinds which I found in the Harvard Library, I happened one day upon a few scraps of paper which furnish illustration of the first steps of the process—paper on which were notes made in Parkman's own hand:

"Deserts covered with bones of buffalo and elk"; "No sign of man from Fort Union to Fort Mackenzie"; "White clay, cactus dried up, grasshoppers"; "Poplars,—wild roses,—gooseberries"; "prairie dogs,—heat, —aridity"; "extraordinary castellated mountains, stone walls,—etc. above Fort Union"; "in 1832 Blackfeet are said to have killed 58 whites, three years before, 80"; "Blackfeet do not eat dogs—Blackfeet Societies —beaver traps lent to Blackfeet"; "wood near Fort Clark chiefly poplar"; "fossils—terres mauvaises"; "maize cultivated by Mandans"; "catching the war eagle"; "Mandans etc. agricultural tribes"; "wolf-pits described"; "Exceptional cold Ft. Clark"; "Wolf attacked three women;—wooden carts no iron"; "Barren

---

[1] "Memoirs of Francis Parkman," in "Proceedings Massachusetts Historical Society, 1892-4," series 2, 8 : 555.

Mts. little dells with water,—gooseberries, strawberries, currants, very few trees, mad river."

But these and many other notes on scraps of blue paper in his hand have significance only in their translation, transfusion into the color or detail of some of his wonderful pictures. Somewhere in his books I felt certain, when reading these notes, I should find those poplars growing on the plains with wild roses and gooseberry bushes not far away; some day I should come to the barren mountains and the dells with water, or should hear the roaring of the mad river and witness the catching of the war-eagle. Indeed, some of these very notes had entered, as I found, into the description of that lonely journey of the brothers Vérendrye as they passed through the bad lands (terres mauvaises of the notes), where the clay is sometimes white as chalk and the barren, castellated bluffs, "carved into fantastic shapes by the storms," stand about.

"For twenty days the travellers saw no human being [see note above], so scanty was the population of these plains. Game, however, was abundant. Deer sprang from the tall reed grass of the river bottoms; buffalo tramped by in ponderous columns, or dotted the swells of the distant prairie with their grazing thousands; antelope approached, with the curiosity of their species, to gaze at the passing horsemen, then fled like the wind; and as they neared the broken uplands towards the Yellowstone, they saw troops of elk (later their bones) and flocks of mountain-sheep. Sometimes, for miles together, the dry plain was studded thick with the earthen mounds that marked the burrows of the curious marmots, called prairie dogs from their squeaking bark. Wolves, white and gray, howled about the camp at night, and their cousin, the coyote, seated in the dusk of evening upright on the grass, with nose turned to the sky, saluted them with a complication of yelpings, as if a score of petulant voices were pouring together from the throat of one small beast."[1]

It is impossible to know how much of this came from his own actual seeing (for in his journey over the Oregon trail he had passed near the trail of the Vérendrye brothers) and how much came from those scraps of color and incident picked up in his blindness from varied sources; nor is it of consequence, except as it connotes something of the quality and character of his genius, for it is all accurate and the brave brothers Vérendrye move as living men across it. He was able to revivify a dusty document as well as a personal experience. "To him," as Mr. Barrett Wendell said out of an intimate acquaintance with him and his work, "a document of whatever kind,—a state paper, a Jesuit 'relation,' the diary of a provincial soldier, the record of a Yankee church,—was merely the symbol of a fact which had once been as real as his own hardships among the western Indians, or as the lifetime of physical suffering, which never bent his will."[2] I have never read "The Oregon Trail" with the same keen enthusiasm as his other books, largely, I think, because it is a mere report of personal adventure and not a composition fused of his imagination. It is an excellent photograph by the side of a master's painting.

But all this accuracy of detail, this revivifying of dead Indians, knights, voyageurs and soldiers, this painting of prairie, forest, and mountain, was not in

[1] Parkman, "Half-Century of Conflict," 2 : 23, 24.
[2] "Proceedings American Academy of Arts and Sciences, 1893-4," 29 : 439.

itself to put him among the world's great historians. And, indeed, there are those who, appreciating the artist's skill, have expressed regret that he gave this skill to no great theme. It is as if he were (they would doubtless say) writing of the labors of sacrificing missionaries in Africa, or of colonial administration in Indo-China, or of forest adventure along the Amazon. In the Boston Public Library I found that every work of his had duplicate copies in the boys' department. (And how great the reading is to this day is intimated by my inability one evening to get a copy of "Pontiac's War," though there were several copies in the possession of the library. A reserve had finally to be called in.) But I should say that this double classification intimated rather the genuine human interest of his story, appealing alike to men and to boys (as the greatest of human writings do)—a work "for all mankind and for all time."

But I should go beyond this. His books are not merely of elemental entertainment. He has seized the most fundamental, far-reaching, and consequential of themes. He found going on in his forest, of which he set out to write, not merely flame-lighted scalpings and official rapacities and picturesque maraudings and quixotic pageants and the like. His theme was even greater than the mere gathering of all these raids and rapacities and maraudings and pageants into an informed racial, national struggle for the possession of a continent. It was nothing less than the grappling, out on the frontier of the world, between two principles of organized human life. The forests are so demanding, the incidents so stirring in themselves, that many have doubtless missed the high theme that expressed itself there. But that theme possessed its author, and it possesses every sensitive reader as some fateful, recurring, tragic melody in an opera full of diverting incident and picturesque figures.

Parkman is more likely to keep his generalizations within the overture, but frequently one gives summary to an act or scene, so that even he who comes for entertainment can hardly miss the significance of it all; though, as Mr. Wendell has said, to borrow again from his, the best, brief tribute: "Parkman was very sparing of generalization, of philosophic comment," whether from overconsciousness or from the intrusion of his malady which forbade long-continued thought. He made the course of events carry its own philosophy.

Several noble and notable generalizations have, however, already thrust themselves into these chapters to illustrate his appreciation of the loftiness of his theme, his candor, and his genuine sympathy with those to whose ill-fated heroism he gave such "precious testimony."

One has only to associate with the persistent, clearly outlined purpose of a half-century a realization of the completeness of its achievement to be stirred, as by the victory not of a fortuitously reckless assault but of a long, carefully planned campaign.

Among his papers (in the fleur-de-lis cabinet of which I have spoken) there are the first prophecies: two maps of the Lake George (Champlain) region drawn by him on the inside of a red portfolio cover, marked 1842, when he was nineteen years old; and next an odd-covered blank book in which he began his note-making on the "Old French War," with such notes as these: "Rights of the two nations"; "When did Marquette make his discoveries?" "When did La Salle settle?" "Had not the French a right both of prior discovery and prior settlement?" "The English never settled"; "The letters patent to Louisiana are preposterous, perhaps, but not more so than the English claim from coasts back of the Mississippi"; "The first blood was spilt by Washington. Jumonville would seem to have been sent with peaceful intentions. His orders charged him to attack the French."

The title is written in a strong hand, but before he has half filled the little book he makes entry that the "French War" is laid aside, for the time, for the history of "Pontiac's War," and thus the latter part of this thin note-book grew into "The Conspiracy of Pontiac," and that in turn became sequel to the whole series of which it also was the promise, a series of books so closely related that John Fiske speaks of them as "one book."

The scope, to be sure, is a restricted one. He has two great wildernesses to cover, but it is a century and a half after the epic narrative begins before enough people enter to prevent one from keeping track of all of them. It is as if he were writing the history of man, from the last day of creation forward, starting with a few transmigrant souls still under the control of their oversea existence. He begins at the beginning, with not even a twilight zone of tradition and with a stage "far more primitive than that which is depicted in the Odyssey or even Genesis." Cartier's route is as well known as that of the steamship that sailed yesterday through the "Square Gulf," if the ice permitted, and the incidents of his first days beyond the gates of the first wilderness have been as accurately recorded, to say the least, as are yesterday's events yonder in the morning's papers here.   And when his story ends, there are not as many people in the two great valleys along the St. Lawrence and the Mississippi as in a good-sized city to-day.   But none the less, as I have said, are the forces (fighting in and through these few representatives of civilization) age-old and world-important.   Never has historian had such fascinating theme—such "epic theme," says Fiske—"save when Herodotus told the story of Greece and Persia, or when Gibbon's pages resounded with the marshalled hosts through a thousand years of change."   And Parkman met one of what Lowell calls "the convincing tests of genius" in the choice of this subject.

When John Fiske said at the Harvard exercises in memory of Parkman that he was one of the world's greatest historians, I subtracted something because of the occasion and the nearness of view.   But a year later he is saying of Parkman's work, in a critical review: "Strong in its individuality and like to nothing besides, it clearly belongs, I think, among the world's few masterpieces of the highest rank, along with the works of Herodotus, Thucydides, and Gibbon."[1]

There will never be such a story to write again, for the frontier of forest and prairie has disappeared.   It is now in the midst of cities where civilizations grapple in their smoke and turmoil.   So shall we hold even more precious his gift and thank Heaven for "sending us such a scholar, such an artist, such a genius before it was too late to catch the fleeting light and fix it upon immortal canvas."

---

[1] *Atlantic Monthly,* 73 : 674; "A Century of Science and Other Essays," p. 264.

Among the writings of Francis Parkman there are a few pages—known not even to a score of his readers, I suppose—which might very well be printed in summary of his great work—though they find no place in any volume—for the symbol they carry of his achievement. These few pages make a leaflet—a reprint of a paper contributed to the *Botanical Bulletin* in 1878 by "Francis Parkman, late Professor of Horticulture at the Bussey Institution," and entitled "The Hybridization of Lilies." In this brief paper is related the story of Parkman's own attempts, extending through seven years, to combine certain well-established varieties of lilies, and especially two superb lilies—the "Speciosum" (*Lancifolium*) and the "Auratum,"—the pollen of the latter being carried to the deanthered flowers of the former. The patient, anxious, exquisite care with which he carried on these experiments suggests the infinite pains with which he gathered and classified and sifted and weighed his historical material (his material of "France Speciosum" and of "France Auratum"). The result of his floral experiment, the wonderfully beautiful flower which he produced, described in a London horticultural magazine as the "grandest flowering plant yet introduced into our gardens," and known as the "Lilium Parkmanni," is suggestive of his achievement in so depicting and defining that civilization which is symbolized by the lily, the fleur-de-lis, in its strange, wild, highly colored flowering on the prairies and by the rivers of Nouvelle France, as to make it for all time identified with his memory and name. He lived among roses of his own growing, through his later invalid years, in the outskirts of Boston. He even wrote a book about roses.

But his peculiar triumph (the one flower that lingers in gardens carrying a memory of him) is a "magnificent" lily. And though he lived amid the heritages of the English, in the new continent, with fair mind and most acute and industrious, he has preserved the hybrid heritages of the French spirit in the American regions —heritages that, save for his research lighted by imagination, might never have blossomed in the pages of history.

INDEX

Addams, Jane, 268; "Spirit of Youth and the City Streets," 356.
Aeroplanes, 208.
Agricultural colleges, 342–345.
Agricultural experiment stations, 342–345.
Agricultural extension, 342–345.
Agricultural machinery, importance of, 334–341; saving effected by, 338–340; affects size of farms, 340–341.
Allouez, Claude Jean, Jesuit priest, 37; at Ste. Marie, 48; oration at Ottawa council, 51–54.
America, origin of name, 391–392.
André, Louis, Jesuit priest, at Ste. Marie mission, 48.
Animals, first road-makers, 174–175.
"Aramoni," a typical western town, 184–185.
Aramoni River, 183.
Architecture of Mississippi Valley, 86–88.
Arnold, Bion J., on future population of Chicago, 265.
Art, lack of appreciation of, in Mississippi Valley, 333.
Artaguette, Pierre d', French officer, 89; murdered by Chickasaws, 115.
Arthur, Chester A., 298.
Aubert, Thomas, navigator, may have discovered Gulf of St. Lawrence, 6.
Aubry (Captain), expedition to relieve Fort Niagara, 117.
Aubry, Nicolas, secular priest, lost in Acadian forest, 16.

Bancroft, George, "History of the United States" cited, 104–105, 119.

Baseball, 242, 333.
Baxter, James Phinney, historian, "Jacques Cartier" cited, 11, 12.
Beaumarchais, assumed name of Pierre Augustin Caron, 320–321.
Beaver, 378.
Benton, Thomas H., senator, speech on a bill for the construction of a highway to the Pacific cited, 174.
Berthelot, Pierre Eugène Marcellin, 342.
Bessemer, Henry, inventor, 347–348; experiments in iron manufacture, 348; paper before the British Association, 348; invents Bessemer converter, 348.
Bienville, Jean Baptiste le Moyne, Sieur de, 106, 108, 394; founds New Orleans, 110.
Big Horn Mountains, discovered by La Vérendrye brothers, 113.
Birkbeck, Morris, "Notes on a Tour in America, 1817," cited, 139.
Bismarck-Schönhausen, Otto Eduard von, his definition of a state, 305.
Bison, Hennepin pictures, 61; La Galissonnière describes importance as domestic animal, 116; paths made by, 174; disappearance of, 378.
Boll-weevil, control of, 303.
Bonnécamps, Joseph Pierre de, Jesuit, his diary of Céloron's expedition, 223; his map, 223.
Book of Wisdom quoted, 331–332.
Boone, Daniel, 133, 315.
Boston, Massachusetts, in 1732, 314.

426 INDEX

time of purchase, 151–153; cost of considered excessive, 153.

Lumber, commerce in, on Great Lakes, 209.

Lussière, La Motte de, French explorer, 199.

Macarty, Chevalier de, rebuilds Fort Chartres, 116.

McCormick, Cyrus Hall, inventor, invents the harvester, 334–336; given cross of Legion of Honor by Napoleon III, 335; honored by French Academy of Science, 336.

McKinley, William, 298.

McMaster, J. B., "History of the People of the United States" cited, 152–153.

Maeterlinck, Maurice, 330.

Maisonneuve, Paul de Chomedey, founds Montreal, 8, 393.

Makarty, see Macarty.

Mallet, Paul, explores New Mexico, 113.

Mallet, Pierre, explores New Mexico, 113.

Mance, Jeanne, 10.

Maps—
Marquette's map of Mississippi exploration, 44, 73.
Joliet's map of Mississippi exploration lost, 44.
Waldseemüller's, 1507, 1513, 73.
Garay's map, 73.
Bonnécamps map of Céloron's expedition, 223.

Margry, Pierre, historian, "Découvertes et établissements des Français" cited, 97, 101, 109.

Marquette, Jacques, Jesuit priest, 393; at Pointe de St. Esprit, 37; at Point St. Ignace, 38; explores Mississippi River with Joliet, 38–44, 73–74, 249; at Illinois village, 41; reaches mouth of Arkansas River, 42; on Illinois River, 42; second expedition to Illinois Indians, 44; dies at Chicago portage, 44, 76, 258; tradition of, preserved among

Illinois Indians, 44–45; brings Ottawas and Hurons to convocation at Ste. Marie, 49; memorial cross erected to memory of, 259.

Mayflower descendants, 316.

Membré, Zenobius, Récollet friar, 100, 109.

Ménard, René, Jesuit priest, lost in Wisconsin forests, 37.

Michigan, Lake, Nicolet explores, 25; Joliet and Marquette on, 38; La Salle on, 63.

Military grants, 167.

Mineral land grants, 167; withdrawn from private entry, 386.

Mississippi bubble, see Mississippi Company.

Mississippi Company, 85, 111–112.

Mississippi River, 70–98; discovered by Marquette and Joliet, 41; named Rivière de la Conception, 41; named La Buade, 41; La Salle on, 67–69; Indian knowledge of, 70–71; French appreciation of, 75, 85; lack of appreciation by Americans, 86; length, 77; crookedness, 77; width, 77; discharge, 77–78; navigable length, 78; sediment, 78; water-power, 78; stages, 78; drainage basin, 78; sources explored by Le Sueur, 113; by Nicollet, 81–83; mouth of, described by Mrs. Trollope, 83; Hamlin Garland on, 85–87; steamboat traffic on, 90; shifting channel of, 91, 93; difficulty of navigation, 91; control of floods, 92, 94; storage reservoirs, 95, 96; floods, 93; loss by floods, 93; jetties on, 94; hydro-electric development, 95–96.

Mississippi Valley, area, 78, 150; temperature, 79; rainfall, 79; agricultural resources, 80, 189; mineral wealth, 80; future population, 80; described by De Tocqueville, 81; survivals of French in, 88–89; Germans plan settlement in, 92; economic development, 189, 329–353; American settlement of, 138–

Printed in the United States
17812LVS00002B/166-189